The Free Economy and the Strong State

Also by Andrew Gamble

From Alienation to Surplus Value (with Paul Walton)
The Conservative Nation
Capitalism in Crisis (with Paul Walton)
An Introduction to Modern Social and Political Thought
Britain in Decline
The British Party System and Economic Policy 1945–1983
    (with Stuart Walkland)
Developments in British Politics 4 (co-editor)

The Free Economy and the Strong State

The Politics of Thatcherism

SECOND EDITION

Andrew Gamble

MACMILLAN

First edition 1988
Reprinted 1989, 1990, 1991, 1993
Second edition 1994

Published by
THE MACMILLAN PRESS LTD
Houndmills, Basingstoke, Hampshire RG21 2XS
and London
Companies and representatives
throughout the world

ISBN 0–333–59332–4 hardcover
ISBN 0–333–59333–2 paperback

A catalogue record for this book is available
from the British Library.

Printed in Hong Kong

'The part played in history by individuals, which was over-emphasised by Carlyle, and is still exaggerated in our day by his reactionary disciples, tends, on the other hand, to be unduly minimised by those who believe themselves to have discovered the laws of sociological change. I do not believe that, if Bismarck had died in infancy, the history of Europe during the past seventy years would have been at all closely similar to what it has been.'— **Bertrand Russell** (1934)

'The Old Testament prophets did not say "Brothers I want a consensus". They said: "This is my faith, this is what I passionately believe. If you believe it too, then come with me." ' — **Margaret Thatcher** (1979)

'I don't at all mind having enemies. But not too many at the same time please.' — **Margaret Thatcher** (1981)

Contents

Preface

The fall of Thatcher in 1990 and the experience of the post-war Thatcher era has provided the opportunity to make the second edition of this book more definitive in its judgements than the first, completed in 1987. This edition covers the whole Thatcher period up to the ending of the Thatcher era in 1990 with the resignation of Margaret Thatcher as Prime Minister and Leader of the Conservative Party after having failed to win by four votes the majority required on the first ballot of the leadership election for outright victory. Chapters 1 and 7 have been substantially rewritten and Chapter 4 extended to cover Thatcher's last three years as Prime Minister. All the other chapters have been revised and updated where required and I have added a new introduction focusing on the key concepts of 'Thatcherism' and 'hegemony'.

I have altered some of my judgements about Thatcherism, and have also clarified some of the concepts I used to analyse Thatcherism in the first edition. But my broad line of approach is unchanged. Much has been written and continues to be written on Thatcher and Thatcherism. This book offers an interpretation of Thatcherism as a political project of the Conservative leadership which sought to re-establish the conditions for making the Conservativce party the leading force once again in the British state. Thatcherism, however inconsistent, incoherent and contradictory it may have been, was a phenomenon of great significance in British and in world politics, and will rightly continue to be studied. Its legacies remain, and many of the problems it sought to tackle remain unresolved.

I have incurred many debts in writing this book. I should particularly like to thank Martin Jacques for the exceptional intellectual stimulus he provided during the 1980s as editor of *Marxism Today*; Ralph Miliband for commissioning and commenting on the original article that suggested the theme of this book; Steven Kennedy, Gillian Peele and a Macmillan reviewer for reading and criticising a draft of the first edition; and numerous friends, colleagues and students at Sheffield, with whom I have discussed the themes of this book. Special thanks for their help and stimulus in different ways and at different times are due to Henry Drucker, Patrick Dunleavy, Henk Overbeek, Stuart Hall, Bill Schwarz, Bob Jessop, Teddy Brett, Colin Leys, David Baker, Ruth Levitas, David Marquand, Bea Campbell, Zig Layton-Henry, John Ross, Chris Rodway, David Coates, Anthony Arblaster, Steve Ludlam, John Solomos, Bill Jordan, Tessa TenTusscher, Chushichi Tsuzuki, Stuart Walkland, Jack Grainger, Paul Ginsborg, Neil Lyndon, Hugo Radice, Hans Kastendiek, Raymond Plant, Mick Cox, Yoshi Ogasawara, Dave Marsh and TSC.

August 1993   ANDREW GAMBLE

Introduction

This book offers an analysis of the Thatcher era in British politics. This era is defined most simply by Margaret Thatcher's long tenure of the leadership of the Conservative Party, first as leader of the opposition between 1975 and 1979, then as prime minister between 1979 and 1990. The 1980s will be remembered under different names in Russia, France and Iran. But in Britain it will always be the decade of Thatcher and Thatcherism. Having lost four of the five general elections before 1979 the Conservatives won four in a row, three of them under the same leader. The electoral triumph of the Conservatives in the 1980s was so marked that it focused attention on the personality of the leader. Yet a little leader worship was understandable. Margaret Thatcher did not just preside over Conservative success. She personified it. Any leader who survived for as long as she did would have attracted attention. But Thatcher did not just survive; she dominated the political landscape in Britain in a way managed by few of her predecessors. The widespread use of the term 'Thatcherism' was one sign of this. It came to stand for the distinctive ideology, political style and programme of policies of the British Conservative Party after Margaret Thatcher was elected leader in 1975.

Analysis of this political phenomenon has not been lacking. A flood of writing has analysed 'The Thatcher Decade', 'The Thatcher experiment' even 'The Thatcher Revolution'. Few aspects of Margaret Thatcher's policy, ideology and personality have not been dissected and assessed. Many different interpretations have appeared explaining the significance of Thatcherism and its impact on British politics.

The term was taken up by academics, journalists and politicians. Even Thatcher herself started using it.

But despite its ubiquity the usefulness of the term remains controversial. This is because it has been used in so many different ways. Thatcherism has no single unambiguous meaning. Critics of the concept argue that it is misleading either because it directs attention to matters that are trivial and relatively unimportant, or because it attributes a degree of coherence and purpose to the actions and ideas of the Thatcher government that does not exist.

The first type of criticism, associated with Tony Benn, objects to the use of the term on the grounds that Thatcherism is in principle no different from other and earlier forms of Conservatism. The Conservative Party changes its ideology and its leaders to suit the circumstances of each period. Its basic character and objectives remain the same. Thatcherism as a programme of policy is therefore quite separate from Margaret Thatcher herself. Her disappearance did not mean the end of the policies with which she was identified. To term the programme that the Conservatives adopted in the 1970s 'Thatcherism' personalises it, and in doing so distorts its character by directing attention to what is least important about it – the peculiarities of style and belief that are associated with one particular leader.

The second type of criticism, associated with Peter Riddell, is sceptical that the Thatcher government ever pursued clear and consistent ideological objectives, and could have achieved them even if it had. For all governments there is a wide gulf between rhetoric and achievement, and the Thatcher government was no different. Its policies were determined by the particular circumstances that existed in each policy sector rather than by some grand ideological design. The outcome of its policies was far less than either supporters or opponents have at times claimed and does not deserve to be dignified with the use of a grand label like Thatcherism.

Some of these criticisms are sound, but they hardly constitute a case for dispensing with the term Thatcherism. Labels may simplify complex political phenomena, but it would not be easy to do without terms such as Stalinism, Butskellism and Powellism. Such terms are not explanations in themselves but identify phenomena that are coherent enough to warrant further investigation. Thatcher is one of the very few British political leaders whose name has been used to denote the particular ideology, political style and programme for government with which their period in office is associated. No other British prime minister this century has had their name used in quite the way Thatcher has. This alone would justify further investigation of why the term has come to be used so widely.

Critics of the concept of Thatcherism are often reacting to their own interpretation of the term. But after only a short immersion in the writing on Thatcherism it should be apparent that there is no single uncontested meaning. The term denotes a phenomenon for investigation, not a known entity. This investigation can proceed on a number of levels.

One level is Thatcher herself as a political personality. Thatcherism cannot be reduced to the personal project of a single individual because it was not created by one person and is much more than just a style of leadership, but it is still important to remember that it is called Thatcherism because of the personal contribution made by Thatcher. A different Conservative leader elected in 1975 would still have had to contend with Thatcherism in the party, in business and in the media, but might have reacted very differently. What makes the term Thatcherism appropriate for understanding events after 1975 is that Thatcher identified herself with the ideas and the causes of the New Right and used her position as leader to promote the spread of these ideas in a manner that was highly unusual for a Conservative leader.

Thatcher is therefore important to Thatcherism. But an analysis of Thatcherism that only concentrated on Thatcher would be seriously inadequate. Thatcherism is used to refer not only to a style of leadership but also to a set of doctrines and a programme of policies. None of these exist in isolation. Thatcherism arose within a particular context and set of constraints. The way in which these combined created a specific conjuncture of circumstances and events. The different aspects of this conjuncture provide the different vantage points from which Thatcherism has been interpreted.

The circumstances that defined this conjuncture were not only national; they were also global. Understanding Thatcherism requires knowledge of the world political economy as well as knowledge of national political and economic structures such as forms of electoral and interest representation, modes of policy formation and implementation, and patterns of economic organisation.

The political and economic crisis of the 1970s was a global phenomenon. Thatcherism was one particular national response. Like other complex political phenomena it was highly contradictory. Its unity did not depend on simple pronouncements and declarations of will by Margaret Thatcher. In analysing Thatcherism the key problem is to decide what gave it coherence. Was it simply the position of Margaret Thatcher, as leader of the Conservative Party (1975–90) and prime minister (1979–1990)? Most writers on the phenomenon of Thatcherism have thought that there was more to it than that. But they have disagreed on what the correct interpretation should be.

Thatcherism as a political project

The argument of this book is that the most appropriate framework for explaining Thatcherism and charting its development is to view it as a political project developed by the Conservative leadership, which sought to reestablish the conditions – electoral, ideological, economic and political – for the Conservative Party to resume its leading role in British politics. During the 1970s the capacity of the Conservatives to play this role had been seriously weakened, and the legitimacy of the state itself had come into question.

As a political project Thatcherism had three overriding objectives – to restore the political fortunes of the Conservative Party, to revive market liberalism as the dominant public philosophy and to create the conditions for a free economy by limiting the scope of the state while restoring its authority and competence to act. It is because Thatcherism deliberately set out an alternative to the policy regime that had been established since the 1940s that it has attracted such attention. Many explanations have been offered for Thatcher's dominance of British politics in the 1980s – the electoral system, the disarray of the opposition and the political skill and opportunism of the Conservatives are all important factors. But the ideological ascendancy given by Thatcherism to the right wing was important as well.

After 1975 the New Right increasingly set the terms of the political and ideological debate. Its central doctrines could be applied to theoretical issues, policy issues and issues of ordinary life, and its arguments appeared plausible and coherent. It was able to do this both because of the failures and disarray of the Labour government and because of the greater readiness of the Conservatives to respond positively to new issues and new opportunities created by rapidly changing patterns of work and leisure and an increasingly open and interdependent world economy. The initial spur behind the development of Thatcherism was the strong reaction in the Conservative Party against the record and policies of the Heath years. But its momentum was maintained by the flow of ideas and policy discussion that came from the New Right and by fast-moving world events.

The impulse behind Thatcherism was the need to restore the state's authority and reverse the decline of the economy. Although the New Right is made up of many groups, which have tended to become more rather than less diverse, they were united in the early years of Thatcherism by the need to free the economy from the controls and burdens of collectivism, while at the same time strengthening the authority of government by limiting its size and scope. The Thatcherite project was driven by the belief that the postwar accommodation between the interests of labour and capital could no longer be sustained, and that this was leading to accelerating inflation, rising unemployment and a growing burden of public expenditure. The market economy was being buried under an avalanche of controls and regulations, and the state was being paralysed by strong pressure groups. The New Right favoured a return to the principles of classical liberalism – free markets and limited government.

Limited government, however, does not mean weak government. The state has to be strong to police the market order and provide those goods – such as security, competition, law enforcement and stable prices – that the market cannot provide for itself. If the state takes on responsibilities beyond these it risks losing its authority and effectiveness. It has to be above the fray of competing interests in civil society, which means that the state should not become involved in administering major spending programmes, such as education and health, or economic enterprises, such as coal, electricity and telecommunications. Its role is to encourage families and individuals to be self-reliant and independent of the state, relying on the market rather than on public services for the satisfaction of their needs. This image of the good society, based on a free economy, a strong state and stable families was central to Thatcherism. It was the inspiration for many of the policies and strategies of the Thatcher government. From it sprang a number of separate if related discourses – commonsense homilies about the economy as well as sophisticated disquisitions on macroeconomic management and public choice.

Thatcherism is sometimes presented as though in 1979 there existed a set of policy blueprints ready for immediate implementation. No actual policy process could ever work in that way. What distinguished the Thatcher government from its predecessors was not detailed policy plans but its strategic sense of its long-term objectives and its pragmatism concerning the means to achieve them. Many of the policies for which the Thatcher government is noted were not in fact planned in detail in advance but were improvised according to the particular circumstances and opportunities encountered by the government. They include the legislation on trade unions, the abolition of exchange controls and the privatisation programme. Subsequently some of these programmes, most notably privatisation, were dignified with more coherence than they had at the time.

The lack of policy planning does not mean that this government governed in the old Tory fashion, according to circumstances rather than principles. It had principles that it was not prepared to compromise, but it had enough political grasp to realise that short-term tactical retreats and compromises were often necessary. The government – like all governments – had many different objectives, not all of which were compatible. In order, for example, to ensure that the privatisation of nationalised industries proceeded smoothly it had to enlist the support of their existing managements. But this meant giving guarantees about the future shape of each industry that were very damaging to another of the government's main aims – encouraging competition. It had constantly to find the trade-offs that worked politically. More than most governments it proved successful in doing this, while still attempting to present its policies as consistent and coherent.

The Thatcher revolution in policy did not extend to all areas of policy. Defence and foreign policy were untouched. The major area of change has been economic policy. However even many of these changes, such as the turn from Keynesian to monetarist policies in economic management, were already under way before 1979. The influence of events such as the ending of the great postwar economic expansion and the system of fixed exchange rates, as well as changes in the political and intellectual climate of the 1970s, would have ensured that the thrust of policy in the 1980s was away from the mode of state intervention that had characterised the postwar period. The political alternative that Thatcherism represented did not depend uniquely on the election of the Thatcher government. What the Thatcher government did contribute was a fierce commitment to the ideal of a more limited government and freer markets, and a readiness to use the powers of the state to confront those groups that resisted. It achieved many successes against its enemies, most notably its victory in the miners' strike in 1984–5. The ruthlessness and determination it showed in organising victory against opponents became a noted feature of its political style.

Analysing Thatcherism as a political project aiming at a restoration of Conservative ideological, economic and political hegemony in the British state requires appreciation of the many aspects of Thatcherism – as a set of intellectual doctrines, as a popular political movement, as a style of leadership, as a bloc of interests and as a programme of policy. It also requires an understanding of the historical context and the structural constraints within which the Thatcherite project arose.

The framework used in this book develops concepts first used in my earlier study, *The Conservative Nation* – the politics of power and the politics of support. The task confronting political leaders is twofold. They must win support from voters, organised interests and their own party members, mobilising a coalition than can win elections and establish a claim to political, moral and intellectual leadership. Secondly, having secured government office they must govern successfully, which involves harmonising their popular mandate with the realities of managing the state machine and coping with the pressures placed upon policy by structural constraints of the domestic polity and the world political economy.

Thinking of Thatcherism within this framework suggests a range of questions.

First, on the politics of support:

- How popular was Thatcherism?
- Who voted for Thatcher and why?
- Did Thatcherism succeed in creating a new dominant party system?
- Did the Thatcher government permanently weaken the institutional bases of opposition to Conservative rule?
- How did the Thatcher government succeed in overcoming so much internal and external opposition?
- Which classes and groups did Thatcherism represent?
- How was Thatcherism shaped by the doctrines of the New Right?
- What was the relationship of Thatcherism to Conservatism?
- What tensions existed in the doctrine of the free economy and the strong state?

Second, on the politics of power:

- How radical were the policies of the Thatcher government and how successful was the government in implementing them?

- Was the Thatcher government able to formulate and implement an economic strategy capable of reversing British decline?[1]
- Did the Thatcher government assist the emergence of a new regime of accumulation?
- How far did the Thatcher government centralise the British state, weaken intermediate institutions, and increase the state's repressive powers?
- In what ways did the Thatcher government restructure the state and change the forms of state intervention?
- Was the state rolled back?
- What international role did the Thatcher government promote for Britain?

These questions can all be subsumed under one central question: has Thatcherism successfully restored the conditions for Conservative hegemony? Hegemony means the exercise of political and moral leadership. Applied to a political party such as the Conservative Party, which seeks to operate in the politics of support as well as the politics of power, the concept of hegemony has four main dimensions – electoral, ideological, economic and state. Seeing Thatcherism in relation to the concept of hegemony has sometimes been misrepresented as concentrating exclusively upon ideology. It came to be associated with the journal *Marxism Today* during the editorship of Martin Jacques. But the notion of hegemony always involved class strategies and political calculation as well as ideology. It also involved a keen sense of the need to analyse the conjuncture of specific histories, circumstances and structures that, as argued above, define a phenomenon such as Thatcherism.

In an influential article in 1979[2] Jacques argued that Thatcherism was a response to the convergence of three trends: (i) the long-term structural decline of the British economy and the advent of the world recession; (ii) the collapse of the third postwar Labour government and the consequent weakening of the social-democratic consensus; and (iii) the resumption of the Cold War.

These developments created the space and opportunity for a political project on the right to set out to achieve a new hegemony. This project sought to rebuild the political leadership of the Conservatives, firstly by assembling a sufficiently large coalition of voters and interest groups; secondly by projecting a new conception of the public interest and a vision of the ideal social and political order; and thirdly by defining policy priorities and developing a credible programme of policies, which was in part tailored to the specific fears and demands of voters and organised interests, but which also addressed the main problems of government, particularly economic policy and external relations.

Several political projects with ambitions to establish hegemony may exist concurrently and compete against one another. The establishment of a durable hegemony requires the emergence of a consensus both on the desirable shape of society and on the policy priorities for government. True hegemony comes about when there is no longer serious conflict over the fundamentals of social organisation. In this book Thatcherism is analysed as a project aimed at the replacement of the discredited social-democratic consensus of the postwar period by a new consensus for the 1990s. It involved from the first an intense ideological struggle, but also political calculation aimed at winning and maintaining support, as well as a programme of policies for reorganising the state, improving economic performance, reversing British decline and restoring Britain's standing in the world. It is hardly surprising that with so many and so diverse goals Thatcherism should have had such a contradictory character. As the attempt to carry through the project unfolded, so the ambiguities inherent in it became clear.

The plan of this book is as follows. Chapter 1 analyses the conjuncture of history, circumstance and structure that defined Thatcherism, paying special attention to the new politics which emerged in the 1970s in response to the world recession, the exhaustion of Fordism as a regime of accumulation, the weakening of the hegemonic role of the United States in the world system, and the crisis of social democratic politics and the British ancien régime. (Some readers may prefer to skip this chapter and move directly to the study of the ideological and political origins of Thatcherism in Chapters 2 and 3.)

Chapter 2 analyses the ideological origins of the Thatcherite project, through an examination of the ideas and doctrines of the New Right, and its two main strands – identified here simply as the conservative New Right and the liberal New Right.

Chapter 3 explores the political origins of the Thatcherite project in the various challenges which emerged to the post-war consensus, and discusses the circumstances in which Margaret Thatcher became Leader of the Conservative party and the first phase of Thatcherism during her period as Leader of the Opposition.

Chapter 4 reviews the record of the Thatcher Government and the extent to which it tried to implement the Thatcherite project. It looks at several different policy areas, asks how radical and successful the Thatcher Government proved to be in the light of its own manifesto commitments in 1979.

Chapters 5 and 6 examine the principal right and left interpretations of Thatcherism. Chapter 5 explores the debates on the legitimacy of Thatcherism as a representative of the Conservative tradition, and probes the question: Is Thatcherism Conservatism? Chapter 6 analyses the debates on whether Thatcherism should be understood as authoritarian populism or class politics, and some of the objections that have been made to both interpretations.

Chapter 7 provides an assessment of the successes and failures of the Thatcherite project, in terms of its success in managing the different requirements of the politics of support and the politics of power. It discusses the new policy agenda which the Thatcher Government created and whether the Government succeeded in its primary objective, to turn Britain round and reverse the long decline.

1

A crisis of hegemony

During the 1970s a new politics became established in the West. There were different national variants but many common themes. In the 1980s its most celebrated exponents were the governments of Margaret Thatcher in Britain and Ronald Reagan in the United States. The new politics came to be thought of primarily as a new conservative politics.

It was not however confined to the right. The opportunity and the necessity for new policies, projects, purposes and doctrines was created by the breakdown of hegemony at both international and national levels during the 1970s. At the international level the breakdown occurred with the disappearance of the undisputed economic supremacy enjoyed by the United States since the 1940s, and the world economy was plunged once more into recession. At the national level it occurred when the policies and institutions of postwar social democracy began to be discredited. The authority of the social-democratic state in the fields of citizenship, representation and economic management was undermined. In Britain these crises became linked with the long-term historical crisis of the British state and its ancien régime. All three crises and how they interacted need to be explored in order to understand the conjuncture from which Thatcherism emerged.

The loss of hegemony did not occur suddenly but over a period. Hegemony operates at three levels. At the level of a state, hegemony signifies the fundamental legitimacy and acceptance of the basic institutions and values of a social and political order, including critically those of the economy and the state, which is only questioned in very extreme circumstances, typically those of revolution, invasion or civil war. At the level of the government or regime, hegemony signifies that one particular party or faction has achieved a position of leadership and commands the active support, or at least acquiescence, of leading economic sectors and key social groups. At the level of the world system, hegemony signifies the political and intellectual leadership of a nation-state whose economic and military and cultural capacities allow it to take on state functions for the world system as a whole. In each case the criteria for saying that hegemony has been achieved are not easy to establish, since there are always conflicts and changes. Nothing is ever stable for long. Constant work and struggle are required to achieve and maintain it, for no hegemony is ever complete, and many attempts to establish hegemony are never realised. That is why at the level of regimes and world systems political projects to win hegemony are encountered much more frequently than hegemony itself.

The loss of hegemony in the 1970s occurred at the regime and world-system level. The basic legitimacy of the Western liberal capitalist system was not under threat, although many feared it might be. The radical-right programmes of both Thatcher and Reagan were responses to the breakdown of authority and stability in the world system and in national politics and economic management. From the outset they offered to restore strong national and international leadership on a new basis. They planned to restore the vigour of British and American capitalism through a new economic strategy designed to encourage the emergence of a new regime of accumulation; they planned to rebuild the system of alliances and defences of the West; they planned to change the balance between state and society and reinvigorate their national cultures.

These were new political projects that openly challenged the ideological, economic and state hegemony of British social democracy and American welfarism. Both were seen as having failed. They were rejected as sets of institutions and policies for managing advanced industrial societies and also as models of the kind of good society that political activity should be seeking to create.

The breakdown of hegemony forced a new policy agenda upon governments. As policies began to change so new political doctrines emerged to justify the new measures and to suggest how they might be extended. But the changes in political institutions and modes of political organisation that the new policies often required occurred much more slowly. The new doctrines and political rhetoric ran far in advance of them.

The new politics developed in response to the events and crises of the 1970s. It did not have a single focus or a single driving force. The various crises of state authority upon which it fastened had developed separately, and although there were some interrelationships there was at no time a single problem to which all the others could be reduced. As structures of authority weakened so the task of governing became more intractable. But at the same time it created new space for more active and creative political leadership, the forging of new coalitions of voters and interests, the framing of new policies and the articulation of new ideologies and doctrines, in short the construction of new political projects aimed at winning electoral and ideological hegemony for the new coalitions of the right.

The opportunity for challenging the policies enshrined in the 'Great Society' programme of the United States or Britain's welfare state arose out of events during the 1970s that changed the parameters and assumptions of national politics. The relative political stability and prosperity of the advanced capitalist world that had been painfully established after the years of world war and postwar reconstruction gave way to renewed turbulence, domestic conflict and international tensions.

What all states faced in the 1970s was a growth in the number of problems that did not seem capable of being solved by ordinary political means. The space for asserting national sovereignty was shrinking; economic management was increasingly unsuccessful; the structures for mobilising consent for national policies were no longer adequate; and the bases of social order and national identity were under threat. The inability of governments to find solutions weakened political authority and generated a deep malaise and pessimism about the possibility of rational management of public policy. Governments appeared weak and indecisive.

None of these problems were new. All had figured in domestic political argument from at least the mid-1960s onwards. But what changed in the 1970s was appreciation of their scale. The trigger for this was the collapse of fixed exchange rates in 1971–2 followed by the quadrupling of the oil price in 1973 and the ensuing generalised world recession. The collapse of currency stability and the rise in oil prices did not cause the recession, but such events drew attention to the increasingly precarious foundations of Western prosperity since cheap energy and stable money had been two of the key factors in postwar expansion. The long boom was now definitely over and a period of much slower growth lay ahead. Following the acceleration of inflation after 1971 and the steep rise in unemployment after 1973 it was recognised that managing the economy successfully was going to be much more difficult than in the previous two decades.

The slowdown in growth and the breakdown of fixed exchange rates undermined the policy regimes that had developed in the period of prosperity. Controlling inflation assumed a higher priority than maintaining full employment; public-expenditure programmes no longer seemed affordable and were reined back; and strict curbs on wages and internal demand were applied.

All governments in the mid-1970s were forced to adopt similar crisis packages to deal with the problem of inflation and the disappearance of growth. At first the disappearance of growth was regarded as temporary and an early resumption was anticipated. But it soon became clear that the shocks of the early 1970s were not accidents but signalled deep and permanent changes in the political and economic organisation of the world economy. Waiting for the storm to pass was no longer enough. The world outside was never going to be quite the same again.

The world system

The single most important reason for the development of a new politics was the shift in the political and economic balance of the world system. This had two main features: the exhaustion of the old regime of accumulation known as Fordism and the decline in the position of the United States. The emergence of an increasingly interdependent world economy over a period of several centuries has brought an unprecedented enlargement of production, population, trade and communications. But political authority within this relatively unified world economy has remained fragmented between a large (and increasing) number of states. This modern world economy has never experienced rule from a single centre, and has owed its dynamism to the permanent competition and occasional armed conflict between states as they seek to promote particular national interests within the framework of international cooperation.[1]

The world system follows no fixed cycle or pattern of development. Every succeeding phase brings new possibilities and novel features. Periods of relative stability within the world system have been associated firstly with the establishment and diffusion of a major new technology capable of revolutionising all the major branches of production and secondly with the emergence of a state that enjoys such undisputed industrial, commercial and financial supremacy that it can exercise hegemony. For a time it can act as though it were a world state, a central authority laying down rules and providing services for the world economy.

Both these conditions were realised during the period of exceptional stability and prosperity experienced during the 1950s and 1960s: the diffusion of technologies based on electric motors into new sectors, particularly consumer goods, and the undisputed hegemonic position of the United States.[2]

During the years of prosperity and rapid expansion of national economies the foreign economic policy of the leading capitalist powers settled into a pattern. The intense debates during the postwar reconstruction period gave way at the end of the 1950s to a (belated) acceptance of the agreements made at Bretton Woods. Currencies were made convertible, trade became multilateral, exchange rates were fixed and progress towards reduction of tariffs through successive rounds of negotiation through GATT were endorsed. The IMF and the World Bank were confirmed as the principal international agencies charged with policing and lubricating the system.[3]

Fordism

The ultimate acceptance of a regime of multilateral trade and payments was made possible by the huge expansion of output and markets based on the full development of the technologies and methods of industrial organisation known as Fordism.[4] The Fordist regime of accumulation was based on assembly-line mass production and the gradual elimination of skilled workers through the systematic incorporation of their skills into the production process using the techniques of scientific management.

Mass production entailed mass consumption, which required either rapid growth in exports or enlargement of the domestic market. The latter was achieved through new measures of national economic management designed to maintain high and stable levels of demand, and through the emergence of collective bargaining arrangements, which ensured that wages were high in the leading sectors and that wage increases matched increases in productivity and prices.

There was nothing inevitable about the establishment of such a regime of accumulation. The political conditions for it had first to be created. The internal political battle for the acceptance of interventionist state policies were prolonged, and the trade unions' ability to win a strong bargaining position in the mass production industries was not conceded without a struggle.

There was inevitably a wide variation in how far and when these conditions were realised in different countries. But as the industrial methods of Fordism became established it helped the emergence of social democratic regimes. Social democracy, in its different national variants, subsequently allowed the full logic of Fordism to unfold. Organised labour was successfully incorporated as a support for the modern industrial order and there followed an era of exceptional growth in output, living standards and the public sector throughout the advanced capitalist countries.

The world recession

As the world system developed, states have often experienced difficulty in maintaining their autonomy in the face of changing patterns in world trade and production and in political, military and economic competition from other states. This has been particularly acute when a period of relative political stability and economic prosperity gave way to a period of political conflict and economic uncertainty.

The breakdown of international hegemony and the emergence of a crisis of accumulation in the world economy forces all national governments to reconsider the role of their countries within the world system. They must rethink what their essential national interests are and adapt their policies accordingly. The adequacy of national economic strategies in respect of foreign economic policy, stabilisation policy and industrial policy has to be reassessed in the light of changing world circumstances. Such rethinking can provoke lively internal debate and major social and political conflicts. The merits of greater autonomy versus greater dependence, of protectionism against free trade, of currency blocs against freely convertible currencies, of controlling inflation against maintaining employment, of markets against planning, as well as questions of military and diplomatic alliances, all come under examination.

This was the context of the new politics of the 1970s. The breakdown of the hegemony exercised by the United States and the relative exhaustion of profitable investment opportunities threw the Fordist regime of accumulation into turmoil. The abrupt slowing down of economic growth in the mid-1970s reopened numerous questions that had been thought settled. The foundations of postwar prosperity were put in doubt. The increase in interdependence since 1945 had initially increased rather than diminished the authority of governments because of the growth in the pool of resources available to be distributed through market and political mechanisms. When the pool stopped growing and even began contracting, national governments struggled to retain their authority.

The advent of the recession was triggered by the deflationary measures adopted by many countries to contain the upsurge in inflation in 1973–4 and to reduce their non-oil imports so as to protect their balance of payments.[5] The check to demand and confidence dramatically exposed the obsolescence of many established industries. Investment opportunities in many fields had become exhausted because markets were saturated and in many industries it was difficult to make any further gains in productivity with the existing technology. A huge shake-out of labour began plunging national economies into the kind of mass unemployment that had not been experienced since the 1930s.

It soon became clear that a major restructuring of the world economy would have to be carried out, and that this would involve the liquidation of a huge amount of capacity, the disappearance of a large part of existing employment and the introduction of new technological systems. The deployment of new technology was aimed at preserving the competitiveness of some parts of national and international capital. It was not itself the direct cause of the unemployment, but what it underlined was that previous levels of employment in those industries would never return. New levels of productivity and new standards of competition had been established that all companies and industries in the future would have to match.

Right at the centre of the new politics has been the question of how to handle the process of restructuring that has been forced upon every national economy. Who is to bear the costs of change? What elements of the old institutions and programmes can be rescued? What can be adapted to meet the new circumstances? For many national economies faced with the closure of steel industries, coal mines and car plants the process of restructuring has often appeared a process of deindustrialisation, with the disappearance of their principal industries amidst growing penetration of the home markets by foreign imports, an inexorable increase in their dole queues and pressure on their public finances.[6] The growth of new technologies such as microelectronics has promoted very rapid growth in a few new sectors and fundamental reorganisation in all others. A new post-Fordist or neo-Fordist regime of accumulation based on flexible specialisation, with different patterns of employment and corporate organisation, has begun to emerge.[7]

All this would be hard enough to handle within a single political system. But its management is enormously complicated because the redistribution of labour between skills and occupation is taking place not only within national economies but between them. The restructuring involves some major shifts in the international division of labour. The division of labour that became established in the 1950s involved exchange of manufactures and primary products between advanced capitalist states and Third World countries, and an increasing exchange of manufactures between the developed states themselves. In the 1970s new patterns in the world division of labour began to emerge, spurred on by the rapid development of certain Third World states and by the impact of the oil revenues that now accrued to the oil-producing states.[8]

The impact of the recession has been very uneven both within states and across the world economy. Just as there are regions and industries within national economies, such as the Sunbelt of the United States and the south-east of England, that have continued to grow throughout the recession, so there are regions of the world economy whose growth has not been constrained by what has been happening elsewhere. The worst effects of the slow-down have been borne by the older industrial heartlands of Western Europe and the north-east of the United States and by many areas of the Third World, particularly those dependent on the export of particular commodities. The beneficiaries are those regions and economies bordering the Pacific. This looks set to be the centre of world accumulation in the next phase of expansion.

The decline of the United States

Alongside the disruption of Fordism as a viable regime of accumulation, a second crucial change that has shaped the new politics is the weakened position of the United States.

The inability of the United States in the 1970s to exercise undisputed leadership was a result of the long-term decline in its relative economic strength. This change influenced the calculations made by all states.

The period of undisputed American hegemony over the world system was relatively short – 1945 to 1973. So successful was the reconstruction of the economies of Germany and Japan and so rapid the pace of expansion in the 1950s and 1960s that the productivity gap between Japan, the European Community and the United States had narrowed and in some cases disappeared by 1970. The costs of overseas investment by American firms and the worldwide military forces maintained by America after 1941 could be funded initially with ease in a world hungry for dollars, but in time they created a chronic balance of payments deficit, which undermined the dollar and with it the stability of the international monetary system. The collapse of the gold exchange standard in 1971 brought an end to the system of fixed exchange rates and removed an important barrier to rapid inflation. No new means of restoring long-term stability to the currency markets was devised in the 1970s or the 1980s, nor was much progress made towards the solution of common problems such as coordinating policies of national economic management or reducing Third World debt.[9]

Yet despite the pressure towards a fissuring of the world economy into protectionist blocs, as had happened in the 1930s, the openness of the Western economy was largely preserved and a plunge into depression was avoided during the 1970s and early 1980s, although at times the possibility came dangerously close. The reorganised political and economic system of Western capitalism demonstrated enormous resilience, and after the initial series of shocks confidence began to recover. This also owed something to the new politics. Many on both the left and the right welcomed the new political space created by the recession and the possibilities for refashioning institutions and redesigning policies in radical ways.

The recessions after 1973 sharpened political conflict within and between states but did not shatter the commitment of national governing classes to the preservation of the system of economic interdependence and military alliances that had become so firmly established after 1945. The military position of the United States remained supreme. It was its hegemony in the economic field that had weakened. The political fragmentation of the European Community and the unwillingness of Japan to exercise a political role commensurate with its new economic importance meant that there was no alternative to continued United States leadership, yet in many fields the United States refused to compromise in the pursuit of its national interests, and it no longer had the authority to exercise leadership for the whole world system.

The economic divisions in the Western bloc in the 1970s were overshadowed by the deterioration in relationships between the superpowers and the beginning of the new Cold War. But even here, as events during the Reagan presidency demonstrated, it was no longer always possible to mobilise the Western powers behind a common foreign policy forged in Washington. The differences in interests and perceptions of the Soviet Union were now marked and subjected the Alliance to considerable strains.

With growing pressures within the United States towards isolationism, the future of an Atlanticist foreign policy was thrown into doubt. The possibility of a more equal trilateral arrangement between the three main centres of the Western world was canvassed, as was the possibility of neutrality and isolationism. After a period in which all these questions had seemed to be settled, the political agenda suddenly opened up. National politicians could dream again.

The crisis of social democracy

The crisis in the regime of accumulation and the shifts in the political organisation of the world system that took place in the 1970s were the fundamental changes that made a new politics possible and necessary. But the content of this new politics was often provided by local concerns, specific to the institutions and circumstances of particular countries. Nevertheless here too certain common themes can be seen. The institutions and policies of social democracy came under attack almost everywhere. The challenges were made through ideological debate as well as by new political programmes and movements. Many of these challenges began before the appearance of the global crisis of accumulation and hegemony. But they became much stronger once the political and economic foundations of the postwar order had been undermined.

Social democracy as a form of political regime has many variants but a common feature in postwar Europe was the existence of a democratic constitution under which all citizens enjoyed certain civil, political and social rights. Political participation was not restricted by property, birth, race or gender. Enfranchising the whole citizenry and allowing freedom of speech, association and assembly created powerful pressures for further extensions of rights and the remedying of abuses and disadvantages through government action.

This had been foreseen by those liberals and conservatives who had opposed extending the franchise. They had feared that at worst a democratic regime would allow the rich to be despoiled of all their possessions by the poor and at best that it would create steady pressure towards collectivism in public policy through increases in public-spending programmes and general taxation. Whether or not socialist parties were elected into office all governments would be obliged under the pressure of a democratic electorate to adopt collectivist measures.[10] Liberal democracies would be ineluctably transformed into social democracies.

The programmes most associated with social-democratic regimes are those to combat unemployment and those that guarantee welfare by ensuring minimum standards of support for all citizens. Social democracy has been associated with a progressive enlargement of the public sector, whether measured by assets, spending, taxes or employment. The range of public responsibilities has been steadily expanded. The impulse behind such policies has been to mitigate the pressures towards inequality stemming from the way markets operate, although how far social-democratic regimes have succeeded in remedying inequality has been a matter of debate.[11]

The existence of a social-democratic regime does not ensure progress towards socialism or even greater equality in the final distribution of resources, but rather the mobilisation of pressure from below for state policies and programmes to correct extreme inequalities and disadvantage. Such pressures often coincided with pressures from above for state intervention to meet particular needs for the system as a whole that private initiative was unable or unwilling to supply.

The growing support for collectivism during the twentieth century across the political spectrum allowed accommodation to be reached eventually between established dominant interests and the interests of the new popular movements. In some countries social-democratic regimes emerged out of the strength of the organised working class. In others they developed despite the weakness or absence of such movements. But in almost all cases they represented some form of accommodation between the demands for political and economic democracy from below and the needs of capital.

In this way stable political regimes, many of them explicitly social democratic, emerged in most advanced Western capitalist states. A regime of accumulation based on Fordist principles of mass production and mass consumption only reaches its full potential upon the establishment of political mechanisms to ensure a high and constant level of demand and mechanisms to transfer many of the social costs of accumulation to public agencies. In many states governments also explicitly accepted responsibility for maintaining the legitimacy of the entire social order. Recognition on both the left and the right that such extensions in the range of responsibilities for government had become desirable and necessary greatly smoothed the path of internal accommodation and allowed the consolidation of a durable policy consensus over a wide range.

In many European countries the popular forces most identified with social-democratic programmes were the parties and trade unions of the organised industrial working class. But collectivist measures in economic and social policy were also sponsored by many other political agencies. In states where the industrial working class was less strong and less well organised many of the programmes and policies that elsewhere would be termed social democratic were still introduced.

One of the consequences of a social-democratic regime has been the raising of expectations about entitlements and rights. The claiming of new rights and the defence of existing ones becomes an essential part of politics. Those groups denied rights or discriminated against have the opportunity to organise and mobilise to demand them. The ideal of universal participation makes it difficult to defend the exclusion of such groups.[12] Nevertheless powerful forces can mobilise to prevent it. The full development of social democracy is heavily constrained by the existence of racial, gender and religious divisions.

The extent to which the goals of social democracy were achieved varied greatly between states, but most social democrats continued to believe that the drift of events was in their direction. This was all changed by the events of the 1970s, which saw the emergence of a pervasive crisis of social democracy. The authority of national governments was rapidly eroded, and the institutions and assumptions of social democracy came under sustained assault from both the right and the left. The impact was uneven. The states that were hit hardest were those whose economies were relatively weak.

The crisis of hegemony that threatened social democracy in the 1970s was precipitated by the exhaustion of the Fordist regime of accumulation and the new instabilities in the world system. The global crisis reinforced the challenges that were already under way to the authority of the state in three main areas: citizenship rights, representation and economic management.

Citizenship

The challenge to the social-democratic concept of citizenship took the form of attempts to block the extension of equal civil, political and social rights to all citizens. This attacked one of the fundamental ideas of the social-democratic state.

Demands for equal rights encountered resistance because
they threatened some of the most entrenched relationships of
power in society. The reason why such demands came to be
raised was partly the working out of the logic of social democracy and partly the impact on national economies of the global Fordism of the 1950s. The need for supplies of new labour
led to large-scale migration from Third World to metropolitan countries and a major expansion in the employment of
women. At the same time a capitalism based upon mass consumption facilitated the development of new leisure interests
and lifestyles, many of them incompatible with the maintenance of a traditional family structure and traditional sexual
division of labour.[13]

The cultural explosion that took place in the 1960s created a powerful feminist challenge to the patriarchal family
and to the continued subordination of women throughout
society. It brought into question for the first time one of the
unquestioned assumptions of the postwar order – the nature
of the family structure. This posed unwelcome questions for
many social democrats in all parties since to take the claims
of the women's movement seriously would involve radical
reform of both state and civil society.

Faced by this challenge most social-democratic parties
moved very slowly indeed, but the mere threat that they
might was sufficient to galvanise a movement in defence of
the patriarchal family that focused upon permissiveness,
crime and education. The family was presented as under
threat and its authority breaking down as a result of social-
democratic doctrines and policies that were undermining
standards in schools and destroying the ethic of hard work,
personal responsibility and abstinence.

Racial divisions have also contributed to the erosion of
the social-democratic hegemonic project in several countries. The large movement of migrant labour that played
such an important part in the postwar boom introduced permanent ethnic minorities into a number of countries. Some,
such as the UK, had previously had few ethnic divisions. A
key political issue became the citizenship status of these
workers and their dependants, whether they possessed full
citizenship or were only 'guest workers' and therefore what

rights they could claim when they encountered discrimination. Their demands were fiercely contested by anti-
immigrant groups within the dominant white communities.

The threat to the patriarchal family and the white nation
in the 1960s seemed to be expressed most openly once
women's groups and black groups became active in press-
ing their demands for equal rights. The real threat came
from processes central to the Fordist regime of accumulation. The conservative wing of the New Right, however,
was not disposed to make the world economy a scapegoat.
Social democracy was a far more tempting target. Social-
democratic politicians might not actively encourage the
aspirations of either feminists or immigrants, but they were
seen to be tolerant towards them. They conceded the case in
principle, pleading expediency as to why faster progress
could not be made. Many on the right concluded that the
social-democratic state now offered no protection against
the forces that were attacking the patriarchal family and the
white nation; indeed often its agencies seemed in alliance
with those very forces.

In several countries the attack on social democracy first
took shape through an emphasis on the politics of gender,
race, national identity, and social and public order. The failure of social-democratic administrations to keep order in
the schools, to control immigration, to halt the rise in crime
and to protect the family fuelled growing discontent among
vocal minorities.[14] This erosion of the consensus on citizenship occurred before the dislocation in the world economy
had damaged the engine of postwar prosperity and discredited the techniques and many of the institutions and policies
by means of which Western capitalist societies had been
managed. Once this occurred the politics of race and the
politics of gender took on further significance.

The extent of the world crisis of accumulation meant that
all governments needed to achieve a major internal redistribution of resources. Those with least political power were
most vulnerable. Within the working class the groups that
stood to lose most were women, blacks and particular
regional communities. The costs of restructuring the economy, however, could be loaded much more easily on to such

, if the political credibility of their case for equal
had first been destroyed. If social-democratic arguments retained their dominant place in public debate on
welfare provision it would be less easy to ignore the claims of
blacks, women and other disadvantaged groups for assistance and subsidy from the state.

The advent of recession therefore has made the onslaught
on social democracy more rather than less necessary for the
new conservatism. A central goal has been to discredit the
social-democratic concept of universal citizenship rights,
guaranteed and enforced through public agencies, and to
replace it by a concept of citizenship rights achieved
through property ownership and participation in markets.
In this way a class of sub-citizens is created, consisting of
those who, being unable to participate in markets, are
forced to remain dependent upon the state. Such dependency becomes a stigma and allows the demands of these
groups to be disregarded.[15]

Representation

The second challenge to social democracy arose over the
representation of interests and the determination of the
public interest. One of the permanent problems for any
state is how to mobilise consent. During the 1970s the
characteristic social-democratic modes of representation
began to appear inadequate for the task of legitimating the
complex ensemble of agencies, institutions, powers and
responsibilities that make up the modern state. As the size of
the state sector has expanded, so the need has grown to find
ways of ensuring that all powerful interests and bodies of
opinion are given appropriate channels of representation,
so that the legitimacy of the state is maintained and the
implementation of policy decisions is made as effective as
possible.

The traditional route for achieving this has been through
elected legislatures or parliaments. By choosing representatives the people can exert control over the laws that are
passed and make the executive accountable for its actions.

The complexity of modern government business, however, makes scrutiny of the executive by elected representatives exceptionally difficult to perform, while the rise of the party has severely limited the scope for independent judgement. In Britain, for example, it has transformed MPs into supporters of the executive rather than representatives of their constituents.

The deficiencies of party government either as an effective check upon increasingly powerful executives or as a reliable representative of volatile electorates have been frequently rehearsed.[16] Reform of parliaments and electoral systems are often canvassed but everyone is aware that the root of the problem is the relative power of executives and legislatures, which executives are little disposed to change. The imbalance that has developed renders most of the traditional accounts of democratic government inoperative.

A second form of representation is the system known as corporatism. Instead of attempting to aggregate the opinions and votes of all individual electors, representation of interests is performed through organised interests and their direct contact with government agencies. By discussing in detail the content of new legislation with the parties most directly concerned governments can hope to ensure successful implementation of their policies.[17]

In this mode of representation accountability to the people is indirect but more effective. It takes place, however, mostly in secret and works through continual compromises and the achievement of a consensus on the limits of acceptable policy, for which politicians must then achieve support in their parties and among voters through the use of modern media methods of persuasion. Parliamentary elections and parties become auxiliaries to the great engine of corporate power, and the compromises worked out between the representatives of labour, capital and the central bureaucracy.

Systems of corporate representation grew up or were installed in most social-democratic regimes. They eased the problem of governing but they never completely solved the problem of legitimacy. They were also required to deliver more and more. At the extreme, as in Britain, the strain became too great and corporatist structures collapsed.

The only alternatives to legitimating policies through the endorsement of organised interests and the media is either to return to endorsing them through party and parliament, or by instituting a presidency above both legislators and special interests. The charismatic president speaks to and on behalf of the people directly.

Corporatist modes of representation were held responsible for many of the failures of economic management in the 1970s. They had given vetos on policy to special interests and were too inflexible in coping with the demands of adjustment to the changes in the world economy.[18] Conservative critics of corporatism argued that it produced weak government. They wanted a new, strong state that did not need to bargain with organised interests. They wished to assert a national interest beyond the sectional interests of the pressure groups and lobbyists. Restoring the authority of the state was a priority. The way to achieve it was through strong and decisive political leadership, and an end to compromises and concessions.

Economic management

The most direct challenge to social democracy came over the conduct of economic policy. If there had been one boast of postwar social democrats it was that mass unemployment had been eliminated and that the kind of problems that had plagued capitalist economies were things of the past. The discovery of the secret of perpetual growth was thought to make possible a long-term strategy for redistributing resources and making equality of opportunity a reality.[19]

The policy of full employment and the major new welfare programmes were regarded as major reforms that had permanently altered the character of capitalism. The enlargement of the public sector, the safeguarding of the private sector, the extension of public ownership and social security, the widening of public responsibilities and powers, the guaranteeing of political, civil and social rights for all citizens – these provided a domestic package that social democrats and many politicians from all parties thought secure against attack from either the left or the right.

What was ignored was how dependent the edifice of social democracy was on continued good performance by the world economy and how that good performance of the 1950s and 1960s was much less dependent on Keynesian techniques of economic management than many had supposed.[20] The ability of Keynesian measures to maintain full employment depended crucially on the political strength of social-democratic institutions. When that strength was available, during the 1940s and 1950s, a Keynesian programme for unemployment was not needed. When it was needed, social democracy was no longer strong enough to deliver it.

The Keynesian approach to economic management was assailed by the new doctrine of monetarism. Monetarists argued that the Keynesians not only had an incorrect model of how the economy worked but also that their policies were leading to a progressive acceleration of inflation.[21] The question of inflation and the inability of social-democratic regimes to control it was taken as symptomatic of the policy stance of social-democratic governments. They were presiding over an erosion of market disciplines and institutions such as sound money. The failure to control inflation by means of demand management in the late 1960s and early 1970s led many governments to experiment with increasingly strict controls on prices and incomes, often trying to use corporatist structures in a bid to win consent for the policies and to make them work.

During the 1970s full employment was formally subordinated to the control of inflation as a policy priority, and this victory of the new politics over the old was reinforced by the major restructuring of public sectors that accompanied it – with spending on many programmes being drastically reduced – and the attempts made to end universal entitlements and the provision of services on any basis other than ability to pay. The failure to maintain full employment and the principle of an expanding public sector greatly damaged confidence in social-democratic governments and cast doubt on whether social democracy as an ideal was any longer either achievable or desirable. In the 1970s there were many prepared to argue it was neither.

The crisis of the British ancien régime

The crisis of hegemony reviewed so far was an international crisis of the world political economy and of social democracy. But although there were common themes the forms these crises took in each country were heavily influenced by local institutions and historical structures. In Britain the crisis was exacerbated by the longer-term crisis of Britain's long-established political institutions, its ancien régime.

Three features of this ancien régime will be noted here. The first is the constitution.[22] Britain's uncodified constitution, with its doctrines of unlimited parliamentary sovereignty and the unitary state and its preservation of premodern institutions such as the Crown and the House of Lords, has been grafted on to a modern mass democracy, with its political parties, universal suffrage, vigorous civil society, professional bureaucracy and enlarged public sector. Liberalism, imperialism and Fabianism breathed fresh life into this remarkable political corpse for more than one hundred years, but with the faltering of all three visions for Britain in the 1970s questions of representation, accountability and competence, as well as the viability of preserving the United Kingdom as a multinational state, came to the fore.[23]

A second feature was Britain's role in the world. Under the ancien régime Whigs, Imperialists and Fabians had all fashioned their own version of Britain's imperial destiny, which reflected three hundred years of overseas expansion, colonisation, trade and investment. Many distinctive features of British economy and society, as well as the British state, come from this history and still shape its politics. The imperial phase may be over, but its legacies are powerful. These stem not just from Britain's formal empire of colonial possessions, but also from its informal empire of trade and investment. They have shaped the overseas orientation of many British institutions, the internationalisation of leading sectors of the British economy and key spending programmes such as defence. They have also left Britain poised uneasily between a European and an Atlanticist identity, between the new drive towards a regional European union and a global Anglo–America.[24]

A third feature was the relative decline of the British economy. Britain's eclipse as a great power and a world empire came to be seen as unavoidable. But the failure of the British economy to remain competitive was less expected and generated fierce debate as to the causes and remedies. Although the absolute wealth of Britain continued to grow, the experience of the elites was that they were administering an enterprise that was steadily becoming more enfeebled in comparison with Britain's main rivals. By the middle of the 1970s the resignation of many in the British elites to continued failure and genteel decline had become deep-seated.

This multifaceted crisis of Britain's ancien régime fused with the crisis of the world political economy and international social democracy to create a deep structural crisis of hegemony in Britain. Social democracy and the world political economy were blamed by the left and the right for problems that really derived from the structures and legacies of the old imperial constitutional state. It was in this conjuncture of legacies from the past and the problems of the present that the political project that became Thatcherism was conceived.

2

The New Right

Surely it is high time for us to cry from the rooftops that the intellectual foundations of socialism have all collapsed.

F. A. Hayek

Tracing the ideological origins of the Thatcherite project requires an exploration of the ideas and doctrines of the New Right. The new politics of the 1970s spawned many political movements and political programmes across the whole political spectrum. The most powerful and influential of these new forces has been labelled the New Right, although many question whether it is new and a few who find themselves labelled New Right question whether it is right. What the term certainly does not signify is either a unified movement or a coherent doctrine. A wide range of groups and ideas make up the New Right, and there are many internal divisions and conflicts.[1] The most important division, which is explored in this chapter, is between a liberal and a conservative tendency.

What all strands within the New Right shared, however, was the rejection of many of the ideas, practices and institutions that had characterised social-democratic regimes in Europe and the New Deal and Great Society programmes in the United States. The New Right was radical because it sought to undo much that had been constructed in the previous sixty years. New-Right thinkers questioned many of the assumptions that had become accepted for the conduct of public policy, while New-Right politicians sought to

34

build electoral and policy coalitions that challenged key institutions and key policies.

As a political programme the New Right has been closely identified with opposition to state involvement in the economy, or at least to the kind of state involvement that had become the norm in most advanced capitalist economies. They were fierce critics of Keynesian policies of economic management, and of high public expenditure on welfare. But New-Right politicians also became renowned as advocates of national discipline and strong defence. They argued that the programmes of both social democrats and socialists had been discredited by experience. Social-democratic policies had led to the morass of inflation, mass unemployment, excessive taxation and a swollen public sector. As the state became more and more interventionist so the authority of governments became progressively weaker in the face of powerful trade unions and other sectional interests.

The operation of social democracy itself therefore created a climate in which the foundations of social and public order were rapidly undermined, and the prospects increased of their restoration through authoritarian means. Many on the New Right in the apocalyptic climate of the 1970s believed that an authoritarian outcome to the crisis of hegemony was inevitable. The only question was whether the authoritarianism would be of the right or the left.

If it came from the left the immediate disorder would be suppressed but at grave long-term cost. An authoritarian government of the left would only create another inefficient, overmanned centrally controlled economy of the Soviet type.[2] What was needed was an authoritarian government of the right. Apart from the anarcho–capitalists on its libertarian fringe all strands of New-Right opinion believed that to preserve a free society and a free economy the authority of the state had to be restored.

The key doctrine of the New Right and the political project it has inspired is therefore the doctrine of the free economy and the strong state. Different meanings are attached to these two terms and they are given different weight by liberal and conservative tendencies within the New Right, as will be shown below. But what gives the New

Right a unity and helps to distinguish it from previous 'rights' is the combination of a traditional liberal defence of the free economy with a traditional conservative defence of state authority.[3]

The idea of a free economy and a strong state involves a paradox. The state is to be simultaneously rolled back and rolled forward. Non-interventionist and decentralised in some areas the state is to be highly interventionist and centralised in others. The New Right can appear by turns libertarian and authoritarian, populist and elitist. This ambiguity is not an accident. It derives in part from the fact that the New Right has two major strands: a liberal tendency, which argues the case for a freer, more open and more competitive economy, and a conservative tendency, which is more interested in restoring social and political authority throughout society. What makes matters more confusing is that not only do those within the New Right regard the importance of these tendencies differently, but those who have written on the New Right often concentrate upon one of them to the exclusion of the other.[4]

This in part reflects the different meaning the term came to have in different countries. In the United States the New Right became strongly identified with the network of single-issue groups that mushroomed during the 1970s and 1980s, campaigning on issues such as abortion, and positive discrimination.[5] In Britain the New Right was used most often to denote monetarist and free-market economic arguments. But in another usage, which became more pronounced during the 1970s, it was used to refer to a set of arguments and movements around race, gender and culture.[6]

It is important to avoid making the New Right an omnibus term for every political development on the right. But a fairly broad definition is probably inescapable. The aspect of the New Right that is of greatest interest and importance for the analysis of a political phenomenon such as Thatcherism is that it was not just a set of doctrines, it developed into a political movement that united diverse ideological strands, created a discourse about strategy, organised interest coalitions, formulated policy programmes and ultimately helped elect governments that were pledged to a distinctive New-

Right agenda. The New Right made the impact it did because of the creativity and skill of its political leadership, and its long-term impact will be judged by the extent to which the assault on the institutions and policies of social democracy in the 1980s was successful and allowed the New Right to determine the political agenda for the 1990s.

What is new in ideological terms about the New Right is that during its ascendancy it was rare to find politicians who supported order and authority and who were also protectionists and collectivists. The social-imperialist wing of modern conservatism has retreated to the margins of right-wing politics; the only substantial remaining manifestations of it are the fascist parties. Conservatives have appropriated the liberal ideas of a market order and a free economy, adapting them to conform to the requirements of conservative discourses about politics. There are many liberals and libertarians associated with the New Right, and many of the New Right's most distinctive ideas have been contributed by them.[7] But as a political phenomenon the New Right has been predominantly a conservative movement, to the embarrassment of some of the intellectuals who contributed to its early development.

The original sense of the doctrine of the free market and the strong state took its meaning from a liberal discourse. The liberal conception of a free economy denoted a spontaneous harmony of interests generated through the voluntary exchanges of free autonomous individuals within a framework of agreed rules. A state was needed, to safeguard the order spontaneously generated by the market, but a state minimal in its functions and limited in its powers. Although the state was to be limited, however, it needed to be strong in carrying out its functions. Policing the market order required vigilance and firm action to enforce laws impartially so that competition might be fair, exchange voluntary and the fruits of enterprise secure. Liberals wanted a state that was both limited and strong.

Limited is not the first word that suggests itself to describe the defence budget of the United States in the 1980s. Yet the Reagan administration was considered to be a New-Right one, deploying a discourse that stressed the desirability of limited government. The doctrine of the minimal state was not considered any obstacle to unlimited defence budgets.

Contrast this with nineteenth-century liberal discourses. Many liberals, such as Cobden, wished to limit public expenditure on armaments and defence as much as any other form of public expenditure. The military budget was regarded as highly wasteful and an abuse of the state's powers. The strong state wanted by radical liberals had nothing in common with the strong state of the old imperial states of Europe, which were dominated by their landowning classes and inspired by dreams of military conquest and territorial aggrandisement. Liberals saw the spread of the principles and practice of the free economy and the establishment of economic interdependence throughout the world as the means of breaking down national boundaries and national rivalries and securing peace.

What changed in the twentieth century is that, starting with liberal imperialists, many supporters of the free economy have also been supporters of large and permanent defence sectors. The conversion of the British Conservatives to free-market arguments was assisted by the increasing interdependence of the capitalist world that led to a decisive shift of conservative opinion in all countries away from national protection towards military and economic cooperation under United States leadership after 1945. The advent of the New Right in the 1970s marked a further stage in this development. For many British conservatives the free economy came to signify not just a national but an international economic space. Its defence was indissolubly tied up with preserving the leading role played by the United States and with maintaining strong military forces against the threat of Soviet aggression.

The free economy and the strong state

The doctrine of a free economy and a strong state is therefore capable of several different interpretations, but at its heart is a conception of the political and economic institutions appropriate to a free society. The right balance between force and consent is always a political question. The state may be considered strong because of the means of repression at its disposal and its willingness to use them. But more durable strength comes from widespread acceptance of the legitimacy of the institutions and policies of the state, with force only used as a last resort. What the doctrine of the free economy and the strong state affirms is that the use of force is justified when it is employed to defeat and contain those interests, organisations and individuals that threaten the survival of the free economy, either by flouting its rules or resisting the outcomes that flow from market exchanges.

If the state makes the protection of the institutions of the free economy its priority then it creates the basis for its own legitimacy. Once all illegitimate functions and responsibilities are stripped from it the state is no longer the weak state of social democracy, overburdened by ever-widening responsibilities and infested by special interests, which seek to use the political process to portray their sectional interest as the public interest. It can concentrate on defending what is the true public interest – upholding impartially the rules of the market order.

The theorists of the New Right are quite clear about the correct balance between the strong state and the free economy in their ideal world, but they face the difficulty of how that ideal is to be realised in the world they actually inhabit. They would have liked to be conservatives but they were obliged to become radicals. They saw their task as struggling against the forces that had gravely undermined the market order and which if left unchecked would destroy it. The existing state had to be reformed in order to permit the restoration of the rules, the institutions and the culture of the free economy. Since the condition of the social-democratic regime of social democracy was judged to be so serious, brought about by its high-spending policies and modes of intervention, radical measures were necessary for recovery. But success depended on a party pledged to a New-Right agenda first obtaining a mandate for reform in a political market corrupted by decades of state intervention, and then carrying it through with the assistance of the agencies of the extended state.

The New Right had to believe simultaneously in the malign and perverse effects of democratic politics on the free economy, and in the possibility of using that same democratic politics and that same interventionist state to reverse the process of creeping socialism.[8] This created considerable tensions between New-Right theory and the practice of New-Right governments, and also produced a range of different arguments on the balance between force and consent in the conception of the strong state.

The state had to be strong firstly to unwind the coils of social democracy and welfarism that had fastened around the free economy; secondly to police the market order; thirdly to make the economy more productive; and fourthly to uphold social and political authority. The first argument commanded agreement throughout the New Right. To restore a free economy firm and decisive action was necessary to cut public-spending programmes and taxes, to privatise public assets and public services, and to abolish interventionist and regulatory agencies. The idea of a radical rupture in public policy, and therefore the need to be prepared to deal with resistance whether from the central bureaucracy or from organised interests, were central themes in New-Right deliberation during the 1970s. There was talk in Britain in Margaret Thatcher's circle of advisers of the need for the next Conservative government to 'prepare for a confrontation with the trade union Left'.[9]

Implementing a radical programme was seen to require a power struggle. The state had to be prepared to take firm measures to reduce state spending and state subsidies, and then had to be determined enough to resist the challenges to its authority that came from those who were disadvantaged by the changes. The political calculations involved in fighting a major strike such as the British coal strike in 1984–5 were complex, but all variants of New-Right opinion were agreed that this was the kind of struggle that had to be won if there was to be any chance of implementing other New-Right policies.

This need to clear a space for the implementation of radical policies was a constant theme in New-Right writing. The state had to be strong in order to reverse the trend towards collectivism, which had become established, and to break the resistance of all special interests, including the new class of public-sector professionals who were likely to oppose the radical policies of a New-Right government. Trials of strength with major interests and entrenched lobbies were welcomed because they provided opportunities to assert the authority of the government and to signal its intentions.

Reducing the size of the state and the range of its responsibilities commanded assent from all parts of the New Right, and it is hard to see how this could have been accomplished without the use of strong government. But the other justifications for a strong state were more controversial even within the New Right. Policing the market order means maintaining a central authority strong enough to maintain formal exchange equality between all economic agents. At a minimum this requires the enforcement of laws that protect property and persons and enforced property rights. But more controversially it also legitimates action by the state to suppress private coercion, monopoly and discrimination. If formal exchange equality does not arise spontaneously – if for example there is persistent discrimination against individuals on the basis of gender, race or religion – does this justify the state intervening to ensure that free and equal exchanges can take place? Few on the New Right will so argue. Economic liberals, who might be expected to be most sympathetic, wish to protect existing property rights, whatever their origin, but they are much more wary about the use of state power to extend rights.[10] Their suspicion of the state generally overcomes their desire to see the basis of the market order extended. Conservatives have fewer problems. There is no good reason in their view why claims of abstract rights should be allowed to undermine important social and political institutions.[11]

A further difficulty is how involved the state should become in policing the market order. There is a conflict between protecting the private sector from state interference and ensuring that market rules are properly enforced within the private sector. The degree of regulation implied by the latter can be considerable. The Thatcher government faced criticism in that by denationalising some public-sector companies, such as telephone and gas, it was creating new private-sector monopolies. The reluctance of the Thatcher government to report mergers to the Monopoly Commission and to introduce statutory regulation of the activities of the City of London also indicated that the government was less interested in policing the market order than in enlarging the private sector and giving companies free rein within it. A liberal state that is weak in regulating private capital and enforcing the rights of market agents may lose legitimacy. Its ability to protect the public interest will be questioned if in practice it adopts a policy of laissez-faire towards whatever is done in the private sector.

The third justification for a strong state concerns efficiency. The rolling back of collectivism is not enough. What is also required is a forceful and imaginative state policy aimed at modernising the economy by speeding up the pace of change and making the whole of society more competitive and enterprising. On this view markets are a valuable instrument of policy for forcing through change. They are not valued primarily because they guarantee individual rights but because they offer the best way of allocating resources, providing incentives and stimulating growth. The overriding goals of economic policy become efficiency and modernisation. Other questions such as the size of enterprises or the rights of particular groups or whether government should be centralised or decentralised are subordinated to them. Reform of institutions such as the central bureaucracy and the education system become priorities.

This view is highly interventionist. It is not concerned merely with using state power to break resistance during a process of disengagement from the commitments of social democracy. It seeks to reshape the institutional framework of the free economy. Citizens have to be forced to be free and enterprising, otherwise there is no guarantee they will be so. By seeking to overhaul many existing institutions in radical ways, such views come into conflict with the conservative disposition to defend existing institutions and established privileges. This disagreement produced some of the greatest conflicts inside the Thatcher government. If the government proved laissez-faire in its attitude to the private sector, it was far from laissez-faire, at least in its aspirations, towards state and public institutions. In this respect the New Right was a radical and a modernising force, capable of inspiring policies that were far removed from the popular conception of laissez-faire and involved the Thatcher government in highly interventionist and centralist policies.

The fourth argument for a strong state is the conservative argument. A free economy is seen as a prop for a strong state instead of the other way round. The authority of the state is all-important and no principles or policy goals, such as the sanctity of individual rights or the need to maximise economic efficiency, can be allowed to override it. The task of the state is to ensure that authority is upheld throughout society because this is the basis upon which its own authority rests. Private property is an important bulwark of social authority and it is for this reason that a free economy must be preserved. But there is disagreement over whether social institutions like the family comprise a private domain from which the state should be excluded or whether the incursions of collectivism have so weakened key institutions that an interventionist policy to restore traditional standards of morality and behaviour is justified.[12]

Sanctioning widespread social engineering, even in the cause of restoring authority and traditional standards throughout society, was not welcome to many Conservatives. They hoped it would not be necessary. Despite the long night of collectivism in the twentieth century, many of them clung to the hope that the character of the nation was still sound. If only the grip of collectivism and social democracy could be prised loose the vigorous virtues of enterprise, patriotism and independence would reassert themselves. But pessimists in the Conservative-Party ranks did not expect the poison of dependence and alien doctrines to be expelled easily or swiftly. A long period of vigilance and struggle would be necessary, as would the reestablishment of a strong state prepared to act illiberally to stamp out undesirable behaviour and attitudes, to rebuild social and political authority and to reeducate the people in the duties and values expected of them.

Despite their disagreements all strands of the New Right accept that one of the main reasons for seeking the restoration of state authority is the maintenance of a free economy. This linking of conservatism and liberalism in a common programme owes much to political changes that have come about through the development of the world economy. As economic interdependence through an international division of labour has become more pronounced, so powerful domestic lobbies have developed in every country to preserve the international order and the openness of the world economy. The autonomy of national governments has decreased and the attractiveness and feasibility of autarchy as an option for national policy has weakened.

The commitment to economic liberalism was much stronger in the 1980s than it was in the 1930s. The breakdown of the world economy in the 1930s destroyed faith in capitalism and gave a significant boost to collectivist doctrines of both the right and the left. In the 1970s and 1980s, however, it was these collectivist doctrines and institutions that came under attack. The new politics that emerged had a double thrust – on the one side the upholding of the principle of the international economic order and cooperation, on the other the unceasing effort to modernise each national economy to make it more effective in international competition. The doctrine of the free economy and the strong state not only expresses the strange partnership of liberalism and conservatism that finally flowered at this time, but also the core elements of state policy as it developed during the period of slow growth and recession in the 1970s and 1980s.

Capitalism is the most dynamic and productive of all economic systems known to history. But it must still depend upon institutions that the market itself cannot generate spontaneously. This leaves a major role for government. Each national government is obliged to maintain relatively open markets but must be prepared to cope with the effects of openness on its domestic economy. These pressures become acute in a period of recession. It is not only protected economies that require strong states. Defending a position within the world market requires a commitment to openness to ensure prosperity and to intervention to ensure competitiveness.

The doctrines and the political movements that have been grouped under the label New Right have revived many old liberal and conservative ideas. But the New Right does not represent a simple return to a nineteenth-century politics of liberal political economy and Victorian values. It is an expression of the new politics of the 1970s. The quest for a free economy and a strong state is a response to the changed circumstances of the world economy and the internal disarray of social democracy. This was how the New Right themselves saw it. Their doctrines were not intended to recreate some lost golden age but to make the free economy the new utopia that could guide the development of contemporary industrial societies.

The liberal New Right

The liberal tendency in the New Right is itself a broad spectrum. It embraces monetarists and supply-siders, followers of the Austrian school and anarcho-capitalists, students of public choice and public welfare, and apostles of privatisation and deregulation. The causes espoused in recent years by free-market economists include strict money-supply targets to reduce inflation, negative income tax, floating exchange rates, indexation, constitutional rules to enforce balanced budgets and limit government spending, abolition of trade-union legal immunities, reduction of income tax and abolition of progressive tax rates, privatisation of all enterprises in state hands, introduction of education vouchers, private health insurance in place of state support, and many more.[13]

This writing represented a major revival of the themes and concerns of liberal political economy. The liberal New Right developed theories of how the capitalist economy functions, theories of the political system and the policy-making process, and theories of social institutions. On this basis they felt able to make very precise recommendations about which government policies were needed to sustain and develop the market economy and which policies injured it. They developed a coherent and plausible economic strategy, which became extremely influential, and helped shape the economic policies of several governments in responding to the recession and the restructuring of the world economy.

The central question for theorists of the liberal New Right is always: what are the conditions under which markets function best? It is taken as axiomatic that markets are inherently superior to any other way of organising human societies. The problem is seen to be creating the conditions in which markets can function by removing whatever obstacles exist or may arise to their operation. The economies presided over by social-democratic regimes are clearly market economies, but in the view of the New Right they are fettered and unable to realise their full potential and in danger of being transformed into something else entirely, the command economies of state socialism. To counter this the New Right have campaigned for sound money, a major reduction in taxation and public expenditure, and a programme of deregulation and privatisation.

Sound money

The call for the restoration of sound money was central to the New Right's criticism of social democracy. It was the economic policy issue upon which the New Right first made a major impact. The doctrine of monetarism, which began to be advanced in the 1960s by Milton Friedman and others, was a restatement of the quantity theory of money and a major theoretical and policy challenge to Keynesianism. The intellectual arguments about how the economy works have not been settled; indeed the divisions between proponents of different macroeconomic theories have tended to widen[14] and much doubt has been thrown on the theoretical and empirical foundations of monetarism. But what gave monetarism its ascendancy was the marked deterioration in economic performance in the 1970s. Governments no longer seemed able to manage economies successfully. The acceleration of inflation in the late 1960s was followed by a steep rise in unemployment after 1973, which undermined confidence in Keynesian methods and techniques.

The monetarist critique was available and plausible. It was widely disseminated through academic and media channels and it began to be voiced by leading politicians.

What gave monetarism its practical importance, however, was not its coherence as a doctrine nor its academic credentials nor even its conquest of the financial press. What was decisive was the breakdown of the regime of fixed exchange rates in 1971–2. Keynesian economic management could be practised either within closed economies or in an international economy in which the degree of openness remained limited. One of the critical tests of openness was the exchange rate. If rates were fixed and the exchanges successfully policed by the central banks, then the limits within which demand could be managed in any domestic economy were tightly fixed. The money supply was necessarily under firm control. Overexpansion of the money supply would result in a balance-of-payments crisis and an exchange-rate crisis. The agreement by governments to maintain fixed exchange rates and to devalue only in exceptional circumstances ensured relatively stable monetary conditions throughout the Western economy during the period of the long boom (1951–67).

Once the system of fixed exchange rates became unsustainable due to the financial weakness of the United States, the major external constraint on domestic financial prudence was removed. The opportunity was created for an unlimited inflation, as countries sought to expand domestic demand in order to sustain employment and prosperity while allowing their currencies to depreciate to keep their costs in line with their competitors. Such a situation did begin to unfold in 1973, a year of very rapid growth throughout the Western economy, fuelled by large injections of domestic demand and increases in money supply. Prices in certain sectors began to rise rapidly.

At the end of the year oil prices were quadrupled by OPEC, which punctured the bubble of speculation and optimism and triggered a recession. Output began to fall but the inflationary pressure the monetary expansion had created was still increasing. The adoption of a new set of international monetary rules became urgent to prevent a plunge into depression and the collapse of the international economy. No return to fixed exchange rates was possible given the political disunity of the leading Western powers and the undermining of the United States' economic hegemony. But what did prove possible with the cooperation of national governments, often assisted by pressure from the IMF, was the adoption of monetarist policies to contain inflation and satisfy the international financial markets.[15]

Formal abandonment of expansionist demand management policies, the publishing of strict money-supply targets and the announcement of major cuts in public-expenditure programmes became the tests applied by the financial markets to the policies of national governments. Maintaining the confidence of the financial markets was critical for maintaining the value of the national currency. The price of remaining within the international economy came to be acceptance of the sound money policies imposed by the financial markets, although the vulnerability of national economies to dictation by the markets varied, depending in part on the character and extent of their integration into the world economy and in part on the strength of corporatism within their domestic politics.

No one appointed the financial markets to the role of makers and breakers of governments. It arose simply through the way these markets themselves worked in an era of recession and floating exchange rates. It was made possible by the huge volume of mobile liquid capital and by the ever-increasing sophistication and integration of the financial circuit.

The imposition of sound money policies on national governments in the mid-1970s gave an enormous boost to those domestic lobbies who were arguing for the adoption of monetarism. The international political and financial climate was no longer favourable to national Keynesianism, and those countries – such as France after 1981 – that tried to practise it experienced a major flight of capital and an exchange crisis. Such outcomes were generally sufficient to return errant countries to the new orthodoxy.

It was convenient for monetarists that their campaign for a basic change in the methods of macroeconomic management should coincide with the external pressure for sound money imposed by the financial markets. But monetarists' belief in sound money was much more than just a technical argument for how best to reduce inflation in a time of recession. Monetarists believed that the full employment objective of postwar stabilisation policy was fundamentally misconceived. Trying to achieve it was leading to accelerating inflation and the undermining of one of the essential requirements of a market order – the role of money as a stable medium of exchange and store of value.[16]

Monetarists argued that the control of inflation should become the top priority of any domestic stabilisation policy, regardless of any increase in unemployment that might be caused. In the years before the recession monetarists predicted that the unemployment that would be created by applying monetarist policies would be small and transitional, the unavoidable price that had to be paid to put the economy back on a sound footing. But some New-Right economists were already recognising that a major restructuring of the world economy was in prospect and predicted that very high levels of unemployment might be experienced for a long period unless radical measures were taken not merely to control inflation but also to tackle many of the distortions that had crept into the market economy.

The key political point that monetarists made against Keynesians was that maintaining the fundamentals of the market economy was far more important than trying to ensure particular market outcomes. No monetarist ever said that full employment was not desirable. But the pursuit of full employment could endanger the free economy if, for example, a government decided to introduce controls on wages and prices in a bid to suppress the inflationary effects of its management of demand. Unemployment was preferable if that was the price that had to be paid to prevent a creeping politicisation of the economy and the suspension of markets in the determination of wages and prices.

Kalecki had argued at the beginning of the Keynesian era that if full employment were accepted as a reform within capitalist societies it would tilt the balance of power significantly towards labour, since it would remove one of the main levers by which government policy was kept within parameters acceptable to the business community. Effective measures to reduce unemployment had always produced a crisis of confidence in the financial markets. Confidence was restored when the measures were dropped. Acceptance by the business community of measures to make full employment permanent meant dispensing with the discipline on the workforce that was imposed by the threat of unemployment.[17]

Many economists have argued that it is a mistake to attribute the high levels of employment in the postwar period to Keynesianism. There would have been a low level of unemployment almost regardless of the stance of macro-economic policy. The political and economic reconstruction of the Western world that took place under American guidance in the 1940s saw the decisive defeat of those political forces that wished to extend social democracy and national Keynesianism. The regimes that emerged from this period represented compromises between the demands of organised labour and the needs of capital. Some advances were registered but the international order that was established ensured that these gains would be limited. How limited was only revealed in the 1970s when the return of mass unemployment was seen as signalling the end of Keynesianism rather than the occasion for its application. The traditional doctrine of sound finance in the new fashionable guise of monetarism reasserted itself. Keynesianism when it was tried was not needed and when it was needed was not tried.

The importance of sound money is acknowledged by all New-Right economists. A stable medium of exchange and store of value is essential for markets to function. If the commodity that is used as money becomes unstable rational calculation becomes much more difficult and in many instances impossible, exchange starts to break down and all manner of distortions, such as speculation and the search for hedges against inflation, creep in. Inflation makes market outcomes appear even more of a lottery than they in fact are, and this can have a corrosive effect on many of the values and attitudes, such as trust and honesty, that are essential for the smooth working of an exchange economy. Stable prices are therefore the foundation for prosperity. They do not guarantee prosperity but they make prosperity possible.

There is considerable dispute, however, within the New Right as to the means by which sound money is best achieved, and also as to the priority that should be given to it in relation to other New-Right objectives. Three important debates have been carried on: between monetarists and Austrians; between advocates of the gold standard and floating exchange rates; and between monetarists and supply-siders.

The protagonists in the first debate were Milton Friedman and F. A. Hayek, two of the most influential New-Right theorists and publicists.[18] Friedman quite early established himself as the leading exponent of monetarism, while Hayek is the most prominent representative of the Austrian school and is a veteran of ideological struggles stretching back to the 1930s. Hayek has never called himself a monetarist, and has important disagreements with both Friedman's methods of analysis and with his conclusions.

Hayek attaches no less importance than Friedman to the problem of inflation. He wrote trenchant accounts of the dangers it posed and of the follies of Keynesian demand management. But he was strongly critical of the gradualist methods proposed by many monetarists for squeezing inflation out of an economy. This method involved devising a financial strategy that would set targets for key monetary indicators. They would be reduced each year until inflation had disappeared. Hayek argued that such a strategy would take too long and would allow hostile political forces time to organise to dilute or overturn the policy. Spreading the unemployment associated with a return to financial discipline over several years would make any government in a democracy vulnerable to attack from the opposition parties. The better way, Hayek argued, would be to be bold from the outset, abolishing inflation at a stroke by introducing a complete reform of the currency, as Germany did in 1923. The immediate level of unemployment would be severe because of the scale of bankruptcies. But the recovery, Hayek believed, would be extremely swift and it would take place from the outset on the foundation of stable money.

A second controversy has centred on the rival merits of the gold standard and floating exchange rates.[19] Partisans of the former have always argued that the world economy can

only enjoy lasting financial discipline if there is an objective foundation for the exchange of currencies that is not
open to political manipulation. Former admirers of the gold
standard, such as the long-serving governor of the Bank of
England, Montagu Norman, thought that one of its main
advantages was that it was politician proof. It provided an
automatic mechanism for ensuring that the domestic price
level of each country participating in international trade
remained relatively stable, and that deficits and surpluses on
the balance of payments were rapidly corrected.

For supporters of the gold standard the postwar gold
exchange standard, which linked currencies to the dollar
and the dollar to gold, provided many of the advantages of
the gold-standard system, but it depended heavily on the
ability of the United States to underwrite it. The breakdown
of this system after sustained pressure on the dollar came
when the dollar's convertibility into gold was suspended in
1971. This obliged all currencies to float against one
another, and supporters of the gold standard freely proph-
esied that the removal of external constraint would produce
a major inflation.

They were not mistaken. The supporters of the gold
standard, however, were very much in a minority in the New
Right. Far more in evidence were the supporters of floating
exchange rates. Economists such as Milton Friedman and
politicians such as Enoch Powell were advocates of floating
exchange rates in the early 1960s, and even some long-
standing advocates of a gold standard, including Hayek,
changed their minds.[20] The reason is that, desirable though
a gold-standard system might be for an international market
order, few on the New Right believe that the political conditions for its reintroduction can be realised. The only feasible
system would be a modified form of the gold exchange
standard, but there is no single national currency that is
able to form the linchpin of this system in the way that
the dollar used to do, and besides many of the New Right
feel that there are some major drawbacks. It gives too
much power to central banks and imposes a straitjacket on
the world economy that may hinder its restructuring and
development.[21]

The advantage of floating exchange rates is that they establish a market for currencies and allow buyers and sellers to
determine their price. Provided that governments adopt
monetarist policies internally there will be no reason for continual currency depreciation or for inflation to accelerate.
The system of floating exchange rates relies on internationalisation of monetary disciplines by national governments, but
in any case the way in which the financial markets operate
severely penalises any country that does not follow sound
money policies.

Hayek carried this argument still further by suggesting
that the most effective way of ensuring internal financial
discipline was not by entrusting it to some regulatory body
such as a central bank but by allowing a free market in all
currencies. This would mean extending the reach of the
international financial markets into every national economy by ending each national government's jealously
guarded monopoly over the issue of the legal form of
money. If all national currencies become legal tender, citizens would choose to hold their savings and even make
their transactions in those currencies that are expected to
keep their value best. The success of a government's stabilisation policy would no longer be judged infrequently and
haphazardly at the time of a general election. It would be
subject to a daily plebiscite. The good money would drive
out the bad.[22]

Supply-side economics

A third debate that developed within the New Right concerned the rival merits of monetarism and supply-side policies.[23] Supply-siders did not dispute the importance of
sound money, but they claimed that far too much attention
had been paid to the task of restoring financial stability and
not enough to the problem of getting the economy moving
again. They gave priority to reawakening enterprise and
restoring incentives rather than to rebuilding the monetary
circuits that underpin exchange. They urged major reductions in public expenditure and taxation as the priority for
economic policy, because they believed that it is the high

taxes required by social democracy to finance its programmes that was stifling enterprise, depressing productivity
and leading to high inflation and high unemployment.

Supply-siders argued that what was of real importance was
creating a successful capitalist economy. Central to capitalism in their view was not money but enterprise and production. The task was to liberate energies by cutting taxes and
deregulating economic activity. Then the budget would balance and prices would stabilise if only production could be
stimulated sufficiently. Monetarism was condemned for
being deflationary and restrictionist, and for failing to break
out of the vicious cycle of decline that was the legacy of
social democracy and big government. The Thatcher government in its early years was criticised in precisely these
terms by leading American supply-siders.[24]

Yet despite this difference of emphasis and the contrasting assessments of the implications of the huge American
deficit that emerged after the partial implementation of
supply-side policies by the Reagan administration, the gap
between monetarists and supply-siders was not vast. Milton
Friedman was a firm believer in the need to cut taxes to very
low levels (20 per cent was his target), and he wrote extens-
ively on the need for a major reduction in government
spending programmes. The issue was over what should
come first, and whether a government was justified in taking
risks with funding its budget and therefore with inflation
and the value of its currency, so long as it had a clear
strategic grasp of how to reinvigorate a capitalist economy.

The concentration by monetarists on the control of inflation, and their argument that this was a technical question
of economic management, sometimes obscured the crucial
political dimension of New-Right thinking. The more politically sophisticated monetarists, as well as non-monetarists
such as Hayek, had no difficulty with the central proposi-
tions of monetarism: inflation is a monetary phenomenon;
it has to be cured by monetary means; it is always caused by
the supply of money expanding faster than the output of
goods and services; governments are responsible for the
money supply; therefore it is governments that are primarily
responsible for inflation.

They pointed out, however, that this analysis suggested that governments acted as they did because they were stupid or ignorant or the victims of poor advice. For Hayek the real issue was why governments felt obliged to expand the money supply. What were the political pressures that created a continual bias towards inflation? The technical reasons why inflation occurred and how it might be halted were trivial beside this question.

New-Right economics provides a comprehensive critique of state intervention in market processes. State intervention is criticised on three main grounds: because in practice it produces worse results than do market solutions; because administrative and bureaucratic methods are inherently inferior to markets as a means of allocating resources; and because it is objectionable on moral grounds. None of these arguments are new; all of them were deployed in the long intellectual struggle against socialism and collectivism in the 1920s and 1930s.[25] But at that time socialism and collectivism were relatively untried systems and doctrines. This was no longer true by the 1970s; the experience of collectivism in practice had by then revived the appeal of the free market.

At first this writing took the form of polemics against particular kinds of state intervention. Such arguments were often highly specific, related to particular policies and problems. The Hobart Papers of the Institute of Economic Affairs, for example, provided a series of case studies in public policy, showing that there were always market solutions available and that they worked better than the established administrative solutions.

A particular target was controls of every kind, particularly price controls and rent controls. Controls were criticised because, while they might give short-term benefits, they produced long-term damage and ended up making the situation worse than it had been at the beginning. Controls worked by freezing or regulating prices and therefore prevented markets from functioning. If markets could not function some other method was needed for rationing resources, and this meant using either administrative rules or administrative discretion. The flaw in any system of rationing is that it tends to perpetuate the original shortage. It brings into play no mechanism by which the shortage might eventually be overcome. The great merit of markets for their protagonists is that the rationing is done through prices rather than administratively. High prices discriminate against those without money, but they also encourage the entry of new producers. Supply increases until both the high prices and the shortage that occasioned them are eliminated.

The detailed case against particular controls was used to build a general argument against intervention. The hallmark of New-Right economic thinking is a distrust of all solutions to problems of public policy that do not involve markets. In those cases where the principle of state intervention is accepted, such as government control of the money supply, New-Right economists argue strongly that policy makers should apply general rules rather than use administrative discretion because the former are likely to cause less long-term damage to markets. Yet even here the difficulty of ensuring adherence to general rules on the part of the policy makers themselves leads some to prefer market solutions, such as Hayek's scheme for choice in currency discussed above.

Public expenditure

One of the most important areas where this approach was applied by New-Right economists lay in the field of public expenditure and taxation. The existence of a substantial sector in which services were provided by public bodies meant a large area where administrative rather than market criteria held sway. New-Right economists endeavoured to show that market solutions would in every case be superior to the established public provision, and that there were very few goods that could not be supplied through markets.[26] This claim was made most controversially for health and education, but it extended to all services in the public sector, even defence. The argument was that good intentions and high ideals were not enough. Any service would be more efficiently provided if it was subject to competitive tender and free from administrative controls and political interference.

Another crucial argument was that any system of administrative rationing necessarily conferred privileges on those groups best able to lobby the bureaucracy. The most disadvantaged groups derived least benefit from the services set up to help them. If services were provided through markets then not only would there be less waste and inefficiency, there would also be greater choice.

The New Right criticised public-welfare programmes not only because of their expense, but also because services provided collectively were regarded as inefficient in meeting the needs of the people they were designed to help. They destroyed choice and they entrenched dependency. The attack on the public sector drew on the traditional liberal preference for self-help, independence and financial prudence, but it also set out to demonstrate that the poor would actually get a better deal if they had to rely for the provision of essential services on making discretionary decisions about how to spend their income, instead of being forced to rely on the discretionary decisions of administrators. These arguments were always controversial. But the fact that they were put at all indicated a new self-confidence and a new assertiveness by the advocates of free markets and competition. The universal welfare programmes, the extended public sectors and the institutions and policies of corporatist economic management that had grown up piecemeal over many decades became a major battleground.

The achievement of the New Right was to place the supporters of public provision and public services on the defensive. The New-Right attacks on the grounds of cost and efficiency were predictable, but what was less expected was the New-Right claim that they had a superior moral vision of what a free society should be like. Their concept of citizenship saw freedom and equality being achieved through the daily plebiscite in the market, not through the infrequent plebiscite in the political system. This combination of morality and efficiency proved irresistible to many Conservative politicians, who were instinctively hostile to high welfare spending. New-Right economics supplied them with a well-developed set of principles for the discussion and analysis of all public-policy questions. Liberal political economy became intellectually fashionable again in the 1970s. If anything its scope and potential were now enhanced since its adherents were not afraid to develop it by extending their analysis to the public sector and the problems of public choice, the activities of politicians and bureaucrats, as well as the traditional focus on the behaviour of buyers and sellers in markets.[27]

Much of the confidence of the new breed of New-Right ideologues who filled the research institutes and colonised parts of the financial press and some university departments derived from the rediscovery of the analytical properties of liberal political economy. The intellectual case for markets appeared overwhelming, much as the intellectual case for planning had appeared overwhelming to an earlier generation of intellectuals. It was the universal cast of liberal political economy that appealed – not the case for this market solution or that, but the case for markets in general.

Milton Friedman was a key figure in the debate that developed around monetarism and macroeconomic management, as well as being a key protagonist in the arguments about the superiority of market solutions to administrative solutions. But the case for the inherent superiority of markets over all other forms of social organisation was made by Hayek and the Austrian school, by the theorists of public choice and by political philosophers such as Robert Nozick.[28]

One of Hayek's major contributions was his emphasis upon markets as a discovery process, the constant search for new methods, new needs and new sources of supply. All the Austrians put great emphasis upon the role of entrepreneurs as the creative force in a market economy. Hayek's market economy was not an economy of perfect equilibrium, perfect competition and perfect knowledge. Instead it was characterised by uncertainty and imperfect knowledge, constant shocks and adjustments. Hayek's argument against socialism and collectivism was not that markets offered a painless and frictionless method of allocating resources, but simply that markets were the method that worked best because it utilised the dispersed and fragmented knowledge that was available only to individuals in their particular local circumstances.[29] The conclusion for policy from Hayek's deliberations on law and society was that instances of 'market failure' needed to be tackled not by suspending markets by attempting to centralise knowledge and decision-making in a planning agency, but by removing the obstacles that prevented markets from functioning and new entrepreneurs from emerging with new ideas on how to satisfy whatever needs existed.

The economics of politics

The public-choice school applied the methods of economic analysis to the behaviour of public actors. They identified numerous shortcomings in the way in which political and administrative systems operate, comparing them unfavourably with the way in which economic markets operate. The chief defect of political and administrative systems lay in the way in which they aggregated preferences. Voters were allowed only one decision every few years, and then were unable to discriminate between the different policies presented to them. Instead they had to vote for a candidate or a party presenting a package of policies covering a wide spectrum. Voters were also fundamentally irresponsible. They lacked the kind of budget constraint faced by all consumers, even those armed with the magical properties of credit cards. As Milton Friedman explained:[30]

> The fundamental defect of the political mechanism [is that] it is a system of highly weighted voting under which the special interests have great incentive to promote their own interests at the expense of the general public. The benefits are concentrated; the costs are diffused; and you have therefore a bias in the market place which leads to ever greater expansion in the scope of government and ultimately to control over the individual.... In the economic market ... each person gets what he pays for. There is a dollar-for-dollar relationship. Therefore, you have an incentive proportionate to the cost to examine what you are getting.

The contribution of public choice as an intellectual discipline to the development of the New Right was that it provided powerful theoretical arguments against any notion that public bodies were disinterested and enlightened, while private individuals and companies were self-interested and rapacious. Public-choice theorists started with the assumption that politicians and bureaucrats had their own interests, which they pursued with the utmost vigour. The difference between private and public bodies was not that one had a special relationship to the public interest denied the other; but that the pursuit of self-interest by private bodies was qualified by the existence of a framework of rules and by competition. These constraints did not exist for public bodies.[31]

The conclusion drawn by many in the New Right was that markets were far superior to democracy in representing and aggregating individual choices. It was only a short step to arguing that democracy needed to be hedged around with restrictions to ensure that it did not permit encroachments upon the private sphere. A key theme of New-Right writing was the necessary limits of democracy and how different areas of policy could be removed from democratic control. Much ingenuity was spent on devising constitutions and entrenched bills of rights. Such reforms would remove from democratic governments the right of taking certain decisions and would require them to operate certain polices within prescribed limits. The idea that there should be a constitutional amendment to oblige the United States government to balance the budget was one of the more modest of these proposals.

Theoretical arguments that stressed the creativity of markets and the defects of administrative systems were further buttressed by the revival of moral arguments against equality. Robert Nozick's restatement of contract theory was the best known of these, but it by no means stood alone.[32] Hayek was also extremely keen to show that there was no moral basis for redistribution and that the pursuit of equality was a chimera that did untold damage to markets.[33]

A significant feature of these arguments was the abandonment of the claim that the pattern of rewards and incomes that was the outcome of markets was in any sense just. Hayek denied that the question had any relevance. The set of general rules that defined the market order could be considered just, but not the outcomes themselves because these depended on luck, chance, accident, effort, skill, inherited wealth, inherited talents and many other factors. For Hayek and many of the New Right the market is a lottery. There is no necessary link between effort and reward. What should be important to every individual is not the justice of the outcomes but the range of outcomes and therefore of choice that the market makes possible. Any attempt to enforce a particular pattern of distribution must destroy many of the benefits that flow from an unhampered market.

Nozick adds the further twist that provided all property holdings have been acquired without coercion there is no moral basis for redistributing property against the owner's consent. American libertarians such as Murray Rothbard argue similarly that all redistribution, including all forms of taxation, becomes a violation of individual rights and is therefore illegitimate. This requires the privatisation of all state functions, including the police, the courts, the bureaucracy and the military.[34] Nozick is more circumspect. He defends the case for a minimal state, and therefore for some taxation. It is anything beyond the minimal state, including the 'extended' state of social democracy, that he wishes to rule out.

The conservative New Right

The second major tendency in the New Right was the conservative. As a doctrine conservatism has always been characterised by its emphasis upon the conditions that are required for the establishment and maintenance of social order. These conditions include the need for authority, hierarchy and balance. Conservatives have generally been fierce critics of liberal doctrines of individualism that justify the removal of all restraints in the path of individual freedom. In conservative eyes such ideas are dangerous since they can lead to the erosion of essential institutions that promote social order.

The hostility conservatives have always displayed towards liberal ideas of freedom made them at one time critics of capitalism and individualism. It was the progress of the new ideology of liberalism that first led to the articulation of conservatism as a doctrine. But once collectivist forms of liberalism and socialism began to emerge the basis for a convergence between some strands of liberalism and conservatism was created. What made this convergence possible was the common respect of both traditions for property. Conservatives have always placed great emphasis upon property as one of the foundations of authority and order. Their suspicion of laissez-faire capitalism has not disappeared, but it has been moderated by the greater dangers that collectivism is seen to pose.

Conservatives gradually began to acknowledge the contribution made by capitalism, as an economic system, to the preservation of a good as well as a free society. Over a long period conservatism gradually came to terms with capitalism and has emerged in most countries as the staunch defender of the free-enterprise system. For the New Right to include a conservative tendency is no accident because of the recognition by conservatives that there are very different forms of liberalism, and that the advanced form known in Europe as social democracy constitutes a major threat to conservative values and institutions. Conservatives could make common cause with the liberal tendency in the New Right because they shared a common enemy. Both saw the destructive impact of social democracy upon the institutions that sustained capitalism. Liberals might express this concern in terms of freedom of the individual, while conservatives emphasised the erosion of authority. Both however regarded as pernicious the trends established by the growth of public sectors and the kind of government intervention practised since the 1940s. Both focused on the rise of a 'new class' of public-sector professional employees who staff the agencies of the public sector and who have a vested interest in its continued growth.[35]

For the conservative New Right no less than for their liberal counterparts the postwar compromise was a major mistake and had to be reversed. The special interests that infested government had to be confronted and their power reduced. The authority of the state itself and authority within all major social institutions had to be restored. Under the promptings of the new class the state had expanded into areas that should be left to other institutions. In usurping their role the state had overburdened itself and undermined precisely those institutions, particularly the family, upon which it depended for its own support. Social democracy destroyed the balance between state and society, threatening the creation of an atomised mass society, the rise of an authoritarian state and the shrinking of the domain of private life.[36]

Conservative writing is often less systematic, and certainly less voluminous, than liberal writing. One of its hallmarks is moral discourse about the good society and the enemies that threaten it. These enemies are numerous and they come from within and from without the social order. Often the two are linked in the conservative mind.

Enemies without

The origins of the conservative New Right lie in the reorientation of foreign policy in the years of postwar reconstruction following the defeat of fascism. Foreign policy became dominated by the perception of a new threat – the Soviet Union and international communism. Conservatives had always regarded protection of their societies against external assault as one of their most important priorities. This made them the protagonists of strong defence. In the postwar context strong defence was not conceived in national but international terms. It was the whole Western economy lying outside the Soviet sphere of influence that needed to be organised and defended. Countries could no longer stand on their own, so extensive alliances were concluded and an era of unprecedented cooperation between states in the Western sphere opened. At its core was the United States.

The establishment of NATO in 1949 marked the start of a major internal and external mobilisation against communism. For conservatives the containment of communism rapidly became their overriding priority. Defence of the free world against totalitarianism involved a new recognition of the virtues of the free-enterprise system and democratic politics. A substantial realignment of political forces took place, with a further splitting of left-wing parties and the coalescence of liberal and conservative forces. The terrain of domestic politics in the countries of the NATO alliance was founded on the exclusion of the communists from government office and the establishment of a consensus between right and left on the main lines of foreign policy – the necessity for whole-hearted participation in the Atlantic Alliance to guard against the Soviet threat.[37]

The consensus on foreign policy underpinned the accommodation on domestic policy that was reached in many states, but it also set limits to further moves towards collectivism. The ideological war against communism weakened the legitimacy of all socialist ideas, placed socialists on the defensive and created a climate of intolerance towards the left that at times involved persecution of those with radical and liberal opinions.

There exists a clear continuity between the resurgence of right-wing influence in the 1950s and the subsequent emergence of the New Right. Some of those who were later to become leading figures in the New Right in both Britain and the United States broke from the left during the early period of the Cold War.[38] The loss of their former faith in the Soviet Union and socialism was given as the main reason for changing their allegiance. A major stimulus to the emergence of the New Right in the 1970s was the renewed perception of a Soviet threat following the breakdown of détente between the superpowers.[39]

The new ideological onslaught against the Soviet Union and international communism was fuelled by fears of a major shift in the strategic balance, which, it was alleged, was giving the Soviet Union the military initiative. The loss of South Vietnam and the establishment of Soviet client-states in Africa and the Middle East reawakened fears of Soviet domination and led to charges of appeasement and the need for increased military preparation. Conservative politicians such as Ronald Reagan and Margaret Thatcher campaigned tirelessly for major increases in the arms budget and a much more aggressive stance towards the Soviet Union, not just to halt any further expansion but to begin rolling back the tide of international communism.

Central to the conservative New Right was this perception of renewed danger from the Soviet Union. It was accompanied by much writing on the theme of the weakness and decadence of the West. Conservatives argued that what was required was not merely a large increase in military rearmament but ideological and political rearmament as well. The disarray of the Western Alliance had to be remedied and military and political unity restored. This was an urgent priority. But as important was the need to combat internal subversion. For the conservative New Right the greatest threat to the survival of the free world lay in the erosion of national will and political authority that was the legacy of postwar social democracy.[40]

The new element in right-wing discourse in the 1970s was this linking of the external threat to the Western democracies with the internal threat created by social-democratic policies and institutions. In *The Road to Serfdom*, published in 1944, Hayek had argued that there was no halfway house between even the mildest socialist measures and full-blown totalitarianism.[41] The idea that social democracy was a Trojan horse for communism had long been popular in right-wing rhetoric. Conservatives in the 1970s, however, took this one stage further by arguing that the dismantling of many aspects of social democracy was now necessary if a successful resistance to communism was to be mounted. Effective defence against enemies without meant first hunting down enemies within.

Enemies within

The decadence of democracy is a major theme for the conservative New Right. The permissiveness and tolerance promoted under liberal and social-democratic regimes allows subversives and militants the space they require to attack the soft underbelly of Western society. Enemies of the free society penetrate the universities, the schools, the media, the unions, the churches, the civil service and even the security forces. From these vantage points they seek to stir up discontent and to undermine the institutions of a free society by challenging authority. The society is propelled towards chaos, and as authority breaks down everywhere the scene is set for a take-over by the left and the imposition of an authoritarian state.[42]

The most urgent task identified by the conservative New Right in the 1970s was to reverse the drift towards chaos and authoritarianism by restoring authority at all levels of society. This became first of all a call for tough government. The coercive power of the state should be used against the most visible agents of chaos and disorder – strikers, criminals, demonstrators and vandals. Public order and essential services should be maintained at all costs. The enemies of democracy should be shown that the government was strong enough and determined enough to use the power at its disposal. The government had to demonstrate that it could not be coerced by any direct challenge to its authority.

As important, however, was the need to combat the forces that sapped the will of democratic governments to resist challenges to their authority. It was necessary to change the climate of ideas that shaped the political agenda and the assumptions that governed the formulation and implementation of policy. The main threat here was posed by the growth of the 'new class', the army of public-sector professionals and ideologues whose tentacles reached into every corner of the modern state and who exerted enormous influence on how the politically practicable and the politically desirable were defined. The attack on the new class was spearheaded by the group of American intellectuals who have been dubbed the 'neo-conservatives'.[43] They criticised the assumptions and ambitions of postwar social and economic policy. They argued that too much of the modern planning by public agencies failed to observe the limits that are inherent in human action, limits both of understanding and of knowledge. They were sceptical also of the optimistic expectations held by so many of the new class about the ability of government to change the nature of both human beings and society.

The attack on the new class continued the critique of rationalism and the Enlightenment that has long been a key theme of conservative thought. Much of this writing is pessimistic and reflects unhappiness at the nature of contemporary society and the forces that are moulding it. Capitalism is not endorsed with any great enthusiasm. But it is endorsed. An influential essay by one of the leading American neo-conservatives, Irving Kristol, was entitled *Two Cheers for Capitalism.*[44] Capitalism is defended as the best available economic system, which, despite its flaws and its inability to inspire allegiance, must be preserved. Capitalist institutions, in particular private property, are regarded as a vital line of defence in the protection of individual freedom and the private domain.

But there were other conservatives who felt no such pessimism. For them there was nothing 'unheroic' about capitalist civilisation. On the contrary they marvelled at its achievements and its dynamism. For them it was the most remarkable economic and cultural system known to history. The working of capitalism itself generated a moral and political system whose watchwords were individual responsibility, freedom and democracy.[45]

Whether they were pessimistic or optimistic, however, all parts of the conservative New Right were agreed that what was most important were the institutions that sustained capitalist economic activity. This placed them closer to Hayek than to Friedman. Markets and free competition were not ends in themselves for New-Right conservatives but only means to those ends. Roger Scruton ridiculed the idea advanced by Nozick and other New-Right libertarians that taxation is necessarily coercive and therefore in almost all cases unjust and an abuse of power.[46] Conservatives argued that, important though it is to protect the private domain from arbitrary power, the authority of the state is as important a principle as the rights of individuals. The proper level of taxation cannot be decided by abstract a priori reasoning about the rights of the individual, it can only be decided in relation to the actual circumstances of government.

For conservatives the crucial need was to restore the balance between the different parts of the social order and to prevent the undermining of authority. The causes they took up and the campaigns they helped launch reflect this. Capitalism in the sense of the free-enterprise system and competitive markets was only a part of their good society. As important were the institutions that underpinned the workings of markets. This explains why New-Right conservatives in contrast to most New-Right liberals and libertarians were preoccupied with the problems of civil society and political culture. They placed great stress on the problems of the family and the erosion of patriarchy; on the schools, and the standards and content of education; on the multiplying threats to public order; on the problems of racial and sectarian divisions; on the churches and the threat to public and personal morality; and on the limits of democracy.[47]

These two strands of the New Right – liberal and conservative – helped create the intellectual ferment that was part of the context in which Thatcherism emerged, and played a major part in shaping its concerns and objectives. It supplied ideas for challenging the dominant ideas within British politics and the Conservative Party. It suggested a novel political strategy for the conservatives that broke away from the assumptions and limitations of the 1940s settlement; and it offered a new strategy for reversing economic decline. In the hands of a major political leader making the economy free once more and the state strong were to be welded into a powerful political programme, capable of reversing the decline in the Conservative Party's electoral fortunes and seizing the new agenda of British politics for the right.

3

From Butler to Thatcher

> The greatest task of the statesman ... is to offer his people
> good myths and to save them from harmful myths.
>
> Enoch Powell

The political origins of the Thatcherite project lie in the
postwar history of the Conservative Party. The novelty and
shock of Thatcherism as it began to unfold after 1975 was
due to the contrast with the style and the policies of postwar
conservatism. Some conservatives, such as Sir Ian Gilmour,
argued that the Thatcherite wing of the party had repudiated
the British conservative tradition of non-ideological politics
and pragmatic statecraft that stretched back to Disraeli.[1] But
the particular quarrel of the Thatcherites was with the attitudes, assumptions and policies to which conservatives had
become committed in the 1940s and 1950s.[2] It was the acquiescence by conservatives in the social-democratic hegemony
over domestic policy that they most wished to challenge.
They always claimed that they were the true Tories, restoring
the party to its traditional principles. To understand why
Thatcherism became so controversial in the 1970s it is necessary to place it in the context of developments in British politics, and in particular in the Conservative Party, since 1945.

Postwar reconstruction

The 1940s marked an important watershed in British politics, both because of the war and because of the election in

1945 of the first majority Labour government. The failure of the policy of appeasement in the 1930s was not only a serious defeat in foreign policy; it was also a serious reverse for the Conservative Party's domestic policy. The successful prosecution of the war demanded a coalition government, and although the majority of its supporters in the House of Commons remained Conservatives, the leadership of the coalition passed to elements hostile to many of the assumptions of prewar policy. The opponents of appeasement also tended to be opponents of balanced budgets and sound finance. They were receptive to the ideas of Keynes and Beveridge for radical changes in the orientation of economic and social policy after the war.

The political momentum behind reconstruction was powerful. Labour ministers tended to see it in terms of an explicit bargain between the working class and the British state. But many Conservatives also accepted the desirability and the inevitability of a major extension of government responsibility surviving into peace-time. Some, such as Harold Macmillan, had already been strong critics of the negative and passive stance of government policy before 1939. Others, such as R. A. Butler, recognised the new circumstances the war had created and became enthusiastic reformers.[3]

The existence of a progressive element within the Conservative Party leadership and among their MPs in 1945 did not mean, however, that they formed a majority. What completed the education of the party was the substantial defeat it suffered in 1945. At the previous general election, held in 1935, the Conservatives had polled 11.8 million votes, which represented 53.7 per cent of the total vote, and won 432 seats. In 1945 they polled only 9.9 million votes, 39.8 per cent of the vote, and won only 213 seats.

The loss of more than half the parliamentary party in the election and the size of the Labour majority made the defeat appear more overwhelming than it actually was. The demoralisation of the Conservatives was certainly profound, in part because of the widespread expectation before the poll that with Churchill at its head the party was certain to win. What the defeat did was to strengthen the hand of those elements in the party who wanted to see a major change in the party's policy. They were quite content to accept the reconstruction plans prepared by the coalition government, which the new Labour government began to carry into effect, as a new permanent framework for domestic policy. In this way the social-democratic hegemony began to take shape.

The major changes in domestic policy to which the Conservatives became reconciled in the 1940s were firstly the changed position of the trade unions, which was achieved partly through the repeal of the 1927 Trade Disputes Act and partly through their greater involvement in national policy-making; and secondly the enlargement of the public sector through the new measures of nationalisation, the improvement of welfare and education programmes, and the setting up of the National Health Service.

The rise of the new conservatism and the ascendancy of the progressive wing of the party was made easier because the limited domestic accommodation with organised labour became combined with a new, bipartisan, foreign-policy consensus in the late 1940s. The commitment to the Atlantic Alliance and the fight against international communism reinforced the need for domestic peace. Though the political rhetoric of the 1940s, particularly Churchill's, was extreme, portraying all social-democratic governments, including the British Labour government, as half-way stages to communism, there was no programme for rolling back socialism. There was no need for one. All the Conservatives desired was that they and not Labour should be administering the new, swollen, state sector. Once they had achieved that aim their ambitions to 'Set the People free', proclaimed in the 1951 election, rapidly subsided.

The contribution of the new conservatism of Butler and Macmillan to policy was slight. It was never a coherent doctrine. But it gave the leadership legitimacy and provided time for the essential work of party reorganisation. The rebuilding of Conservative electoral strength and the reemergence of the party as a strong contender for government was aided by the demonstrated readiness of its leaders to accept much of the programme that Labour had implemented.

Labour politicians found it hard to believe, and predicted the return of mass unemployment and the wholesale dismantling of welfare services. The electorate was not convinced. The Labour vote held but the Conservative vote recovered strongly in 1950 and 1951. In the second election, despite running second to Labour in terms of votes, the collapse of the Liberal vote gave the Conservatives a clear parliamentary majority.

Returning to government only six years after having suffered so major a defeat testified to the great powers of recuperation of the Conservative Party and its ability to subordinate all other considerations to the pursuit of office. The new conservatism perfectly fitted the need of the party in the 1940s. A reactionary Conservative programme could have been suicidal for the party. Instead its new leaders saw clearly that the party needed to adjust its perspectives to win back lost electoral ground and to present itself as the party best suited to manage the enlarged public sector.

The party succeeded to an extraordinary degree, winning three elections in a row and increasing its parliamentary majority each time (although its share of the vote rose only marginally). Macmillan and Butler, two of the principal architects of the new conservatism when in opposition, now emerged as the dominant figures in the government. They advanced a generation of younger politicians such as Macleod, Maudling, Powell and Heath. They presided over an economy that was enjoying the benefit from the great surge of growth in the world economy that began in the 1950s and was based on the generalisation of the production methods of Fordism throughout the capitalist world.

Very little that was inherited from Labour was dismantled by the new Conservative government. Ministers had to be pressed to proceed with even the limited measures of denationalisation proclaimed in their manifesto.[4] While they wanted commercial disciplines encouraged in the new nationalised industries they felt there was no danger or special problem with retaining these industries within the public sector now that Conservatives were back in charge of the government. There was no crusading zeal to roll back the frontiers of the state and revive enterprise. The level of taxation and the level of public expenditure were little altered.

What did stop was the momentum for further state control and ownership. The Conservative government, while it did not disturb the fundamentals of the new social-democratic order, believed at first in consolidation rather than in any further extension of the logic of the new system. It experimented with market policies, most notably by placing much greater reliance on monetary rather than fiscal policy and by easing rent controls. The new role and enhanced position of trade unions was accepted. No proposals for any new legislation on trade unions made any headway during the thirteen years the Conservatives were in power. Unemployment and inflation were both minuscule by later standards. In eight out of the thirteen years unemployment was below 500 000 and it never went above one million. The rate of inflation never reached 5 per cent and in most years it was below 3 per cent. The growth of the economy, although interrupted by balance-of-payments crises and by periodic deflations of demand to protect sterling, was still substantial. It was not spectacular in comparison with many other economies but it still allowed Butler, when he was chancellor of the exchequer, to predict in 1955 that the standard of living in Britain would double in twenty five years.

As the decade wore on, ministers could be forgiven for feeling increasingly complacent about domestic politics. Certainly they felt no pressure from their right wing on domestic issues. The 1950s saw the establishment of the Institute of Economic Affairs and the harrying of the Conservative government by Edward Martell's Freedom League.[5] But despite the threatened revolt of the middle orders of society, hard pressed by the grinding levels of socialist taxation, it obstinately refused to happen. The confidence of the new conservatives can be judged from Butler's remark in his 1953 budget speech: 'Those who talk about creating pools of unemployment should be thrown into them and made to swim', and Harold Macmillan's judgement after the 1959 election: 'the class war is over and we have won it'.[6]

Amidst this relative domestic tranquillity the government was preoccupied with the consequences of Britain's decline as a world power; the disengagement from Empire, the halting steps towards closer involvement with Europe and the continuing contest between the superpowers. The extent of British overseas responsibilities remained substantial in the 1950s; Britain was still a major military power with a network of bases and colonies around the world. At least until the traumatic Suez invasion in 1956 British governments had a clear conception of a British sphere of influence, and could still contemplate acting alone in defence of what were defined as British interests. Britain was a welfare state in the 1950s but also a warfare state. The burden of maintaining overseas military bases was heavy for the British economy because of their cost in foreign exchange and therefore their impact on the balance of payments and the strength of the pound.

The old politics of Empire began to come apart in the 1950s, but the Conservative leadership had some consolation in having found a new politics of the nation that allowed them to claim the mantle of prosperity and to appear before the people as the protectors of welfare and social rights and the providers of growth. The years of the long boom were also the final stage of the British Empire. The success of the new domestic accumulation strategy, which was producing unparalleled prosperity, made the winding down of the external support to the British economy that the Empire had provided seem no longer important. The existence of the Empire and Britain's world position had greatly assisted the constitutional advance of the labour movement. But through the establishment of a Fordist regime of accumulation and the 1940s settlement in domestic politics, a durable accommodation between capital and labour appeared to have been reached and the basis for a stable hegemony created. The Conservatives had once again emerged as its chief political agent.

Despite the problems of foreign policy the Conservative Party achieved remarkable success in the 1950s. The political problem that had seemed so momentous in the 1920s – how the social and political claims of the rising labour movement were to be met – had been solved and in a way which appeared to allow the Conservatives to retain their traditional leading political role. Ever since the advent of mass democracy in the 1880s, which most Conservatives had instinctively opposed, the leadership of the party had been uneasily aware of the frail base of support upon which the Conservative Party rested. In a population already predominantly urban and industrial no secure pre-industrial or traditional social base for a mass Conservative Party existed. The Conservatives had to become a party of the industrial proletariat or it had to face being marginalised. The winning of the working-class votes it needs to be able to form governments has ever since been preoccupied Conservative leaders.[7]

The ferment of the 1960s

The domestic calm did not last. As the dismantling of the British Empire gathered pace so the precarious foundations of British prosperity were exposed. The relative decline of the British economy once more became a focus for concern. Britain had long lost any pretension to being the world's leading industrial power but it was a new experience to find its economic performance so easily outclassed by states with similar resources and populations. British governments had committed themselves to an accumulation strategy based on encouraging the spread of the production methods and consumption patterns of Fordism throughout the economy, while maintaining and gradually increasing the openness of the economy to trade and capital flows. But the performance of Fordist industries in Britain in most cases never began to match the performance of similar industries elsewhere.[8]

The unease that began to grip political and administrative circles in the late 1950s about Britain's stuttering economic progress (rapid though it was by historical standards), gave rise to a wide-ranging debate on how British society and the British economy could be modernised.[9] To become modern implied rejection of traditional attitudes and established institutions. This was an uncomfortable position for Conservatives to take up, but it was a task that many of the leadership accepted with enthusiasm.

The first major programme of measures to modernise Britain and reverse its economic decline was launched by the Macmillan government in the late 1960s. At the end of his career Macmillan found an opportunity to follow the dirigiste instincts that had been so evident in his writings in the 1930s. The new Conservatives as a group had no inhibitions about extending state involvement and state responsibilities where they thought it necessary and desirable. Most of the available models of modern, high-performance economies appeared to involve either an implicit or explicit extension of links between the state and private capital. This became the basis for the economic strategy of the 1960s.

What is important for understanding Thatcherism is that the first Conservative attempt to grapple seriously with the problem of decline took for granted not only that the solutions could be found within the parameters of the 1940s settlement, but also that they would involve ways of releasing the potential for collaboration between the major producer interests. New tripartite institutions such as the National Economic Development Council, and the first serious attempt at an incomes policy, the National Incomes Commission, were launched. But the modernisation drive was perhaps characterised above all by the additional public expenditure the Conservatives were eager to commit to new programmes to improve health, education and transport. This was accompanied by a commitment to expansion and the preparation of contingency plans to avoid the momentum of growth in the economy being interrupted by sterling crises.[10]

The adoption of this economic strategy to modernise the economy could not bring quick results and the government was an easy target for past errors and past neglect. A reunited Labour Party won a narrow victory at the general election in 1964. The election was remarkable for the closeness of the policies of the parties. All three main parties subscribed to the need for substantial modernisation of British institutions to enable Britain to restore competitiveness and improve the rate of economic growth.

Labour built on the initiatives started by the Conservatives. The Wilson government when it took office enjoyed a wide measure of support for its programme from all major interests. But the government proved quite unable to pursue a coherent strategy in the face of repeated pressure on the pound, and in the end it abandoned its expansionist ambitions. The disappointment of the high expectations of the Wilson government held by many on the left was marked and was to have profound long-term consequences for the Labour Party. But there were important consequences also for the Conservative Party. Conservatives observed the weakness of the government in the face of corporate interests, and many turned against measures of modernisation that involved increasing the quantity and range of government controls, and on involving the major producer groups in economic policy-making. The relative failure of the various corporatist initiatives of the Wilson government, such as the prices and incomes policy, the national plan and the industrial policies, discredited the modernisation programme among Conservatives and helped spur the birth of a new kind of right-wing opposition in the party.[11]

This response was all the greater since, although the Labour government failed to deliver its 'New Britain' through a reversal of economic decline, the pace of change in the 1960s was rapid, particularly in cultural terms. Many of the Conservatives who were critical of increased state intervention were also worried about threats to the family, public order and national identity.

This period saw the first emergence of a New Right in Britain. It embraced the growing misgivings of economic liberals about the direction of government economic policy, as well as the new concerns of moral entrepreneurs such as Mary Whitehouse, who launched her National Viewers and Listeners Association to monitor the output of the media in 1965. It was plainly post-imperial with its focus on domestic issues, and it challenged the authority of the Conservative leadership to determine the direction of party policy. The politician who united its different strands and who provided a clear challenge to Edward Heath and his supporters in the party leadership was Enoch Powell.

Powell's career has been much studied.[12] Before Thatcher rose to prominence he was the most important right-wing figure produced by the Conservative Party since 1945. He had been a new conservative and one of the recruits to the powerhouse of the new thinking, the Conservative Research Department, over which Butler presided in the 1940s. He always remained obstinately loyal to Butler, even refusing to serve in Alec Douglas-Home's cabinet in 1963 after Butler had been denied the premiership for the second time.

Even in the 1950s he was noted for his commitment to free-market ideas. He resigned as a treasury minister in 1958, along with Peter Thorneycroft and Nigel Birch, because of a cabinet decision to increase expenditure by £50 million against Treasury advice. Powell ever after argued that that decision was the beginning of the great inflation that reached its climax in the 1970s.[13]

His reputation as an adherent of liberal economics did not inhibit him as minister of health between 1960 and 1963, when he participated fully in the modernisation drive and supervised a large expansion of the hospital-building programme. But once he had resigned he began to be noticed more and more as an exponent of what was abusively termed 'laissez-faire economics'. His hostility to high levels of public expenditure and taxation and to all forms of government intervention in the workings of free markets made him often appear very isolated within his own party, and still more in British politics. In the early 1960s his arguments for unfettered markets marked him as an oddity. The tide of opinion was flowing very strongly in the other direction.

Powell resumed front-bench responsibilities when the party was defeated in 1964. In 1965 he contested the party leadership – the first open election the Conservatives had ever held – and polled 19 votes. The new leader, Edward Heath, appointed him defence spokesman. Powell, at one time an ardent imperialist, now emerged as the advocate of a drastic reduction in Britain's overseas military commitments to create a defence more in line with Britain's reduced capacities in the world. These ideas did not endear him to the traditional imperialist right in the Conservative

Party, which was still arguing strongly for the maintenance of British bases east of Suez.

What transformed Powell's standing with the electorate as well as his relations with the Tory Party was his intervention in the debate on immigration and race relations, which had been gathering pace through the 1960s. In his speech at Birmingham in 1968 he was careful to say nothing that was not party policy but the language he used to say it made the speech an intervention the party leadership could not ignore. Powell became the first major politician to break the bipartisan consensus that had grown up on immigration. By using his speech to publicise the fears expressed by his constituents he took on the role of a tribune of the people attacking the conspiracy of silence of the progressive establishment.[14] Powell's speech was of decisive importance in launching a new politics of the nation, and in demonstrating the possibilities of a populist assault upon some of the central aspects of postwar social democracy. In April 1968 1 per cent of those questioned by Gallup wanted Powell to be the next leader of the Conservative Party; in May after the speech it rose to 24 per cent. As many as two thirds of those questioned by pollsters said they agreed with what Powell had said. He received 105 000 letters of congratulation and East End Dockers demonstrated in his support.[15]

Powell touched off a minor explosion in public sentiment. The frustration and anxiety of white working-class communities at the growing number of immigrants was not being represented by either major political party. Powell's concern with the identity of the nation and the need to preserve its essential character and continuity provided him with a popular cause, which free-market economics would never have done. Powell's espousal of this cause, however, was not primarily a cynical manoeuvre aimed at advancing his own career and claims to leadership. It flowed from a particular conception of politics, one which emphasised above all else the importance of the nation and its preservation. Powell was drawing on a very old Conservative insight. Making appeals to non-rational instincts and emotions could often elicit a much deeper response than a politics of incentives and material benefits. Even before the boom had cracked Powell showed the potential for reconstructing British politics on very different terrain. He rejected the idea that the only way the Conservatives could compete with Labour was to provide faster economic growth. The claim of the Conservatives to be the national party, able to appeal to all classes and particularly to the working class, depended in Powell's view on its ability to protect the nation from its enemies.

Expelled from the front bench Powell became the severest critic of the Conservative leadership, but Heath's election victory in 1970 ensured that he would remain outside it. Powell's new nationalism found new causes in the 1970s alongside race; opposition to Britain's entry into the Common Market and the defence of the union with Ulster. Isolated from so much of the political establishment Powell became increasingly strident in his denunciation of it. He attacked the enemies within, not merely those who by their violent actions and protests were undermining public and social order, but also those in the civil service, in the media and in government who were persistently thwarting popular demands. The gulf between the progressive elite and the people, which was a common theme in radical-right rhetoric elsewhere, was deployed with great vigour and skill by Powell.

In appealing to national feeling and attempting to mobilise opinion against the opinion-formers of the progressive establishment Powell did not neglect his other obsession – the market. Once freed from the restraints placed upon him by membership of the shadow cabinet, Powell once more became a savage critic of all the assumptions and priorities of the modernization programmes of the 1960s and which were still deeply embedded in the thinking of the Conservative leadership. He was particularly scornful of incomes policies and of all tendencies towards corporatist arrangements between government, unions and employers. He also called for wholesale denationalisation of all public enterprises, for income tax to be reduced to 4s 3d (21p) in the pound, and for drastic reductions in public expenditure by ending state intervention in the economy and privatising welfare.[16] Above all he was a strong supporter of sound money to prevent the drift towards faster inflation, and he was an early advocate of floating exchange rates.

Powellism, as it emerged, always contained this mix of free-market economics and nationalism. Powell was the first politician in Britain to advocate the doctrine of the free economy and the strong state, which was to dominate the New-Right debate in the 1970s and 1980s. Yet Powellism was always more coherent than Thatcherism as a set of ideas, in part because of the kind of politician Powell was, in part because the package never became the policy of either the party or the government and so was never tested by the kind of pressures to which Thatcherism was subjected.

Powellism was important for later developments because it demonstrated not only that there was a coherent intellectual alternative to the modernisation programmes of the social-democratic state, but also that there was an alternative politics of support available to the Conservatives. The right did not need to be imprisoned forever within the social-democratic hegemony, much of which was not of their making. If the old politics was breaking down, the opportunity could be seized to forge a new course.

Apart from a few clues, such as her speech to the Conservative Political Centre in 1968, there is little evidence of what Margaret Thatcher thought of the potential of this new politics. But she was known to admire Powell. She was the only member of the shadow cabinet to wish him well in the 1970 election and it is difficult to believe that his example and his ideas did not leave a deep impression.[17]

The Heath government

The Conservative government that was elected rather unexpectedly in 1970 lasted less than four years, but it proved a critical episode in the emergence of Thatcherism. In retrospect it appears both as a first attempt to introduce a 'Thatcherite' programme and as the last phase of the interventionist modernisation programme of the 1960s. Although it seemed radical at the time and was regarded as marking a sharp break with the policies that had been established during the 1960s, in retrospect the government belonged more to the era that was closing than to the era that was about to be born.

What was radical about the Heath government was not that it had abandoned the objectives of postwar economic management, which had underlain the modernisation programmes of the 1960s, but that it was proposing new means to achieve them. The profound disillusion with the effects of Labour's interventionist policies, the increasing pressure from Powell and his allies in the party and the need to differentiate the party from its opponents all combined to promote a policy of disengagement of the state from the economy.[18]

The Heath government began by dismantling many of the interventionist agencies used by Labour to implement its policies. The Prices and Incomes Board, the Industrial Reorganisation Corporation and the Ministry of Technology were all axed. The government declared that it would not intervene in industry, 'lame ducks' would be allowed to go bankrupt to make the economy more efficient, and no pay and price controls would be introduced. A more competitive and more enterprising economy was the goal.

The emphasis upon competitiveness and efficiency was linked to the commitment to as rapid an entry into the EEC as negotiations would permit. Membership of the EEC was expected to open the British economy to fiercer competition from European industries and made the achievement of higher levels of investment and productivity in British companies essential for survival. It was also the next stage in the gradual adjustment of British policy to the withdrawal from Empire. Heath had been in charge of the negotiations in 1961–3 and despite their failure, and the subsequent failure of the Labour government's bid in 1967, he had never wavered in his commitment to Europe.

Apart from Powell and a small number of backbenchers the party had become reconciled to membership of the EEC by 1970. For Heath and many leading Conservatives the bid to join Europe was an essential part of the bid to modernise the British economy and improve the British version of Fordism. It offered a new and challenging environment in which British industrial practices would be shaken up and their deficiencies exposed. It offered an end to the illusion that Britain was still a great power able to do without cooperation with its closest neighbours and able to rely on its 'special relationship' with the United States. Heath's pro-Europe stance and his coolness towards aspects of the relationship with America made him the least Atlanticist British premier since the war.[19]

Heath's conception of what a modern Britain would be like was drawn from the models of the successful EEC member states. He wanted to reform British government and British industrial relations and to inject more competition into industry. The policy of disengagement and the plans for a new legislative framework for industrial relations were integral parts of this strategy.

Entry into the European Community was achieved very smoothly. Heath was able to give the kind of reassurances to the French about Britain's future role in Europe that were necessary to at last removing their veto. But in their domestic policies the government faced mounting problems, particularly over Northern Ireland and the trade unions. The worsening disorder in Northern Ireland was to have momentous domestic political consequences for the Heath government. The decisions taken by the government to impose direct rule, abolish Stormont and set up a power-sharing executive eventually brought the severing of the link between Ulster Unionism and the Conservative Party. The refusal of Ulster Unionist MPs to take the Conservative whip in 1974 prevented the Conservatives from being the party with the largest number of seats after the February election.

Still more traumatic for the Conservatives, however, and still more decisive for Heath's loss of the party leadership in 1975, was the course of industrial relations. The attempt to impose a comprehensive legal framework upon the unions badly misfired. The degree of union resistance and the inflexibility of many of the new institutions (in particular the National Industrial Relations Court under Sir John Donaldson) led to a series of major confrontations with the unions and often to embarrassing climbdowns for the government. The refusal of the unions to cooperate with the

Act made much of it ineffective, and by 1974 even the CBI was acknowledging that the Act had harmed rather than helped the evolution of better industrial relations.

The central problem with the Act was that it was designed to deal with the problem of unofficial strikes and the growing power of shop stewards in some major industries, and it sought to do this by giving greater authority to the national union leaderships. The refusal of the trade unions, however, to trade some loss of their privileges for greater authority over their members destroyed the plan and soured relations between unions and government.

The industrial relations reforms of the Heath government were misconceived in another way. They did not address the central problem faced by the government – holding down the rise in labour costs. The government was determined at first to do without an incomes policy, preferring instead to set a good example by restraining pay in the public sector and encouraging a more competitive atmosphere in industry. It had some early successes in public-sector pay disputes but it then suffered a major defeat in 1971 against the miners.

The policy of disengagement also had some hard knocks, first from the collapse of Rolls Royce in 1971, which had to be rescued by being nationalised, and secondly from the long campaign by workers on Clydeside to resist the closure of Upper Clyde Shipbuilders. Events like these, combined with the sluggishness of the economy and the rise of unemployment towards one million during 1971, created pressures for policy changes. The changes when they came were interpreted by Heath's critics in the party as a U-turn.

The term is very inexact to describe what took place in 1972.[20] In many areas of policy there was no significant change, in others there was a slight shift of emphasis. But there were also three more substantial changes. The government changed its macroeconomic stance, deciding that a substantial reflation was necessary to achieve the kind of rapid growth rate the government hoped would become routine once Britain was a full member of the EEC. The government also chose to implement the decision to reflate by increasing public-spending programmes. The attempt to hold down or even reduce public spending was substantially modified after 1971. The government also became much more actively in favour of state intervention to restructure industry. Sweeping new powers were given to the secretary of state under the 1972 Industry Act.

The biggest change of all, however, and the one which excited the loudest shouts of betrayal, was incomes policy. The manifesto in 1970 had been quite specific that the Conservatives would not introduce a compulsory incomes policy and in the first phase they had remained true to that pledge, dismantling the incomes policy apparatus they inherited from Labour. The experience of trying to manage the British economy convinced ministers that some formal controls on pay were essential. It was very difficult to envisage such controls without the active consent and participation of the trade unions.

A peculiarity of the British political system is that the trade unions are not just allied to one political party but are a key element in its internal organisation and finance. This has always made Labour governments much better placed to secure cooperation from the unions and has made the Conservatives more wary of corporatist institutions. The position was especially difficult for the Heath government since its handling of the Industrial Relations Act and its abrasive style during its early period in office had greatly depleted the goodwill upon which the government could draw.

Nevertheless, despite the unfavourable climate, in the summer of 1972 the Heath government came very close to securing a comprehensive agreement with the TUC and the CBI over the management of the economy and over the control of pay and prices. When the talks finally broke down the government moved to impose through legislation a statutory incomes policy. This was the most far-reaching statutory incomes policy ever achieved in peacetime.[21] Trade unions and employers initially acquiesced to it. Stage 1 and stage 2 of the policy were successful. Only when stage 3 was reached did the policy come unstuck due to the mishandling of negotiations with the miners. This precipitated another clash with the NUM, with dire consequences for the government. But no general trade-union offensive materialised against the pay policy. Most workers settled under the phase 3 limits.

The complaints of the government's critics were voiced most strongly by Enoch Powell. During the short life of the Heath government he managed to vote against the Conservative whip on no fewer than 113 occasions. He argued that the government was pursuing policies that were quite contrary to the prospectus upon which they had been elected. He deplored the turn to a compulsory incomes policy and to greater intervention in industry and he predicted that by so lightly abandoning their principles they were heading for disaster. The decline of the Conservatives was made all the more certain, Powell thought, because they seemed prepared to abandon their customary role as the national party, embracing the EEC and forsaking their friends in Ulster.

The Heath government would have had no difficulty in shrugging off these charges if it had more luck or if its policies had been more successful. The Conservative attitude towards incomes policy had always been pragmatic. Powell had clashed in 1964–5 with Maudling and other senior Conservatives over whether Conservatives should favour an incomes policy. The balance of opinion in the party had swung against incomes policy in the late 1960s due to dissatisfaction with Labour's record. The pragmatic revival of incomes policy by the Heath government was not a betrayal of a deep Conservative principle.

What hurt Edward Heath's leadership more than the charge of treachery was the charge of failure and incompetence. So much happened between 1970 and 1974 that in retrospect the record of the government looks incoherent. It also appears to have failed in several of its major objectives. Popular memory of the period was of a period of great turbulence. The government had been forced to declare five states of emergency in those three and a half years. At the height of the miners' overtime ban it had been forced to impose a three-day week on industry. It had confronted the trade-union movement and ultimately it was judged to have lost. The government proved unable to defeat the miners industrially, and by calling and then losing an election in February 1974 it proved unable to defeat them politically either.

The Heath government left behind it an image of failure and incompetence. The government had failed in the end to impose its authority. Union power, far from being less, seemed to have received a significant boost. Legislation on industrial relations proposed by successive governments had been successfully resisted. The performance of the economy had not improved but deteriorated. The country was coming to seem ungovernable. The decision to impose the three-day week in January 1973 to cope with the shortage of power supplies, and the announcement of major new expenditure curbs shortly before, dramatically signalled the end of the hopes of the Heath government for a new era of rapid economic growth. The much faster rate of growth that had been achieved in 1973 was cut short by the quadrupling of the oil price and the onset of world recession.

The misfortune of the Heath government was to have presided over the British economy during the last phase of the long boom when the ground was already beginning to shift. The breakdown of the Bretton Woods system in 1971 and the acceleration in commodity prices and domestic cost pressures made the monetary and fiscal policies of the post-war policy regime quite inadequate to contain them. A major increase in the rate of inflation was already under way when the Heath government came into office. A much larger increase was bequeathed to its successor.

The critics of the Heath government subsequently singled out the reflation of the economy in 1972 as the cause of the high rates of inflation in 1974 and 1975. The record of economic management under the Conservative government was taken as vindicating the monetarist critique of Keynesianism. To a greater extent than any British government since the war the Heath government attempted to spend its way back to full employment during 1972–3. It was able to do so because the constraint afforded by fixed exchange rates had disappeared. But to keep the momentum of the expansion going the government found itself more and more obliged to intervene in markets and to try to control wages and prices directly.

For a time the policy had seemed to carry all before it. But the collapse of the boom in the world economy and the

resistance of the miners wrecked the policy and the hopes
that were attached to it. Heath called an election and made
the main issue 'Who Governs Britain?' To be refused a parliamentary majority on the basis of such a call was a severe
rebuff and threw the Conservative Party into despair and
demoralisation. The political initiative now passed to
Labour, which formed a minority administration and subsequently won a small parliamentary majority in a second
general election in October 1974.

At this second election the Conservative vote fell to 35 per
cent, the lowest percentage they had polled this century.
The beneficiary was not Labour but the Liberals and the
nationalist parties. Nevertheless the Conservative electoral
coalition had been severely weakened, and yet one more
major modernisation programme had been shipwrecked.
The Conservatives seemed more marginal to British politics
and to the new centres of power than at any time since 1945.
In these circumstances, whatever the degree of blame
attaching to him, it would have been remarkable if Edward
Heath had remained as leader. The challenge was not long
in coming.

The ascendancy of Margaret Thatcher

In 1974 the Conservative Party lacked any procedure for
challenging an incumbent leader. It was only nine years previously, in 1965, that the party had adopted a method of
direct election for the party leader in place of the informal
processes of consultation by which Conservative leaders had
previously emerged. Heath was the first leader to owe his
position to direct election by the parliamentary party, but
nothing in the rules obliged him to seek reelection.

The peculiar circumstances of 1974, when the Conservative Party lost two general elections, created great pressure
for Heath either to resign or to renew his mandate. Heath
soon made it clear that he had no intention of resigning and
his friends in the party then tried to persuade him to submit
to an early vote of confidence by the party. Their reasoning was that there was no serious challenger in sight. The

Shadow Cabinet was mostly filled with loyal Heathmen. Enoch Powell had put himself out of the running first by refusing to stand as a Conservative in February 1974 and advising his supporters to vote Labour, and secondly by reentering the House of Commons in October 1974 as an Ulster Unionist.

The only senior Conservative who seemed likely to challenge Heath was Sir Keith Joseph. He emerged during 1974 as the leading critic inside the party of the policy errors of the Heath government. In a series of speeches he began to develop a free-market and monetarist programme, proclaiming that the Conservative Party needed to rediscover its principles. He disowned Keynesian economic management, state intervention, high public spending and incomes policies. In one speech, received with some incredulity by his former Cabinet colleagues, he announced his conversion to conservatism. He had always thought of himself as a Conservative, he said, but now he realised he had never properly understood what being a Conservative entailed.[22]

Sections of the Tory press, notably the *Spectator*, became strong supporters of Joseph and launched a fierce anti-Heath campaign. The anti-Heath forces were considerable because Heath had antagonised many Conservatives during his period as leader. The defeat of the Conservative government gave all these elements the chance they needed to begin mobilising against the leadership. Those who had criticised some of the policies of the government at the time now appeared to be vindicated. Keynesianism and interventionist policies were badly discredited, and to that was added widespread disquiet about the state of the country, the loss of authority and the drift towards ungovernability. The extent of disorientation in the British establishment was very marked. Strange vigilante groups like GB75 were springing up, pledged to protect the public against trade-union militancy, *The Times* ran a leader on the possibility of a military coup, and the elements of the secret service began actively plotting to discredit the prime minister, Harold Wilson, in the hope of bringing down the government.

In these circumstances the New Right, with its vigour and ideological conviction, was able to take the initiative. In

1974 Joseph and Thatcher showed their distrust of the Tory Establishment and the central party institutions, including Central Office and the Conservative Research Department, by setting up an alternative source of policy advice, the Centre for Policy Studies. This was to become the key Thatcherite think-tank of the 1970s.

But despite the new ideological strength of the New Right, Heath's critics seemed in no position to launch a bid for control of the party. Keith Joseph had an uncertain touch as a politician and torpedoed his own chances of becoming leader by making a speech in which he gave the impression that curing the problems of poverty and deprivation required restrictions on the right of the lower-income groups to have children. A second difficulty was that any leadership contest would be settled by the votes of the Conservative MPs. This was an electorate unlikely to be swayed by ideological arguments of the kind offered by Keith Joseph, but by pragmatic and hard-headed assessments of where their interest and the party interest lay. Joseph's deficiencies as a politician were unlikely to recommend him.

Although there appeared to be no convincing challenger to Heath in 1974 there was deep unease in the party about his leadership and a strong body of opinion in favour of a change. The problem was that the most promising successors were all loyal to Heath and would not agree to stand if they had to fight him. The curious situation had developed where those who wanted a leader other than Heath only had a chance of getting who they wanted by voting initially for someone they did not, namely a candidate from the right of the party who had no inhibitions about challenging Heath.[23]

Heath was eventually persuaded to submit himself to a new election under a new set of rules drawn up by the former Conservative leader, Lord Home. This at last provided for an annual election of the leader. For such an election to take place, however, there had to be someone prepared to challenge. Keith Joseph had seemed certain to fill that role, but once he had ruled himself out, and Edward Du Cann could not be persuaded to stand, the way was clear for Margaret Thatcher to step in.

Thatcher had been a relatively junior member of Heath's cabinet; her ministerial experience was confined to education. In 1974 she had become a front-bench spokesman on Treasury matters and had considerably increased her reputation with MPs by her attacks on the Finance Bill. In opposition she had become associated with Keith Joseph's critical assessment of the record of the Heath government through her sponsorship of the Centre for Policy Studies, but there had been no stream of ideological speeches from her, nor had she opposed any of the policies of the government while she had been in the cabinet.

Her emergence as the standard-bearer of the anti-Heath forces in the Conservative Party was unexpected, but just credible enough to make her challenge a serious one. At the outset few expected her to win, but she did have certain advantages. Her campaign was very skilfully managed by Airey Neave, she had few enemies in the party determined to prevent her election, and she benefited from drawing on the support of all those who did not want her as leader but hoped that a sufficiently large vote for her would persuade Heath to resign.

Her campaign managers skilfully exploited this last factor, playing down Thatcher's chances of winning outright and fanning the fears of those who knew that if Heath got a sizeable majority on the first ballot it might be impossible to shift him from the leadership for a long time. The strategy worked perfectly. When the vote was announced the confidence of the Heath camp that they were heading for an easy victory was shattered. Thatcher had won 130 votes, Heath 119, Hugh Fraser 16.

Heath now departed and the way was open for all his loyal lieutenants to come forward to join the contest. But now another factor operated in Thatcher's favour. She had set up an irresistible momentum. The *Daily Telegraph* headlined an editorial: 'Consider her Courage'. Thatcher had made the all-important psychological break with the Heath era. Her victory in the first ballot had created a quite new situation. As a result her support did not diminish in the second ballot, it increased. She now won 146 votes; Whitelaw received 79, Prior 19, Howe 19 and Peyton 11. It was an extraordinary triumph but it was due mainly to the number of Conservative MPs wishing to vote against Heath rather than to the number wishing to vote for Thatcher. Almost by accident the New Right found they had captured the most important position in the Conservative Party.[24]

Opposition

Margaret Thatcher had become leader of a Conservative Party that was in disarray and still demoralised after its heavy defeat in 1974. The party badly needed a new strategy and a new self-confidence to allow it to restore its former dominance of British politics. It had to rebuild its electoral appeal and had to develop a new programme for government.

There was widespread gloom in the Conservative Party in 1974 and 1975 about the party's future prospects, a gloom that in some parts of the party Thatcher's election did nothing to dispel. Harold Macmillan reflected this mood when he said in 1975: 'The Tory party is not regarded as a national party now. We tried – Churchill, Eden, myself – to make it a sort of jolly for everyone. It was a party for the nation. Now I'm afraid they've lost that'.[25] John Biffen, a leading critic of the policies of the Heath government reflected:[26]

> Today the Conservative party no longer receives the support of MPs from Northern Ireland, its representation in Scotland is lower than at any time in this century and in England it has barely a Westminster toe-hold in the large industrial cities. There is a real danger that the Tories will become the middle class party of the English shires.

What many Conservatives feared also was that their party would be marginalised by the way in which governments responded to the recession. If the trend towards the strengthening of corporatist structures continued, the main beneficiary would be the Labour Party with its close ties to the unions. Labour might be perceived as more relevant and more competent as a party of government. If the

Conservatives could not win trade-union consent how could they govern? And why should voters support them?

The party had climbed back from heavy defeats before, but in 1975 the future did not look hopeful. The decline of the party as a national political force was evident, as John Biffen suggested. The Conservatives had become closely identified with the EEC which seemed to hand the valuable card of defender of national sovereignty to Labour. The Empire had gone and Britain was no longer a great power. Its economy was in a mess and economic performance had been relatively much poorer than many of its closest rivals. The Conservatives had become the advocates of modernisation and rapid social change in the interests of improving industrial efficiency. Their traditional role as defender of national institutions and the English way of life had become blurred. In the recent past the Conservatives seemed to have cut themselves off from many of their natural supporters, and had lost the wider popular support they had gained in 1970 because they had been unable to sustain their authority as a strong and competent government capable of improving the performance of the economy.

Harold Macmillan's advice to the party he had once led was forthright:[27]

> Don't be doctrinaire. Reunite the party at the top. Reunite it in the House of Commons. Invigorate the old Tory machine, which has largely been allowed to collapse. The party is in disorder. The Tories have got to get themselves into a position to fulfil their role, whatever that role may be – we can't tell yet.

Few in the Tory establishment seem to have believed that Margaret Thatcher would be able to reunite the party. Many thought that in electing her the party risked accelerating its decline. Her appeal was regarded as strictly limited. There were numerous jibes about her supposedly suburban and middle-class image, as well as her gender. Ian Gilmour warned during the leadership campaign that the party must not retire 'behind a privet hedge' if it wanted to acquire a broad national appeal.[28] Julian Critchley recalls a fellow Conservative describing Margaret Thatcher soon after her election to parliament as just like the chairman of his Conservative Women's association 'writ horribly large'.[29]

Disdain for the new leader was curiously shared at first by many New-Right intellectuals. Thatcher lacked the intellectual qualities of Keith Joseph; her right-wing views always appeared much more a matter of instinct than rational argument. She was seen by some as comparable to a mid-West American politician, strong on first principles, weak on understanding of the complexities of the modern economy. Her lack of political and intellectual sophistication invited ridicule. The Conservative political class had long despised conviction politics and those who practised it. They prided themselves on their intelligence, flexibility and pragmatism. Thatcher's abrasive, direct style swept all that away and threw into panic the devotees of the Tory political arts.

Her leadership in opposition certainly did not follow in all respects the pattern prescribed by Harold Macmillan. Her election unleashed a remarkable outpouring of doctrine in the party, assisted by the highly doctrinaire tone of most of the leader's own utterances, and there was no reuniting of the party at the top. Thatcher's purge of the shadow cabinet she inherited was fairly modest, considering that only three out of 23 are thought to have voted for her in the leadership election. But the victims included some major figures, such as Peter Walker, who had been a senior minister in the Heath government, had run Heath's campaign and was younger than Thatcher herself.

The most significant absence, however, in Margaret Thatcher's shadow cabinets was Edward Heath. His exclusion advertised the deep division that had opened up in the ranks of the Tory leadership, a division that was to last throughout the Thatcher years, although it was to become less significant as Thatcher's dominance increased. Heath moved steadily into a position of bitter personal antagonism towards Thatcher and denounced many of the policies she adopted and pursued. In a manner that was unprecedented for a former Tory leader he carried on the battle in public – at the party conference, in the House of Commons and through the media.

There was never any question of a Heath restoration. But his vocal opposition to the new leader and the direction she was taking the party did express the views of many of those inside the shadow cabinet. Many of the senior Conservatives whom Thatcher did not consider it prudent to remove from her shadow cabinet were strong supporters, if not of Heath personally, certainly of the policies he advocated. From the start Thatcher moved cautiously. Her supporters were in a minority in her shadow cabinet and in her first cabinet as well. The Conservative leadership was divided by her style of leadership and the policies with which she was identified to a greater degree than at any time since the 1930s.

The pace at which new policies were developed was, however, very slow.[30] The Conservatives were not committed to a radical Thatcherite programme by the 1979 election. Yet by that date the main outlines of Thatcherism were clearly established. A new political agenda had been marked out, and with it the outline of the political project to restore the fortunes of the Conservative Party, through a distinctive economic strategy to reverse economic decline and a distinctive political strategy to rebuild the authority of the state.

Thatcher attracted enormous attention when she became leader of the Conservatives, at first because she was the first woman leader of any major British political party, but subsequently because of her very distinctive political style, which began to emerge in her responses to the events and crises that destroyed the authority of the Labour government and undermined the credibility of its policies. Thatcher took full advantage of this. She used every opportunity during her time in opposition to intervene on particular issues.

A firm image of her objectives and beliefs soon began to crystallise. Her lead encouraged the marshalling of powerful popular and intellectual forces in support of a radical programme. This programme was never adopted as the programme of the Conservative Party, but it became the rallying point for all those groups who wished to overturn the old politics and destroy the old consensus. A thousand flowers began to bloom on the New Right. Enormous hopes and expectations began to be invested in this new leader.[31]

The way in which her image came to be formed can be traced through the major interventions made by her between 1975 and 1979. She focused on those areas where the authority of the state had been weakened. The solutions she favoured and the attitudes she struck defined a new role for the Conservative Party, but it was a very different role from the one envisaged by Harold Macmillan. Instead of cleaving to the centre and rebuilding an image of soundness, competence and moderation, Thatcher provided something much more exciting and risky – a radical assault on the assumptions of the postwar consensus on domestic policy in the name of Conservative principles.

Yet the intervention that first gave content to Thatcherism and expressed Thatcher's new style was not a radical break with the postwar consensus but a return to one of its most central themes. In a speech in Kensington on 19 January 1976 Thatcher launched a major attack on the policy of détente and called for a major new arms build-up by the NATO countries and an ideological crusade against communism.

The speech was one of the opening shots in the new Cold War. It brought Thatcher considerable notoriety, especially after she had been labelled the Iron Lady by the Soviet media. The epithet was gratefully accepted and iron became an essential part of the Thatcher image. In her speech Thatcher denounced the Soviet Union, declaring that its leaders were bent on world dominance and were 'rapidly acquiring the means to become the most powerful imperial nation the world has seen'. A constant theme was impatience at Western weakness: 'They put guns before butter, while we put just about everything before guns'. She warned of the huge gap that she claimed had opened up between the size of the conventional forces on each side. Most striking of all, however, were the constant references in the speech of the need for moral rearmament against the Soviet threat. She quoted Alexander Solzenitsyn approvingly for reminding the West that 'we have been fighting a "Third World War" over the entire period since 1945 – and that we have been steadily losing ground'. She cited the loss of Vietnam and Indo-China and the 'open grab for power' in Portugal, and warned:[32]

Even now the Soviet Union and its satellites are pouring money, arms and front-line troops into Angola in the hope of dragging it into the Communist bloc ... the Russians ... have one great advantage over us – the battles are being fought on our territory not theirs.

Britain must wake up:[33]

The advance of Communist power threatens our whole way of life. It is not irreversible, providing that we take the necessary measures. But the longer we go on running down our means of survival, the harder it will be to catch up. In other words, the longer Labour remains in government, the more vulnerable this country will be.

The first need therefore was to get rid of socialism and social-democratic governments throughout the West. She took comfort from the recent election victories by right-wing parties in Australia and New Zealand:[34]

What has happened in Australasia is part of a wider re-awakening to the need to provide a more positive defence of the values and traditions on which Western civilisation, and our modern prosperity, have been based.

The speech was also notable for its firm support of the Atlantic Alliance and its lukewarm endorsement of Europe – Britain's membership had been recently confirmed in the 1975 referendum: 'We believe in the Conservative Party that our foreign policy should continue to be based on a close understanding with our traditional ally, America'. For the EEC she cautioned 'the interests of individual nations are not identical, and our separate identities must be seen as a strength rather than a weakness. Any steps towards closer European union must be carefully considered'.[35]

This was coupled with the traditional endorsement of Britain's greatness and special mission in the world. Thatcher rejected the idea that Britain was no longer a great power. The decline in Britain's former strength, she declared, was partly inevitable, caused by the rise of the super powers, and partly avoidable, 'the result of our economic decay, resulting from processes that the Labour Government has assisted'. The speech ended on what was to become a major theme of Thatcherism: 'The Conservative Party has a vital task in shaking the British public out of the effects of a prolonged course of sedation'.[36] The shaking was only just beginning.

Thatcher's speeches on foreign policy marked a shift away from the pro-EC stance of the party under Heath and a reaffirmation of the party's commitment to the Atlantic Alliance. This coolness towards the EC had already been demonstrated during the referendum campaign in 1975, when the major Conservative contribution to the pro-referendum campaign had been left to Edward Heath. There was never any suggestion that the party might reverse the commitment it had made to the EEC, but there was no longer such enthusiasm about Europe and no wish to see the Community develop quickly as a supranational body.

In her onslaught on détente Thatcher first demonstrated her ability to define issues in new ways and to change the existing agenda. Her taste for moralising and for seeing problems in simple black and white terms began to delight her followers and enrage her critics. Her interventions on policy were rarely cleared with her colleagues. Reginald Maudling, who had reentered the shadow cabinet as foreign-affairs spokesman after Thatcher's election, became appalled at the way in which Thatcher chose to make impromptu policy pronouncements. One of these appeared to commit the party, without prior discussion, to a major programme of rearmament. His protests were ignored and he was soon removed from his post.[37]

The attack on détente and the reaffirmation that the Anglo–American alliance had greater priority than the EEC were hardly bold positions staked out against the tide of British political opinion. They were attitudes shared entirely by the Labour governments of Wilson and Callaghan. But Thatcher skilfully exploited the new Cold War fears to outbid any position taken up by the Labour government. Labour was condemned for vacillation and weakness in the face of the 'threat to freedom'.

Another area where Thatcher intervened to help shape the agenda of the new politics was economic policy. Once again the radicalism and novelty of the positions taken up by the Conservative leadership can be exaggerated. Much of the replacement of a Keynesian by a monetarist policy regime was the work of the Labour government in response to the crisis in the world economy between 1974 and 1976. What the Conservatives argued was that Labour's conversion to monetarism was produced by circumstances, not by conviction, and would be reversed at the earliest opportunity. They also claimed that it was too little, too late. The monetary cure had to go much further if sound money was to be restored and if new life was to be breathed into the ailing British economy.

What gave the attacks by the Thatcher leadership such edge was the critical state of the British economy in the 1970s. The failure of successive governments to reverse the relative decline by trying to modernise the productive base of the economy in line with best practice in Fordist economies elsewhere was evident. The weakness of many British industrial sectors was now painfully exposed by the world recession.

The Labour government, after dropping its own radical programme after 1975,[38] attempted to cope with the recession by a mixture of pragmatism and opportunism. It used whatever policies and institutions were to hand. It had no coherent economic strategy. Its ambitions were aimed at preventing the situation from getting any worse. The policies of the Labour government were quite successful within their limits. After the first two years and a series of major crises involving inflation, public spending and sterling, the situation was stabilised. Inflation fell sharply, the pound began to rise with the prospect of North Sea oil coming on stream, unemployment did not rise beyond 1.5 million, the incomes policy held and strikes declined to very low levels.

These achievements were, however, scorned by the Thatcherites and the New Right, although for a time during 1978 they were understandably nervous that the economic improvement and the parliamentary pact with the Liberals[39] might help Labour to recover enough electoral popularity to win the election. The basis of their scorn was their conviction that the old political formulas were tired and played out. British decline could not be reversed by Labour's defensive policies: subsidising jobs, propping up or nationalising industries that got into difficulties; protecting and strengthening the position of trade unions; and attempting to control a wide range of wages and prices.

What Thatcher grasped was that the productive base of British capitalism was so enfeebled that it could no longer support the public-sector spending programmes and the tripartite structures of economic policy-making, which gave a veto to producer interests on radical policies. Profitability had to be rebuilt, and to achieve this a new economic strategy had to be pursued that would give priority to sound money, free markets, lower taxes and greatly reduced trade-union power.

Under Thatcher's leadership, through its enthusiastic embrace of monetarism the Conservative Party first began to signal its interest in a radically different economic strategy from the one being pursued by the Labour government, even though its policy statements remained cautious and pragmatic. On becoming leader Thatcher had moved Michael Wolff from his post as head of the Conservative Research Department and had given Keith Joseph the job of coordinating policy and research. Both Joseph and Thatcher had become identified with the New-Right critique of Keynesian economic management, but while Joseph explored the deeper intellectual arguments in favour of a new policy regime, Thatcher was chiefly interested in finding solutions to inflation. She argued passionately in favour of stable prices as the most important economic objective. Monetarist arguments provided a useful justification for a policy objective she felt should be central to any Conservative programme.[40]

The appeal of monetarism was much more than a set of techniques for controlling the money supply. In Thatcher's hands the arguments against Keynesianism became an opportunity to restate the case for a free society. Stable money was one of its foundations, but limits on public expenditure and the removal of obstacles to free competition were also crucial. The major obstacles to a free economy were identified as the spreading network of corporatist institutions, which were encroaching on the functioning of free markets. The main targets were the Labour government's incomes policy, the influence of the trade unions over government policy, the proposals of the Bullock report for legislation to enforce industrial democracy within all enterprises with trade unionists on company boards, the new measures of nationalisation in vehicles, shipbuilding and aerospace, and the level of public expenditure, borrowing and taxation.[41]

Thatcher always made it clear that she intended to break with the corporatist style of economic management practised by both Labour and the Heath government in its last phase. As the party in opposition the Conservatives were obliged to distance themselves from the programme of the Labour government and revive once more the traditional free-market, individualist critique of state power. What was new was that this turn in party policy was not just a matter of electoral expediency but was now also bolstered by a set of doctrines about how the economy worked and how British decline could best be reversed. The Conservatives now had a leadership that was convinced that a major power struggle was going to be necessary before the economy could be turned around and a new and viable economic policy regime installed.

Thatcher succeeded in identifying the party with the assumptions and conclusions of monetarist analysis and made it plain that the party would reject corporatism. One of her chief targets was incomes policy. In her Conference speech in 1976 Thatcher supported the return of free collective bargaining in place of the kind of incomes policy achieved through Labour's social contract with the unions. She argued that the only reason there had been a clash between the unions and the Heath government was because of the imposition of a statutory incomes policy, which the next Conservative government would not repeat.

Throughout the period of Labour's voluntary policy (1975–8) the Conservative opposition indicated it would scrap all controls. When the policy finally collapsed in the wave of public-sector strikes in the winter of 1978–9 Thatcher's stance seemed vindicated. But it had only been maintained against powerful opposition within the party. Many leading Conservatives believed an incomes policy was a vital instrument in the management of the economy, and that the only alternative to it was to permit the creation of much higher levels of unemployment.

Leading figures in the Tory Reform Group urged the creation of a Tory social contract, which would combine understandings on pay with government commitments on industrial democracy and urban deprivation.[42] There were widespread misgivings about abandoning attempts to secure an understanding with the trade unions and relying on a revival of the disciplines of bankruptcy and unemployment to curb prices. This pressure was resisted however. Thatcher's repeated denunciations of statutory incomes policy ensured that by 1979 the party was committed to a return to free collective bargaining and therefore to curbing trade-union power by other means.

What these other means might be was left vague during the years of opposition. The policy documents *The Right Approach* (1976) and *The Right Approach to the Economy* (1977) promised very little new legislation on unions. The opposition spent a lot of time trying to dispel the idea that any future Conservative government would be embroiled once again in confrontations with the unions. The leadership gave considerable thought to the question. Two internal reports were prepared, one by Nicholas Ridley and one by Lord Carrington, to advise the shadow cabinet on its options in the face of major industrial unrest under a future Conservative government. Carrington was more pessimistic than Ridley. In his report Ridley argued for a policy of fighting public-sector strikes in industries where the government was confident of winning, and avoiding them where it was not, until it had built up its strength sufficiently to be sure of victory.[43]

Thatcher made her own characteristic contribution in an interview on *Weekend World* in September 1977. Pressed to say how she would respond if a government led by her were faced with a new miners' strike she said that she would call a referendum. This idea received no favour among her colleagues and was subsequently dropped. The handling of the miners, however, from the payment of subsidy to keep pits open in 1981 followed by the carefully prepared breaking of the strike in 1984–5, showed that Ridley's report was not forgotten.[44]

Thatcher and Joseph seem to have been in no doubt that a major curb on trade-union power was indispensable, but in opposition they trod carefully, preparing the ground rather than drawing up the kind of detailed plan with which the Heath government had entered office in 1970. Important members of the shadow cabinet, such as James Prior, fought a long and successful rearguard action against the rising tide of anti-union feeling in the party. Norman Tebbit, still a backbencher but by now one of four key advisers to Thatcher,[45] denounced the attitude of some party leaders to the unions as demonstrating the morality of Laval and Petain, the French leaders who were prepared to collaborate with the Nazis.

Pressure for commitments by the opposition to tighten the law was particularly strong at the time of the Grunwick dispute in 1977.[46] The party leadership, however, contented itself with denunciations of union power, but made no firm proposals for curbing it. Yet since the party was also committed to do without an incomes policy and to reduce the scope of subsidy and intervention, the need to weaken trade-union power became an inescapable necessity. The opportunity to press for new laws finally came with the Winter of Discontent.

Thatcher and Joseph seized on the events of that winter of 1978–9 as a symbol of the bankruptcy of social democracy. It seemed to confirm everything they had been saying about the impossibility of going on in the old way and trying to keep the old consensus together. Trade-union power could not be appeased. It had to be destroyed if decline was to be reversed and the authority of the state restored. The myth of the Winter of Discontent, with its images of closed hospitals, rubbish piling up in the streets and dead bodies rotting unburied in graveyards, was a masterpiece of selective news management in the Conservative interest and even came to surpass another great myth fostered by the Conservatives, the myth of the 1976 IMF crisis.[47]

It reawakened all the fears about union militancy that had been stilled by the social contract, and it once again raised doubts as to whether the project of social democracy in Britain still had the capacity to be hegemonic. Its economic strategy had proved inadequate to reverse the decline of British capitalism, it had lost the ability to command the support of key sectors of capital and organised labour, and its electoral coalition was visibly fragmenting. It could no longer sustain the authority of the state against challenge. It had produced a weak state and a fettered economy.

Thatcherism offered deliverance from all this.[48] Emboldened by the winter carnival, the Conservatives at last made some explicit if still cautious commitments in their 1979 manifesto. There was no great trumpet call to announce the beginning of the Thatcher revolution. There were few indications in the manifesto of the storm that was about to break.

4

The Thatcher government, 1979–90

> Our country's relative decline is not inevitable. We in the Conservative Party think we can reverse it. We want to work with the grain of human nature, helping people to help themselves.... The Conservative Government's first job will be to rebuild our economy and reunite a divided and disillusioned people.
>
> Conservative Election Manifesto, 1979

The Conservatives' victory in 1979 was decisive but not overwhelming. The party's share of the vote recovered from its low point in 1974 to reach 43.9 per cent. The Conservatives won 339 seats, a majority over all other parties of 43. A Conservative victory had seemed probable after the collapse of the authority of the government during the IMF negotiations at the end of 1976 and the subsequent loss of its parliamentary majority. Labour had trailed the Conservatives by as much as twenty-five points in the opinion polls in some months between the autumn of 1976 and the summer of 1977. The party had suffered some major by-election losses in this period,[1] as well as enormous losses in local government seats.

The by-election defeats had deprived the Labour government of its overall majority in parliament, and the opposition had some hopes of forcing a general election halfway through the government's term. This was avoided by the conclusion of a parliamentary pact with the Liberals in

March 1977. The government's popularity recovered markedly at the end of 1977 and during 1978, but it chose not to call an election as expected in the autumn after the ending of the Lib–Lab pact. It then suffered the second major blow to its authority with the strikes of public-sector workers in early 1979. What brought the government down however was not the Winter of Discontent but its inability to maintain its parliamentary majority. The crucial event here was the failure of the devolution referenda in Scotland and Wales.[2] This allowed the opposition to press a vote of no confidence and to force an election at a time of their choosing.

Before May 1979 it was unclear whether the radicalism of Thatcher and her supporters was merely a tactic in the battle for electoral support that would be quickly discarded in office, or whether it would be carried through in government. Even for those who accepted that Thatcher's intentions were radical there was still doubt as to how far the Conservatives, if elected, would be able to carry through a New-Right programme within the existing state, or how extensive a restructuring of the state they might be forced to undertake in order to overcome obstacles.

Many of the early interpretations of Thatcherism were based on the performance of the Conservatives in opposition, or on the experience of the first term of government. Only now is it possible to see the Thatcherite project in all the phases of its development. Thatcherism turned out to be no brief spasm, no six-months wonder. It dominated an entire decade, and its legacy remains powerful.

The easiest way to divide up the Thatcher years is by the dates of the general elections: Thatcherism mark I, 1979–83; Thatcherism mark II, 1983–7; Thatcherism mark III, 1987–90. The rationale for this approach is that if the governing party is defeated an election can mark major changes in the personnel, the style and the programme of government. Even when the existing government is reelected an election means a new manifesto and a new legislative programme, and usually a major cabinet reshuffle.

What an emphasis on elections fails to capture, however, are the trends, continuities and patterns that are independent of the election cycle.[3] These are often striking even between governments formed by different parties, and are particularly strong in the case of governments that are reelected. They allow different phases in the life of a government to be identified. They may be created by particular events and issues, by particular policies and doctrines, or by the patterns of party support and conflict.

Britain has become so integrated into the world economy that the greatest influence on the electoral and economic cycles of its domestic politics has become the trends in the world economy. Using this criterion there were three crucial phases in the life of the Thatcher government. The first was determined by the slump in the world economy between 1979 and 1982, the second by the recovery between 1982 and 1987, and the third by the new world recession that began to take hold following the stock-market crash in October 1987. The slump, which brought to an end the partial recovery from the earlier recession in 1974–5, was triggered by the rise in oil prices in 1979. The recovery after 1981 was fuelled and sustained by the budget and trade deficits of the United States. The world recession at the end of the 1980s was caused by the collapse of the boom due to the unsustainable growth of debt, which reignited inflation and punished the hubris of the Reagan–Thatcher years.

pride, arrogance

Phase I, 1979–82 : the slump

The monetary cure

The first phase of the Thatcher government lasted from May 1979, when it was elected, to the March budget of 1982 and was dominated by the consequences of the government's determination to maintain a strict monetarist policy in order to bring down inflation. The conquest of inflation was the government's top priority. It had decided to apply a monetary cure for inflation before the onset of the recession, and it persevered with the policy even when the severity of the recession became apparent.

The major rise in oil prices in 1979 reduced world demand and increased industrial costs. At the same time it placed further upward pressure on sterling. The UK became a significant oil producer at the end of the 1970s. Since 1977 the markets had begun to anticipate this fact and sterling had begun to appreciate markedly in value. OPEC's decision to increase oil prices by 15 per cent was announced on 28 June. Two weeks before, on 12 June, the new chancellor, Sir Geoffrey Howe, introduced a budget that had two principal objectives – lowering the rate of inflation through a severe monetary and fiscal squeeze and beginning a major restructuring of the burden of taxation. The rate of VAT was doubled from 8 per cent to 15 per cent, income tax was reduced from 33 per cent to 30 per cent and prescription charges in the National Health Service were increased. At the same time personal tax allowances were raised and the top income-tax rate was lowered from 83 per cent to 60 per cent. Dividend control was abolished, a new higher threshold for investment income was announced and development land tax was cut.

These measures were intended to increase incentives and signal the new direction of government policy. They were accompanied by the announcement of new money-supply targets, a pledge to reduce the public-sector borrowing requirement (PSBR) to £8.25 billion and the immediate raising of the minimum lending rate (MLR) from 12 per cent to 14 per cent. Public expenditure was to be cut by £1.5 billion and where annual cash limits on spending programmes were in force they were tightened to reduce planned expenditure by a further £1 billion.

In its first few months in office the Thatcher government made some other crucial decisions that signalled its intentions to break not only with many of the policies of the previous government, but also to dispense with several of the key institutions and agencies through which previous governments had intervened in the economy. It placed its faith in the private sector and the removal of obstacles to the working of free markets.

In July and October 1979 all remaining currency-exchange restrictions were removed. This abandonment of exchange controls on capital movements proved permanent. On 19 June the privatisation programme began when the National Enterprise Board (NEB) was ordered to sell assets worth £100 million. On 1 October the British National Oil Corporation (BNOC) was forced to give up many of its interests in oil exploration and its stake in 23 blocks in the North Sea was put up for sale. On 17 July the government announced that the regional support budget was to be cut by £233 million (one third of the total budget) within three years.

These early decisions were taking place alongside a growing number of challenges to organised labour. On 1 November, one week after the removal of all exchange restrictions, the closure of the steel works at Corby was announced by the British Steel Corporation. In another nationalised industry, British Leyland, the management began the start of a major crackdown on the shop floor when they sacked Derek Robinson, the convenor of the shop stewards, on 19 November. The government made plain that in the public sector it was prepared for closures and redundancies, and would back tough management policies to carry through whatever degree of restructuring was necessary to restore profitability and end public subsidies.

By the end of 1979 the general condition of the economy was beginning to deteriorate rapidly. The government responded to evidence that money supply-growth was accelerating by hoisting MLR from 14 per cent to 17 per cent in November. The year ended with decisions by first Saudi Arabia and then Libya to impose major increases in the price of light crude oil.

The government had already shown its strong commitment to monetarism by raising interest rates from 12 per cent to 17 per cent within six months of taking office. In the budget in March 1980, however, it went much further by announcing a medium-term financial strategy (MTFS).[4] This aimed to provide greater certainty about future monetary conditions by indicating targets for both money supply and government borrowing. If the targets were not met there would be automatic fiscal or monetary changes in government policy. The room for discretionary economic management, which was held to have been so destabilising in the past, would be drastically reduced.

The MTFS, as unveiled in 1980, sought to set targets for money-supply growth (using one particular measure of the money supply, sterling M3, as the indicator) over a four-year period. It was planned to decline to 6 per cent by 1983–4. Money supply would be tightened by increasing interest rates when necessary in order to achieve this. At the same time the PSBR would be gradually reduced, if necessary by cutting spending or increasing taxes. The government deficit would not be allowed to increase and would not be financed in ways that increased the money supply.

From the outset the control and reduction of public expenditure was an essential part of the monetary cure for inflation. The new assumptions were clearly spelled out in the White Paper on Public Expenditure in November 1979. With its first sentence, 'public expenditure is at the heart of our current difficulties' the white paper challenged the bipartisan consensus that had existed since the 1940s on the desirability of high levels of public expenditure. Cuts were no longer necessary simply to meet a short-term fiscal crisis. They had to be permanent and deep in order to lay the foundations for economic revival and long-term economic prosperity.

The white paper opened a war on all fronts. Specific proposals included the withdrawal of supplementary benefit from strikers' families, the taxing of unemployment benefit and new increases in prescription charges, excise duties and petrol revenue tax. The white paper planned a reduction in public expenditure of 4 per cent by 1983–4.

During 1980 the recession deepened rapidly. High interest rates and soaring oil prices combined to push up sterling by 12 per cent. The competitive position of British companies declined by 35–45 per cent. Both profits and liquidity were severely squeezed. A mounting wave of bankruptcies, plant closures and lay-offs was the result. Unemployment rose rapidly month by month. By the end of the year it had reached 2.13 million, an increase of 836 000. Inflation was soaring too, peaking at 21.9 per cent in May 1980.

The severity of the recession brought the first modification in the policy in the autumn of 1980. The MLR was reduced to 14 per cent, even though the figures for £M3

Minimum Lending Rate

were running far above the target range. The government argued that the figures had been distorted by the removal of the Bank of England's 'corset' on bank lending in July, and that the strength of sterling indicated that monetary conditions must be tight.

The fiscal targets were also proving hard to achieve. Treasury ministers encountered great problems in forcing through cabinet the cuts they wanted in public expenditure. Some spending ministers argued that it was unwise to cut spending when the country was in the grip of such a deep recession.

However expectations that monetarism would be short-lived and that the severity of the recession would oblige the government to change tack proved mistaken. In the 1981 budget the tight monetary policy was maintained. MLR was again cut and the monetary targets were modified, but what enraged the critics of monetarism within the cabinet was that direct taxation was sharply increased because tax allowances were not increased in line with inflation. This was done to ensure that the borrowing targets fixed by the chancellor the previous year, and which he had been unable to reach through spending cuts, would still be achieved. In the midst of the deepest recession since 1945 the government made progress towards fiscal balance its priority rather than attempting to counteract the fall in demand.[5]

The application of the tight monetary policy and its consequences dominated the first phase of the Thatcher government. The depth of the recession had not been anticipated, but those ministers and political advisers who were strongly influenced by monetarist thinking seized on it as an opportunity for forcing through the radical changes they desired in economic policy and economic structure. An atmosphere of cutbacks, closures and retrenchment pervaded the public and private sectors. By launching a policy blitz and attacking simultaneously on so many fronts the government encouraged the belief that it was bent on radical change of attitudes, institutions and policies, and that it was determined to see the policies through whatever the short-term costs.

During its first eighteen months in office there was a spate of decisions announcing closures and cuts in areas of direct government responsibility.) Many of these decisions were aimed at destroying institutions and reversing policies associated with the Labour government. Fifty-seven quangos were axed, among them the Price Commission. The National Enterprise Board was stripped of most of its functions, and after its directors had resigned en bloc it was merged into the British Technology Group. The July 1979 Education Act withdrew the instruction to local authorities to organise their schools on comprehensive lines. In November 1980 the Community Land Act was repealed.

Trade unions and the public sector

Despite its eagerness to smash icons and break taboos in order to reshape the policy agenda, the government's radicalism was most apparent where decisions could be easily implemented and cost little. Abolishing boards and public agencies were the best example of this. In several key areas of policy, particularly industrial relations and nationalised industries, the government initially moved extremely cautiously.)

The first trade-union bill was put through in 1980. But although it restricted picketing and defined tighter limits for the closed shop, it was a modest measure and was strongly criticised for not going further. James Prior, the employment secretary, was one of the leading anti-monetarists in the cabinet, and although he favoured trade-union reform he was a restraining influence both in opposition and government on those who wanted much tougher measures to be enacted.[6] There was no disposition at first to confront union power directly for fear of presenting the unions with the kind of issue around which they could rally effective protest, as had happened with the Heath government's Industrial Relations Act.

In opposition the Conservatives had anticipated that major problems with the trade unions would arise in the public sector. The strategy recommended in the Ridley report in 1978[7] was faithfully followed. At first the government only picked quarrels where it was sure of victory. It backed the management of BSC when the first national steel strike for more than fifty years began in January 1980. The strike was defeated after four months. But when the miners began an overtime ban in February 1981 over pit closures the government swiftly retreated and found a subsidy to defuse the issue.[8]

Elsewhere in the public sector during this early phase the government attempted to make nationalised industries more efficient by backing a new breed of managers, often imported from the private sector, to put the industries into competitive shape and staunch the flow of losses. Major confrontations with shop floor power followed. Some of the greatest struggles came in British Leyland, as Michael Edwardes, appointed by the previous Labour government, reorganised the company by reducing the workforce, closing plants, changing working practices and investing in new models. In 1980 Ian MacGregor was brought in to do the same for BSC.[9]

One radical option that had been canvassed when the government first took office was for the major lossmakers among the nationalised industries, particularly British Leyland, to be declared bankrupt, and their assets sold off for whatever they might fetch.[10] The government retreated from this option once the implications for unemployment became clear. Sir Keith Joseph, the leading advocate of free-market policies within the government, was obliged as secretary of state for industry to preside over the attempt to make the nationalised industries profitable through state intervention. In the short run this meant a massive increase in subsidies to cover their losses.

Intervention in nationalised Industries.

This appeared at the time a significant retreat for the government, since if the government were successful in making the industries profitable it would demonstrate that public enterprise could work; but if it were not successful it would leave the government still subsidising the losses. In the meantime it meant that the government was forced to authorise more public spending on precisely those programmes it most wanted to see cut. Denationalisation of other public sector assets was pursued in part to offset this.

The first moves to sell off public holdings began when the NEB was instructed on 19 June 1979 to sell assets worth £100 million. The government stakes in the computer company, ICL, Fairey Holdings and Ferranti were all sold over the next year. In addition the government sold 5 per cent of its stake in British Petroleum (BP) in January 1980. This was followed by the sale of 52 per cent of the government's holding in British Aerospace (February 1981), its 24 per cent stake in the British Sugar Corporation (July 1981) and 49 per cent of its stake in Cable and Wireless (October 1981). The government's receipts from these early measures of denationalisation were modest – £377 million in 1979–80 and £405 million in 1980–1, but their success created a momentum for sales that were to be carried much further in future years.

The control of public expenditure

The intractability of the problems in the public sector helped throw doubt on whether a key objective of government economic policy – the need to cut taxation and public spending as a proportion of national income – could be achieved. The control and reduction of public expenditure was seen by the government as an essential part of the monetary cure for inflation.

But the government was blown off course almost immediately by the severity of the recession. It increased the subsidies to nationalised industries and it bore the burden of increased spending on social security as the numbers of unemployed soared. In addition the government was committed to increased spending on a number of programmes. Police and army pay were immediately raised by substantial amounts, as promised in the 1979 manifesto, and the defence budget enlarged. More surprisingly the government decided to honour the Clegg Commission's verdicts on public-sector pay. The Clegg Commission had been set up by the previous Labour government to investigate the gap that had opened between pay scales in the public and private sectors. Its recommendations kept appearing until the summer of 1980 and meant sizeable additions to public-sector budgets.

In the face of this wave of higher spending the government sought every available means to reduce spending.

Major spending cuts were announced in November 1979 and in the 1980 budget. Prescription charges were pushed up sharply, the regional aid budget was slashed, overseas-student fees were raised, the Parker Morris standards for new council building were abolished, and school-meals charges and council-house rents were increased. Major reductions in grants to local authorities were announced and university places were cut. A bruising battle at a succession of summits with the other heads of government in the European Community resulted in the negotiation of a sizeable rebate on Britain's budget contribution. The overall level of public spending did not fall, but the government made very plain its hostility to public spending over a wide area and its determination to cut and squeeze wherever it could.

Foreign affairs and defence   ~Thatcher more interested in the US than Europe.~

The battle over the Community budget was an early sign that the Thatcher government, like its Labour predecessor, would give greater priority to the relationship of the UK with the United States than to its relationship with the European Community. There was little enthusiasm, except in the Foreign Office, for the revival of the pro-European policy of the Heath government.

The worsening of relations between the superpowers after the USSR's invasion of Afghanistan in December 1979 led to the American boycott of the Moscow Olympics in 1980, which action was strongly supported by the British government. Margaret Thatcher's Cold-War stance enabled her to play a leading role in the new ideological onslaught on the Soviet Union. She became still more important following the election of Ronald Reagan to the US presidency in 1980. The close political relationship between Thatcher and Reagan helped underline the continuing importance of the Anglo–American relationship in the political and economic management of the world system. Both were to give each other important assistance in the years ahead.

One tangible sign of the new Cold War was the increase in the tempo of the arms race. In July 1980 the government decided to purchase the Trident missile system to replace Polaris as Britain's nuclear deterrent. The plans to station Cruise missiles in Britain had already been laid by the Labour government and were now confirmed.

The government enjoyed an early success in foreign policy when, despite initial opposition from the prime minister, her foreign secretary, Lord Carrington, successfully negotiated a settlement to the civil war in Zimbabwe. This led to the end of the rebellion, democratic elections and the granting of independence in 1980. The end of the Rhodesian rebellion seemed to mark the final end of the Empire as an important factor in British politics. All that remained was negotiating the hand-over of a few far-flung dependencies. The Falklands were soon to confound that notion.

Public order

During this first phase, as the Thatcher government struggled to make the economy free and to restore the authority of the state, it did not neglect to strengthen the capacity of the state to repress disorder. The government had to face two major challenges – the hunger strikes in Northern Ireland and the inner-city riots.

The government was implacable in its opposition to the republican movement in Northern Ireland, particularly following the assassination of Airey Neave, one of Margaret Thatcher's closest advisers, in March 1979 by the Irish National Liberation Army. In Northern Ireland itself the IRA remained the greatest security threat. In August 1979 came the bombing at Warren Point and the murder of Lord Mountbatten. During 1980 a major challenge developed to the government's authority through the hunger strikes. This protest was organised to win political status for republican prisoners in the H blocks in the Maze prison.

The hunger strikes were led by Bobby Sands who, following the death of the sitting MP, was elected MP for Fermanagh and South Tyrone at a by-election in April 1981. The strikes were an early test of Thatcher's political will. She refused to make any concessions to the strikers, despite the sympathy the strikes enabled the IRA to attract both in

Ireland and in the United States. After several of the hunger strikers had died, including Bobby Sands, the strikes were called off.

The inner-city challenge came from the riots that erupted in several major cities, including Bristol (St Paul's), London (Brixton) and Liverpool (Toxteth). These riots helped justify a large increase in the range of police equipment and changes in police training. The burning of the cities at the depth of the recession, with unemployment climbing towards three million, was seen by many as a direct result of the kind of policies the Thatcher government was pursuing. Thatcher vigorously denied this, arguing that the problem had nothing to do with either race or unemployment, but was a problem of public order.[11]

Party and electoral support

In 1980–1 the British economy appeared to have gone into a nosedive and one easily identifiable target for blame was the government's insistence on maintaining a rigid monetary policy. This brought the government great unpopularity and created considerable dissension within the cabinet.

During the first parliamentary session, 1979–80, the main beneficiary of the government's unpopularity was the Labour Party, which saw its opinion-poll ratings leap. In the Southend by-election in March 1980 Labour came close to snatching the seat. In the autumn of 1980, however, a major internal rift developed in the Labour Party. At the Labour Party Conference two of the three constitutional changes sought by the left were passed. This was followed by a leadership election in which Michael Foot defeated Denis Healey and a further Conference at Wembley, which decided on the composition of the electoral college to elect the leader. The largest share, 40 per cent, was given not to the MPs, as the leadership wanted, but to the trade unions. Several prominent Labour MPs, including David Owen and Shirley Williams, then left the party and set up the Social Democratic Party (SDP). Altogether 27 Labour MPs and one Conservative crossed the floor to join the new party in the first six months of 1981.[12]

This major split in the opposition was eventually to work to the advantage of the government. During 1981, however, the new challenge from the electoral alliance concluded between the Liberals and the SDP proved formidable. The Alliance soared in the polls, reaching 40 per cent in some months. In October 1981 it won two major by-election victories in Conservative seats – Croydon NW and Crosby. Government popularity fell at the end of 1981 to the lowest level ever recorded by the party in government. Thatcher was also briefly the most unpopular prime minister since the war.

The economic blitz, the inner city riots and the crumbling of government support caused great unease within the Conservative Party. In her first period as prime minister Thatcher faced a divided cabinet and strong opposition to some of her key policies. She compensated for this by concentrating her main supporters in the economic ministries (she took special care with the choice of her Treasury team). She also used the cabinet committee system to ensure that she retained control over the policy agenda in crucial fields. Nevertheless the dismay of some ministers with the direction of policy found expression in an extraordinary spate of leaks about cabinet discussions and coded messages of opposition in ministerial speeches.[13]

The cabinet opposition were dubbed 'wets' by the media after a phrase of the prime minister. The term was used indiscriminately to denote those who, either on grounds of principle or grounds of expediency, opposed Thatcherite policies. With its public-school overtones of spineless opposition 'wets' came to mean those who lacked the political will and the political courage to take and carry through the hard decisions required by the Thatcher revolution. Thatcher's own personal political style encouraged a cult of toughness, inflexibility and conviction politics. Scepticism was equated with weakness.

The main battle between Thatcher and her cabinet critics came over public spending. In the autumn spending round in 1980 the wets had some success in resisting the full cuts sought by the Treasury. This meant that the government could no longer achieve its targets for government borrowing. To remedy this the Treasury team clawed back what had been lost by deciding not to raise tax allowances in line with inflation in the budget. This meant a sizeable increase in direct taxation at a time when the recession was at its most severe.

In line with the normal convention the 1981 budget proposals were not revealed to the cabinet until the morning of the budget speech. Several ministers contemplated resigning on the spot but none did so. Nevertheless the criticism from inside the government of the direction of government policy grew. The isolation of Thatcher within her cabinet and within the party appeared to be increasing, especially after coded speeches by two senior figures – Francis Pym, the leader of the House, and Lord Thorneycroft, the party chairman.

Thatcher's response was characteristically defiant. In September she launched a major reshuffle of her cabinet, bringing in those committed to her policies and removing or sidelining several of her most prominent critics. Gilmour, Soames and Carlisle resigned and Prior was removed from Employment and made Northern Ireland secretary, although he retained his seat on the cabinet 'E' Committee, which discussed economic strategy. Norman Tebbit, at that time one of Thatcher's most trusted allies and advisers, became employment secretary, while Cecil Parkinson became party chairman and Leon Brittan chief secretary to the Treasury.

Thatcher now had a cabinet more balanced in her favour, although it still contained leading critics such as Prior, Walker and Pym. She also had critics in the party. The 1981 Conservative Party Conference witnessed a fierce denunciation by Edward Heath of the government's economic policy. At the nadir of the government's electoral fortunes in late 1981 prospects for the government's survival looked slim. Most observers thought a Conservative defeat at the next election was certain, and the ability of Margaret Thatcher to survive as prime minister and Conservative leader for much longer was questioned. The Thatcher government seemed to be the latest in a long line of governments that had suffered irreversible damage as a result of bad judgement and ill-fortune. It appeared that the Thatcher experiment would be short-lived.

Phase II, 1982–7: the recovery

These years were golden years for the Conservatives. The government won two general elections by comfortable margins and emerged victorious from a series of major confrontations with its enemies: the Argentinians over the sovereignty of the Falkland Islands; the miners over pit closures; local authorities over ratecapping and the abolition of the GLC and the metropolitan counties; and the peace movement over the stationing of Cruise missiles in the United Kingdom.

The world economy

Underlying the growing confidence and ascendancy of the Conservatives during these years was the recovery in the world economy. The Thatcherites claimed that the recovery after 1981 was due to the monetary stabilisation achieved between 1979 and 1981. The recovery was, however, not confined to Britain but was general throughout the capitalist world economy. It was sustained by the supply-side policies pursued in the United States that reflated the American economy and increased world demand. This created a boom that brought unemployment down to very low levels and fuelled domestic consumption. This boom was kept going by allowing the budget and trade deficits to rise without check. With the other major economies still pursuing tight monetary policies and refusing to reflate, the world economy became increasingly unbalanced. The position was widely regarded as unsustainable. The financial crash finally came in October 1987, threatening the world economy with a new world recession and a collapse in the value of the dollar.

Foreign affairs and defence

The Conservative government profited not only from the world economic recovery but also from its victory in the Falklands war in June 1982. A potential disaster for the government that might have brought its downfall was transformed into a popular triumph. It produced a major improvement in Conservative poll ratings. The display of resolve and the success it brought lent credibility to other government policies. When the British flag was raised again over Port Stanley Thatcher's reputation as a tough, resolute and trustworthy leader became greater than any British leader since Churchill.

The dispatch of the task force to reconquer the islands after the Argentinian invasion appeared a simple exercise of British power and resolve. But the reality was more complicated since Britain's freedom to act in the South Atlantic depended on the tacit agreement of its allies and the active assistance of the United States. It demonstrated the continuing importance of the Anglo–American relationship rather than the reassertion of British national sovereignty.

The close relationship between Britain and the United States was symbolised by the close ties between Reagan and Thatcher. Throughout this phase of the Thatcher government Britain confirmed its traditional postwar role as principal ally of the United States. Britain gave full support to American policy towards the Soviet union, Central America and the Middle East. The most striking instance of British support came in April 1976 when the British government gave permission for American bombers stationed at bases in England to bomb Libya.

In its defence policy the government gave full support to the deployment of cruise missiles. It fought a major propaganda battle with the revived peace movement over the stationing of these missiles at American bases in Britain. The deployment went ahead, despite the demonstrations at Greenham Common and Molesworth. Strains in the relationship came mainly as a result of unilateral American actions that were not cleared in advance with their allies. Prominent examples included the invasion of Grenada, a Commonwealth country, in 1984 and the Reykjavik summit in 1986. At the latter Reagan appeared prepared to agree to Soviet proposals for a nuclear-free Europe. The British desired to retain nuclear weapons as a deterrent.

The relationship with the European Community improved during this second phase of the Thatcher government, although the British were still obstructive on many issues. Thatcher continued to veto British participation in the

European Monetary System (EMS) and to resist increases in the regional-aid budget and other community programmes. On many foreign-policy issues Britain more often lined up with the United States than with its European partners. Examples included the boycotting of UNESCO, support for the contras in Nicaragua, support for American action against Libya and resistance to sanctions against South Africa.

The higher priority given to the United States than to the European Community was clearly seen in economic policy. Despite the very different emphases of American and British policy there was no public criticism from the British government at the growing American deficits. Similarly there was little encouragement to those attempting to strengthen the European economy. The economic strategy pursued by the Thatcher government did not ignore Europe, but at no time did the needs of European capital become its focus.

The Westland affair in 1985–6, although it only concerned a small company, illustrated this. Michael Heseltine, the defence secretary, fought inside the government for a European solution to the problems of Westland helicopters. He wanted the government to reject the bid from the American firm Sikorski, which Westland itself wanted, in favour of a bid from a European consortium of helicopter companies. Heseltine broadened the issue into the question of how to ensure the survival of an independent European manufacturing base. Blocked by the prime minister Heseltine resigned from the cabinet on this issue in 1986, and the decision subsequently went against him.

Economic management

After 1981 it became clear that the worst of the recession was over. Unemployment ceased to rise rapidly, inflation fell sharply, the pound dropped back and a slow recovery in industrial output began. The devastation of large parts of the economy, particularly the areas of old traditional industry, still loomed large. But the decline had stopped. From 1982 onwards the dominant feature of economic policy and debate was not the recession but the recovery and how far it would go.

Government economic policy in this phase shifted from a concern with monetary targets and the control of inflation to the supply-side remedies that were considered necessary to spread prosperity and revive economic activity. Monetarism became steadily less important in government thinking. Zero inflation remained the government's objective but it no longer appeared willing to make the sacrifices to achieve it. The medium-term financial strategy still figured prominently in every budget speech but its targets were now often revised upwards, and the government began to use more than one indicator of monetary conditions. In this way the main complaint of the wets – that government policy was far too rigid – was overcome. Discretionary economic management was reinstated. By 1987 monetarism was quite unimportant as a guide to what the government was doing.[14]

With unemployment relatively stable at three million and the rate of inflation falling below 5 per cent, the government began to experiment with supply-side changes to widen the scope of markets and incentives. The first objective was tax cuts, in the belief that this would provide the incentives that were needed to revive enterprise. Tax cuts and tax reform had long been central to Conservative economic thinking and had featured prominently in the first budget. But the need to cope with accelerating inflation and the deepening recession had deflected ministers away from this part of the strategy. The emphasis had become narrowly monetarist. Many American supply-siders were strongly critical of this orientation arguing that cutting taxes to stimulate enterprise should come before control of the money supply. The Thatcher government, however, continued to emphasise that tax cuts would only be made when it was safe to do so. This meant when spending had been cut or revenue increased.

The government's hopes of achieving a major change in the balance between the public and private sectors depended on its success in holding down public spending and finding new sources of public revenue. Certain areas of spending, notably the health and social-security budgets, were judged too sensitive for major direct cuts. The principal targets in this second phase came to be local-authority spending and subsidies for nationalised industries. The government became involved in major confrontations with local councils seeking to protect their spending and with the National Union of Mineworkers (NUM), seeking to protect jobs and communities.

On the revenue side the government, already a major beneficiary from North Sea oil revenues, found that the easiest way to increase its income was by selling public companies (denationalisation) and privatising public services. After a slow and hesitant start this programme, which the government misleadingly referred to as its privatisation programme, became a significant factor in the planning of the budget.[15]

Local government

After its earlier failures to control local spending through grant penalties, central government now attempted to achieve control through ratecapping. This involved the government drawing up a list of councils it deemed to be overspending and placing a ceiling on the amount by which they could legally increase their local property taxes (rates). This brought about a long struggle with many Labour-controlled councils who tried to avoid the effects of rate capping by refusing to set a legal rate or by creative accountancy to raise additional money.[16]

Relations between central and local government, particularly in the large urban centres, deteriorated so badly that the Conservatives began to seek ways to bypass local councils and take responsibilities from them. In their 1983 manifesto they included a pledge to abolish the GLC and the six metropolitan councils. Some of the functions of these councils, such as transport, were to be removed from local-authority control altogether. A major battle was waged against the abolition of these councils, which caused grave embarrassment to the government, but ultimately the abolition was pushed through in 1986.

By the 1987 election the Conservatives were growing even more hostile towards local government and were proposing a range of new measures to limit the responsibilities and the

power of local authorities) These included the replacement
of rates by a poll tax, to be known as the community charge,
the setting of a uniform business rate, educational and
housing reforms that would allow schools and council
estates to opt out of local authority control, and proposals
on inner-city redevelopment designed to reduce local-
authority involvement.

Trade unions and the public sector

A second major area of confrontation arose over support for
industry. The government was determined to use its control
over nationalised industries to force them to become profitable. The big test came with the mines. After giving way in
1981, faced by the threat of a major stoppage over pit closures the government carefully prepared for a major show-
down. Little was left to chance. Coal stocks were built up at
the power stations, alternative sources of supply were identified, the security forces were alerted, detailed contingency plans were drawn up by Whitehall, and a new tough
chairman, Ian Macgregor, was appointed.

The strike began in March 1984 and lasted eleven months.
It was enormously costly for the government. But it ended in
complete defeat for the miners, once they had split and been
successfully isolated from the rest of the labour movement.
By crushing the miners the government was able to demonstrate to the whole Labour movement that nothing was to be
allowed to stand in the way of restructuring industries to
make them profitable and internationally competitive.[17]

The greater the government's success in hauling nationalised industries back into profit the more attractive the
option of denationalisation. The years 1982–7 saw a series of
major sales of public companies, including British Telecom,
British Gas and British Airways. These sales were justified on
a number of grounds – as a contribution to government revenue, as a means of making companies more efficient and as
a way of boosting popular capitalism by increasing the number of shareholders in Britain. These enormous denationalisations came to be used by the Conservatives as the most
tangible evidence of the Thatcher revolution. In the 1987

manifesto the government promised to denationalise the
water and electricity industries during the new parliament.)

Reducing union power and privileges was given a very
high priority in this second phase of the Thatcher government. Two further pieces of legislation were introduced in
1982 and 1984, aimed at restricting union rights and opening their funds to claims for damages. This legislation contributed to the climate of trade-union demoralisation and
retreat that had been created by mass unemployment. The
government found it increasingly easy to brush aside union
resistance. It imposed strict pay curbs in the public sector
through cash limits, and it showed itself ready to meet and
defeat any strike in the public sector.

The miners' strike was the major test of this resolve. Other
important disputes included the print-union battles at
Warrington in 1983 and Wapping in 1986–7, and the
teachers in 1986–7. Throughout this period the TUC was
frozen out of participation in central-government decision-
making. The government made it clear that what it sought
was either union-free companies and industries or single-
company unions with no-strike agreements. The new forms
of such an industrial-relations system were foreshadowed in
the experiments promoted by some of the Japanese companies, such as Nissan, now beginning to locate in the UK.[18]

Unemployment rose above three million in January 1982
and did not fall below it until July 1987. The number of
long-term unemployed in the total rose sharply. Controversy centred on the frequent government redefinition of
'unemployed', which had the effect of cutting the headline
total by some 600 000 by 1987. The government's main
response to the problem of mass unemployment was the
expansion of the Manpower Services Commission (MSC),
a quango first established by the Heath government and
developed under Labour. The Thatcher government, in its
first phase, cut the MSC budget and seemed poised to
abolish it altogether. With the rapid rise in unemployment, however, the agency was reprieved and became an
extremely powerful and expansionist arm of government.
It organised major programmes, first for the young unemployed and later for the long-term unemployed, and

began to concern itself with all aspects of training and education.[19]

Public order and security

Throughout this second phase the government continued to arm itself to repress violent protest, breaches of public order and, increasingly, internal dissent. A major initiative on Northern Ireland, the Anglo–Irish Agreement, was signed in November 1985. The agreement was a modest document aimed at increasing cooperation between the Irish and British governments, but it produced fierce opposition from the Unionists and attempts by them to make Ulster 'ungovernable'. The Unionists were faced down. The level of IRA activity in Northern Ireland continued to decline during this phase, but they were still capable of major operations. The most spectacular was the bombing at the Conservative Party Conference in Brighton in October 1984, which came close to killing the prime minister and several cabinet ministers.

There were a number of important controversies about security, amidst fears of growing secret-service involvement in domestic surveillance. They included the decision to ban unions at the government intelligence-gathering centre, GCHQ, in 1983; the revelations of former agents such as Cathy Massiter; the Zircon affair – which involved disclosure of information about the government's spy satellite; and the attempts by the government to prevent the memoirs of a former MI6 officer, Peter Wright, from being published in Australia.

Party politics and electoral support

These years saw a strong recovery of the government's popularity. In the general election in June 1983 it won a crushing victory in terms of parliamentary seats over a divided opposition. Between May 1982, after the commencement of the Falklands War, and the end of the miners' strike in March 1985 the government's support in the monthly opinion polls rarely dipped below 40 per cent.

The new strength enjoyed by the government during this period and the increasing ascendancy of Margaret Thatcher as a national and a world leader owed a great deal to the Argentinians' seizure of the Falkland Islands in April 1982 and the government's response to this unexpected crisis. If the bid to retake the islands had been mishandled and had ended in a costly defeat, or if the government had agreed to peace terms that conceded part of the Argentinians' claims, the reputation of the government and of Thatcher herself would have been severely damaged. The successful recapture of the islands created the kind of national euphoria that had long been absent from British politics. It was the first occasion for a very long time that a British government had succeeded in a major undertaking. The effect upon the credibility of the government in all its other activities was considerable. The Falklands War more than any other single episode restored the authority of the state, and with it the political fortunes of the Conservatives Party.[20]

Throughout this period, from the beginning of the Falklands war to the victory celebration at the Conservative Party Conference in 1987, the Conservatives were generally in the ascendancy. Only during 1985, after the end of the miners' strike, and in the first half of 1986 did Conservative electoral fortunes dip. A succession of events – the Westland affair, the Libyan bombing, the schools' dispute, the mishandling of the bill to abolish the GLC and the attempted sale of part of British Leyland to foreign buyers – put the government on the defensive and made it look vulnerable. But although it lost some by-elections its support never crumbled in the way it had in 1981. Labour gained ground once the miners' strike was over, but although it led in the opinion polls it was never able to rise above 40 per cent support. It never established the kind of commanding leads that oppositions in the past had generally achieved prior to victory in a general election.

The two general-election results in 1983 and 1987 were remarkably similar. The Conservatives polled almost the same percentage of the vote as in 1979. Labour came second, but 12–15 percentage points behind. The Alliance came third with a substantial vote, 22–26 per cent, but not sufficient to win a large bloc of seats. The economic prosperity (and even more important the steady economic improvement) for the majority of those in employment, the divided opposition and the geographical concentration of Conservative support made the Conservative position an extremely strong one. In both elections the Conservatives entered the election as clear favourites and held their position throughout the campaign. Labour had a new leader, Neil Kinnock, in 1987 and fought a superior campaign to the Conservatives, but it failed to make a major inroad into Conservative support.

In the Alliance David Owen had replaced Roy Jenkins as leader of the SDP in 1983, but although the Alliance had many electoral successes it never recaptured the levels of support achieved in its first twelve months. When the election came its vote was squeezed between the Conservatives and a strengthened Labour Party. The attempt to merge the Liberals and the SDP immediately after the 1987 election led to a major split within the SDP, and subsequently threatened to split the Liberals also. The disarray of the centre appeared a direct consequence of the failure of the Alliance strategy between 1982 and 1987.

Throughout this phase the prime minister's position was generally unassailable, particularly after the two election victories. The only moment of real danger for her came with the Westland affair, which brought both her veracity and her competence briefly into question.[21] But this moment of danger passed. With the exception of this dramatic episode cabinet dissent was at a much lower level than in the first phase of the Thatcher government. Critics were steadily purged. Francis Pym was removed in 1983, Jim Prior resigned in 1984, Michael Heseltine resigned in 1986, John Biffen was sacked in 1987. The prime minister appeared to exhaust and then alienate even some of the colleagues closest to her, such as John Biffen and Norman Tebbit, the latter leaving the cabinet and resigning as Conservative Party chairman in 1987.[22]

Despite its share of scandals – Parkinson, Archer, Proctor, Best[23] – the Conservative Party retained its confidence and its unity. The wets disappeared as a visible or coherent force within the party. Thatcherite ideas increasingly dominated the party, and the influence of New-Right doctrines and

truthfulness ; veracity.

libertarian groups became more pronounced, especially in the Federation of Conservative Students, among some of the younger MPs and in the Conference itself. Many doubted how far the bulk of the parliamentary party had become committed to Thatcherite doctrines, however. Two decisive election victories and a steadily improving economy were more than sufficient grounds for loyalty to the incumbent leadership.

Phase III, 1987–90: the fall of Thatcher

One of the curiosities of the Thatcher government was that it became more radical as time went on. On several occasions the government appeared to be losing momentum and direction, but each time it recovered, and instead of heeding the advice to consolidate it plunged into a new round of policy change. This capacity to renew its radical purpose was one of the distinctive features of the Thatcherite project and marks the Thatcher government out from other governments.

The last phase of the Thatcher government started with a time of triumph and ended in disaster and disarray, with Thatcher herself ousted from the premiership in a dramatic election in 1990, leaving a cloud over the achievements of the Thatcher era and the prospects for the future of the Thatcherite project. The reasons for her forced exit were firstly the unpopularity of several of the key policies of her third term, in particular the attempt to reform local-government finance by replacing the rates with the community charge (poll tax); secondly the divisions within the Conservative leadership, most notably over policy towards the European Community; and thirdly the collapse of the economic 'miracle' and the return of familiar economic problems.

The mismanagement of the economy

The government's proudest boast in the 1987 election was to have turned the economy round and reversed decline. For a short period the growth of productivity in Britain outstripped that in all other European economies. Inflation was below 4 per cent and unemployment was falling steeply. The British economy had been growing uninterruptedly since 1982. The monetarist cure appeared to have worked.

The very rapid growth rates of 1987 and 1988 were, however, unsustainable. The government had reflated the economy before the 1987 election by relaxing control of the money supply and allowing public-expenditure plans to grow by £7.5 billion. Private consumer debt rose rapidly, aided by the deregulation of the financial sector pushed through by the Government and fuelled by a property boom, particularly in the South East. The government believed that the boom could be maintained indefinitely and that it had broken out of the cycle of stagflation for ever. Its policies of reducing direct taxes, privatising public-sector assets, deregulating business and curbing trade-union power were seen as the means for achieving a high growth, low inflation, recession-free economy.

The first sign of impending disaster was the crash of the world stock markets in October 1987. The scale of this dwarfed previous crashes, including that of 1929, and raised fears that a great depression was about to ensue. The risk was averted, in part by coordination of policies by the central banks and by finance ministers. But the immediate consequence for Britain was that monetary policy remained loose throughout 1988. The £M3 measure of money supply grew at 40 per cent. The reason was that the government wished to keep the recovery going and to avoid doing anything to push the economy into recession. But it also did more. In the 1988 budget the chancellor, Nigel Lawson, triumphantly unveiled a set of proposals that the Thatcherites regarded as both expressing their revolution and setting it in concrete. Income tax was reduced to 25p in the pound and the top rate to 40p. Personal allowances were raised by twice the rate of inflation, and corporation tax and inheritance tax were cut. The effect was to give a large boost to personal consumption at a time when the economy was already expanding too rapidly.

The consequence of these policies was that they prolonged the afterglow of the great 1987 triumph at the expense of storing up serious problems. By keeping the boom going into

1988 and 1989 the government allowed the economic and electoral cycles to get out of phase with one another. At the same time inflation was reignited (it peaked at 10.5 per cent in 1990) and began to rise rapidly during 1989, while the deficit on the balance payments rose to very high levels. It became clear during 1989 that the economy was in serious difficulty and that a recession was inevitable. A period of rising interest rates, economic contraction, bankruptcies and high unemployment ensued. Talk of an economic miracle disappeared as familiar economic problems reasserted themselves.[24]

The political damage caused by the reemergence first of inflation and then recession was considerable. It broke the Thatcherite spell, and was one of the main causes for the deep unpopularity suffered by the government in 1989 and 1990. It was a critical political defeat.

Europe

The second reason for Thatcher's fall was the divisions over Europe within the cabinet and the party. The signing of the Single European Act in 1985 inaugurated a period of rapid progress towards closer European union. The Act required some 280 separate pieces of legislation to harmonise conditions between the member states in time for the inauguration of the single European market in 1992. A crucial part of the Act allowed many of these new rules to be imposed by a system of majority voting among the twelve member states. It represented a significant addition to the supranational authority of Community institutions.

Thatcher was persuaded to sign the Single European Act partly because the goal of a single market was one that fitted well with the thrust of the Thatcherite domestic economic strategy, and because she did not wish progress towards that goal to be frustrated by vetos from some of the smaller states. But it seems she did not fully appreciate the implications of the Single European Act and the advent of qualified majority voting. It greatly encouraged other moves towards European union, leading directly to the proposals incorporated into the Maastricht Treaty, signed in 1991.

The issue of European union divided the Conservative Party in a way that no issue has done this century since tariff reform.[25] Like tariff reform and the Corn Laws earlier it involved a key strategic choice over Britain's role in the world political economy, which touched questions of national identity as well as economic interest. It posed the question as to whether Britain's priority should be its Atlanticist or its European links. The issue split the Thatcherites, with some like Geoffrey Howe and Lord Cockfield, and to a lesser extent Nigel Lawson, accepting the argument that economic interdependence made pooling of sovereignty at the European level essential to creating a strong public authority to safeguard the European market order. Others, including Thatcher herself, Norman Tebbit and Nicholas Ridley, came to view the moves to create a supranational authority not as the fulfilment of Thatcherite principles, but as opening the way to loss of national independence, and that they presented the possibility of socialism being reimposed on Britain not by the decision of the British people but by decisions taken in Europe. They came to believe that everything achieved by the Thatcherite project was endangered by European union.[26]

This split in attitudes was already one of the factors in the Westland affair in 1986, when Michael Heseltine resigned from the cabinet rather than accept the imposition of a solution that favoured American rather than European interests. But a much deeper split was to emerge over the conduct of economic policy. A key part of the project of European union was economic and monetary union. The exchange-rate mechanism (ERM) had been established in 1979 as a means toward this. Britain had stayed out at that time but by 1985 both Geoffrey Howe, foreign secretary and former chancellor, and Nigel Lawson, the chancellor, had become convinced that Britain should join in order to promote financial stability by tying sterling to the Deutschmark and contributing to regional financial stability in what indisputably was now Britain's key market.

Membership of the ERM was fiercely resisted by Thatcher, assisted by her personal economic adviser Alan Walters. This long-running dispute at the heart of government weakened the conduct of economic policy. Lawson increasingly disregarded Thatcher's opposition, and although he could not commit sterling to the ERM he did the next best thing, which was to shadow the Deutschmark, using the sterling/Deutschmark rate as a key indicator for deciding domestic monetary policy. Thatcher opposed the policy partly because she wished to retain greater flexibility over the choice of economic targets, and partly because she saw the policy as a step to Britain joining the ERM and being sucked inexorably into a currency union. The markets soon sensed that the government had two economic policies and that Alan Walters was being used by Thatcher to undermine the chancellor's position. Eventually Lawson resigned in October 1989, followed swiftly by Alan Walters.[27]

Thatcher was weakened by the loss of one of the key architects of the Thatcher project. She had already sidelined Geoffrey Howe and sacked John Biffen, and Norman Tebbit had left the government in 1987. Now her weakness was exposed. Her new chancellor, John Major, and foreign secretary, Douglas Hurd, combined effectively to persuade Thatcher to swallow her objections and join the ERM in September 1990. But her antipathy to European union remained strong. In 1988 she had raised the banner of national sovereignty in her speech at Bruges. In the summer of 1990 she had been forced to accept the resignation of another minister, Nicholas Ridley, one of her closest cabinet allies, because of remarks he made in an interview with the *Spectator* about German plans to dominate Europe through the EC.

The cabinet rift appeared to have been healed with the announcement that Britain would after all join the ERM. But Thatcher was now deeply unhappy about the direction to which her cabinet was committed. Returning from the Rome summit in November 1990 she began by reading out the prepared government statement in the Commons. But then in response to a question she departed from her script and launched into a fierce assault on the supranational pretensions of the EC Commission. This was the final straw for Sir Geoffrey Howe, who resigned and in a highly damaging resignation speech cited Thatcher's European policy as the key reason for his departure. His resignation gave the opportunity for a formal leadership challenge from Michael

Heseltine, so beginning the chain of events that was to lead to Thatcher's downfall.

The reconstruction of the state

The third factor in Thatcher's fall was the controversial set of policies included in the 1987 manifesto and which helped renew the radical momentum of the Thatcher project in the third term. Having got the economy right, as they believed, and having won a third successive popular endorsement, the Thatcherites saw the reconstruction of the public services as a key task in refashioning the British state and British civil society.

The main proposals were in the field of local-government finance, education, health and social security. But they were allied to what has become known as the 'new public management' – a set of ideas for managing all institutions in the public sector and involving devices such as internal markets, contracting out, tendering and financial incentives. One of the most radical decisions of the Thatcher government was its acceptance in 1989 of the report of the Efficiency Unit – the Next Steps Report – which inaugurated sweeping changes in the civil service. The key proposal was to separate the policy-making and policy implementations of the civil service by setting up new agencies to deliver services independently of the departments advising on policy. The aim was to increase efficiency by giving civil servants greater autonomy and financial incentives to improve service delivery.[29]

While the Next Steps initiative may turn out to be one of the most long-lasting of the Thatcherite reforms, they attracted little public attention. It was quite different with the health and education reforms, and particularly with the community charge. The NHS reforms set out in the white paper *Working for Patients* in 1989 introduced an internal market with fundholding for GPs and trust status for hospitals. The education reforms were unveiled in the 1988 Education Reform Act. They included a national curriculum, a system of national testing and provision for schools to opt out of local-authority control and receive their funding direct from central government.[30]

The most controversial measure however was the community charge, which even Margaret Thatcher on occasion referred to by its more famous name, the poll tax. This was a tax that was primarily political in its conception and went to the heart of the Thatcher project. It was intended to facilitate a further shift of the cost of local-government services from central government to local government, and at the same time to make local government accept responsibility for the burden of taxes they imposed. In this way local democracy was to be enlisted to force down local spending. For the first time all citizens would be required to pay for local services, and therefore forced to decide whether they wanted more spending or lower taxes.

The political problem with the tax from the outset was that there were many more losers than winners, and most of the winners were solid Conservative voters anyway. Even many of these felt uneasy about a tax that was so unrelated to criteria of fairness – the owner of a castle paid the same as the tenant of a cottage. In some regions of the country, such as the north west, the impact of the tax was particularly severe in areas where Conservative support had been strong. The alteration in the tax for many households was not marginal. As the seriousness of the consequences sunk in the government reacted by providing rebates to cushion the impact. But it could not stem the wave of hostility to the tax. Polls found that more than 80 per cent of the electorate were opposed to it in 1990. It was the major factor in the loss of the Mid-Staffordshire by-election in 1990. Margaret Thatcher robustly declared in parliament that the poll tax 'will be popular'. What worried many Conservatives was that the tax had become so closely identified with her. She described it as her flagship. It was Maggie's tax and quickly became the symbol of her ten-year reign.[31]

The leadership election

The circumstances of Margaret Thatcher's fall were some of the most dramatic in recent British political history. It did seem improbable that a leader as dominant as Thatcher had become and who had led her party to three successive general-election victories could be ousted by an internal party vote. The reasons why a minority of her party turned against her and forced her out were partly electoral – they believed that she had become an electoral liability and that the party would not win another election under her. But there were deeper reasons too – above all the split over Europe within the cabinet and the feeling that the Thatcher project was overreaching itself.

One of the features of all the different reforms aimed at reforming the public services was that the government was determined to by-pass public-sector professionals and establish new modes of service delivery. It was prepared to confront what it saw as the vested interests of teachers, doctors and local-authority managers. But the polls showed that these moves were highly unpopular with most voters and raised fears that the government was intent not just on reforming but on privatising health care and education. Polls also showed large majorities opposed to the privatisation of public utilities, such as water and electricity.

The new plunge in the government's popularity ratings began soon after she had celebrated in May 1989 a record-breaking ten consecutive years as prime minister. A series of reverses during 1989 in local elections, by-elections and elections for the European parliament (when the Conservatives lost 13 seats) was followed by a collapse of support for the Conservative Party in the opinion polls and for Thatcher personally as prime minister. The worst period was the early months of 1990, when antagonism to the new community charge was at its height. In this period Labour achieved very high poll leads of 20–26 per cent. For a time it scored above 50 per cent, the highest level of support Labour had ever recorded in opinion polls. Later in the year Labour's poll lead fell back, but it was still between 10 per cent and 20 per cent. As significant was the fact that Labour support had now moved firmly above 40 per cent. During the whole of the 1983–7 Parliament Labour had never scored 40 per cent in any major opinion poll.

The apparent reemergence of a two-party system, and the possibility that the government might therefore change hands at the next election, caused deep dismay within the

Conservative Party. It was heightened by the unwillingness of Thatcher to entertain any significant moderation in the radical policies on health, education, privatisation and local-government finance, upon which the government had been reelected for its third term.

Thatcher would not have fallen, however, simply because of electoral unpopularity and bad economic news. The reason she lost office was that the Conservative Party, and in particular the Conservative cabinet, became divided, leading to the resignations of Nigel Lawson in October 1989 and Geoffrey Howe in November 1990, both of them key architects of Conservative policies through the 1980s.

Lawson's departure in November 1990 allowed Anthony Meyer to challenge Thatcher for the leadership. She won comfortably but thirty-three MPs voted for Meyer, three abstained and another twenty-four spoilt their ballot papers. It was a warning that was not heeded. When Geoffrey Howe resigned in November 1990 he presented the opportunity for a much more serious challenge from Michael Heseltine, who had himself resigned from the government over the Westland affair in 1986. Margaret Thatcher won fifty two more votes than her challenger on the first ballot and only failed by four votes to win outright on the first ballot. She won 204 votes and Heseltine 152. (She needed a majority of the votes and 15 per cent more than her challenger; she received 57.3 per cent and Heseltine 42.7 per cent.) Her decision not to contest the second ballot was due to her calculation that her authority had been so damaged by failing to win outright that either she might now lose the second ballot and hand the leadership to Heseltine, or that in winning narrowly she would be unable to reunite the party behind her. The majority of her cabinet informed her that she could not win; a few told her they would not support her. She therefore chose to resign and throw her weight behind John Major in order to prevent the victory of Michael Heseltine, whom she feared would lead the party in a different direction and undo her legacy.

5

The pursuit of statecraft

> In a progressive country change is constant; and the great
> question is not whether you should resist change which is
> inevitable, but whether that change should be carried out
> in deference to the manners, the customs, the laws, and
> the traditions of a people, or whether it should be carried
> out in deference to abstract principles, and arbitrary and
> general doctrines.
>
> Benjamin Disraeli, 1867

> We cannot really believe that this is the moment for the
> party of Baldwin and Churchill, of Macmillan and Butler,
> of the Industrial Charter and the social advances of the
> 1950s to retreat behind the privet hedge into a world of
> narrow class interests and selfish concerns.
>
> Sir Ian Gilmour, 1975

How did Conservatives understand Thatcherism and the
events of the Thatcher era? Despite the success of Margaret
Thatcher in leading her party to three consecutive election
victories there were always some Conservatives who
regarded Thatcherism as an aberration, a deviation from
the broad highway of the Conservative tradition, and predicted that sooner or later the Conservatives would return
to the political tradition represented by Harold Macmillan
and Edward Heath.

From this standpoint what happened in 1975 was that the
party was 'hijacked' by its extremist wing. Aided by events
and divisions among the other parties it was able to secure

itself in power,[1] and banish or win over its enemies within the party. But all the while it remained illegitimate and those it exiled from influence and office waited the day when the usurper would be gone and they would be restored to their rightful place.

New-Right Conservatives, however, refused to accept that there would ever be such a restoration. They regarded Margaret Thatcher's accession to the leadership as the reassertion of true Conservative principles that had been forgotten during the party's long postwar acquiescence in the regime of social democracy. According to this view it was postwar Conservatism that was the aberration, from which Thatcher rescued the party.[2]

Margaret Thatcher's tenure of the Conservative leadership was therefore accompanied by a fierce debate among some Conservatives over whether 'Thatcherism' reasserted Conservative principles or broke from them. The party was riven by ideological and doctrinal disputes to an extent remarkable for a party that has always prided itself on its pragmatic and non-ideological approach to politics. One leading Conservative lamented that 'the odium theologicum' had come to infect the Tory party.[3] This debate was in the first place a debate between two groups involved in a struggle for position and influence within the party. But the question 'is Thatcherism conservatism?' involved a wider issue than simply which leadership group was to dominate the party. It goes to the heart of our understanding of British conservatism. Does this tradition embody a distinctive ideology and doctrine, or is it better analysed as a practical activity, a form of statecraft, in which ideas and principles are subordinated to political calculation, the pursuit of office and the management of power?

The interpretation of Thatcherism has absorbed a great deal of intellectual energy on the right. The view of Thatcherism as a new ideological doctrine initially commanded most attention. But although there was some debate as to whether Thatcherism was or was not a Conservative doctrine, the real issue quickly became the relationship of this doctrine to the party's new statecraft. Even if the doctrines of Thatcherism were regarded as alien to the Conservative tradition, the Thatcher government could still be judged to be pursuing a Tory statecraft. The finer points of ideological dispute would then become relatively unimportant.

The object of Tory statecraft has always been to ensure that a durable hegemony is achieved and preserved throughout the institutions of state and civil society. Hegemony involves politics, ideology and economics, which is why the agents of hegemony, and the framers of political projects, are generally political parties. Building support and negotiating power, winning the arguments at all levels of ideological discourse, and framing and implementing a viable economic strategy, are all involved in a successful political project that aims to establish and maintain hegemony. Statecraft involves identifying and then bringing about the conditions for hegemony, as conservatives have long understood. Assessing Thatcherism as statecraft was always a key concern for Conservatives.

The perils of ideology

The Conservative Party has had its share of ideological poison in the past, but it has long cultivated an image as a non-ideological party. John Stuart Mill called the Tories 'the stupid party', which was taken by most Tories as a compliment. The squires who thronged the Tory benches were described by Salisbury as 'red hot cannon balls, which they resemble in density if not in weight'.[4] This has not prevented the party from being led by a succession of very able and intellectual leaders, who perceived clearly that doctrine and ideology should have a role, but a subordinate one, in the party. The main purpose of the Tory Party was to govern, and to remain united for that purpose.

This brought many jibes against the party. The Tories were often portrayed as unprincipled opportunists whose only concern was the gaining of office. This was the Tory Party satirised by Trollope:

At that time we had not thoroughly learnt by experience, as we now have, that no reform, no innovation – experience almost justifies us in saying, no revolution – stinks so foully in the nostrils of an English Tory as to be absolutely irreconcilable to him. When taken in the refreshing waters of office any such pill can be swallowed.[5]

Many critics of the British Conservatives, from Winston Churchill to Friedrich Hayek, have also focused on their opportunism and want of principle. In its anxiety to gain office the party's principles have often appeared negotiable, its policies determined by the best means of winning votes. It has seemed at times a party not of principles but of interests. Churchill once called the Tory Party:

> a party of great vested interests, banded together in a formidable confederation; corruption at home, aggression to cover it up abroad; the trickery of tariff juggles, the tyranny of a party machine; sentiment by the bucketful, patriotism by the imperial pint; the open hand at the public exchequer, the open door at the public house; dear food for the million, cheap labour for the millionaire.[6]

Despite his admiration for Margaret Thatcher, Hayek has always had reservations about conservatism as a sound ideological basis for politics. In his postscript to *The Constitution of Liberty*, 'Why I am not a Conservative', he claimed that Conservatives could not be trusted to defend a free society, either because they believed in collectivism, or because, like the British Conservatives, they were opportunists in their political practice and lacked a principled commitment to the maintenance of the conditions for a free society.[7] This made Conservative administrations hardly less likely than Labour ones to embrace collectivist solutions to problems that involved interference and intervention in the workings of markets. Governing according to circumstances meant for Hayek placing public policy at the mercy of the fashions and pressures of the political market-place. All manner of evils, including protectionism, cartels, closed shops and industrial subsidies, could be justified on 'pragmatic' grounds. Conservatives could not be trusted to protect freedom.

Defenders of the British conservative tradition, such as Sir Ian Gilmour, argue that what Hayek derides as vices in conservatism are in fact its virtues. Most of his charges against conservatism are 'merely pejorative descriptions of attributes in which Conservatives take pride. What to Hayek is opportunism, is to Conservatives paying proper attention to circumstances. What Hayek calls the use of arbitrary power, the Conservative calls the legitimate use of the power of the state to promote the welfare of the people'.[8]

This argument is a long one in the history of conservatism. Where Conservative parties have become influential in government Conservative statecraft has generally been seen as more important than Conservative doctrine in explaining Conservative actions. Conservatism is understood more in terms of its orientation to government rather than in terms of specific beliefs.

Samuel Huntington, in his theory of conservatism, drew a distinction between *doctrinal* and *positional* conservatism.[9] The former is seen as arising in periods of social and political upheaval, often precipitated by internal revolution or defeat in war. Positional conservatism in contrast is concerned not with the politics of social breakdown but with the administration of an existing order.

Doctrinal conservatism has been most in evidence in counter-revolutionary movements seeking either to overthrow a radical regime or to safeguard an existing regime from a revolutionary challenge. Such conservatism, tends to embrace an ethic of will and loyalty and seek triumphs rather than reconciliations.[10] It values conviction and commitment, rather than compromise and consensus. It looks for enemies to defeat and thrives on conflict and battle. Positional conservatism in contrast shuns ideological certainty and the cult of conviction and struggle. It cultivates instead the art of ruling in order to maintain a stable social order. Decisions on policy are matters of political calculation, to be arrived at after careful assessment of all aspects of the situation, rather than through a simple-minded application of abstract principles. The need for flexibility is the great virtue.

The opposition between doctrinal and positional conservatives is perennial. It exists in every period, and to some extent in every conservative. Whether doctrinal or positional elements are most prominent depends, however, on the problems conservatives must confront. The argument between trimmers and realists on the one side and diehards and reactionaries on the other goes on in every period, but who gets the upper hand is not determined in advance.

The British conservative tradition has generally been interpreted as one in which the trimmers have won out over the diehards.[11] The English Tories have always been perceived as positional rather than doctrinal conservatives. Many Conservatives thought that Thatcherism broke with this tradition. They argued that the emphasis on doctrine, the dislike of consensus, the lack of concern about being labelled extreme, and the embrace of radical change and experiment, made the Conservative Party under Margaret Thatcher at times resemble in its approach and style a party of the radical left rather than the British Conservatives.

Sir Ian Gilmour in *Inside Right* lists three things the Conservative Party is not: it is not averse to change; it is not a pressure group; and it is not an ideological party.[12] The charge against Thatcherism was that it supported radical and destructive change, that it represented the interests of only one part of the nation and not the whole nation, and above all that this came about because it made the Conservative Party an ideological one, dedicated to the pursuit and implementation of a particular doctrine. In doing so it had abandoned the one-nation perspective that had guided its practice and its programme since Disraeli, and contradicted the fundamental principles of conservative statecraft.

The quest for true Toryism

This debate on the character and future of the Conservative Party was ignited by Margaret Thatcher's election as leader and by the way she then chose to conduct the leadership. The demoralisation and recrimination that followed the two general-election defeats in 1974 increased the factional struggle within the party and led to an outpouring of books and articles attempting to define what the party was about, where it had gone wrong and what its future direction should be. A significant feature of the ideological disputes was the readiness of all sides to describe the party in terms of right and left and to emphasise the fundamental nature of the conflict. Patrick Cosgrave described it as 'a conflict between two wholly different visions of the future, for country as well as party'.[13]

In the past Conservatives generally trusted their leaders rather than their principles as a guide to politics. Dissenters were often counselled to damn their principles and stick to their party. Such attitudes embodied an important political truth. Disunity and splits were generally fatal to a party's prospects of gaining political office.

The Conservative Party, like every other political party contesting the terrain of mass democracy, has from time to time been swept by great causes and doctrines. Every party has its men and women of principle. The Conservative Party has been unusual in the success it has had in keeping them away from the leadership. In electing Margaret Thatcher, however, the Tories had elected a leader who herself became the focus of ideological argument. The question she was alleged to have put when considering appointments – 'is he one of us?' – came to symbolise her style. From the start she was a very divisive leader. She invited Conservatives to declare themselves for or against her.

Thatcher was not an intellectual Conservative in the manner of Salisbury or Keith Joseph. But her interest in questioning the legacy of ideas and assumptions that had guided the party throughout the postwar period created a space in which the ideas of the many variants of the New Right could flourish. The apparent legitimacy being given to such ideas by the party leader was deeply threatening to other elements in the party.

Extravagant language has been used before about shifts to the right in the Conservative Party. After his refusal to serve under Sir Alec Douglas-Home in 1963 Iain Macleod claimed in the *Spectator* that the Conservative Party was now being led for the first time since Salisbury from 'right of centre'.[14] Similar charges were made after 1975. One active member of the Tory left argued in 1978 that the party had been plunged back into the dark days of Salisbury and Balfour.[15] Thatcher's leadership was pictured as regressive, undoing the tradition of the one-nation Toryism of Baldwin, Churchill, Macmillan and Heath. To her supporters in the New Right, however, her leadership offered the first real opportunity for a generation to challenge the ideas and policies of collectivism. Although the New Right did not represent a single coherent perspective, all parts of it were united in rejecting the tradition that Heath represented in the party. While the liberal New Right proclaimed the need to commit the Conservative Party to a programme of freeing the economy and rolling back the state, the Conservative New Right put its emphasis on the restoration of authority.

New-Right institutes, pressure groups and journals sprouted like mushrooms throughout the 1970s and 1980s.[16] The key think-tanks on the liberal and libertarian wing of the New Right were the Institute of Economic Affairs (1957), the Centre for Policy Studies (1974); and the Adam Smith Institute (1981). Long-established campaigning organisations such as the business pressure groups Aims of Industry and the Economic League were joined by the Freedom Association and the Libertarian Alliance.

On the conservative wing of the New Right, Common Cause, founded in 1952, and the Monday Club, which had been a focus for right-wing dissent since 1961, were now joined by the more intellectual Salisbury Club, some of whose meetings Thatcher attended, and by numerous Cold-War, anti-communist organisations, which included the Freedom Association, the Coalition for Peace and Security and the Institute for the Study of Conflict. Many of these organisations, like the Freedom Association, had overlapping membership and sponsorship. There emerged a network of journalists, lobbyists, academics, business executives and politicians committed to spreading New-Right ideas and supporting Thatcher against her enemies in the party.

For all sections of the New Right a crucial ideological task was to establish the legitimacy of their ideas within the British conservative tradition. The Conservatives among them especially wanted to claim that they were the true Tories.

The search for 'true Toryism' promised endless writing and rewriting of history. The great conservatives from the past were scrutinised to determine whether they should hold their place in the Conservative Pantheon or be cast from it.

The Salisbury Club and its journal, the *Salisbury Review*, edited by Roger Scruton, where this kind of writing was particularly noticeable, were named after the former Conservative leader who was least admired by one-nation Conservatives. A general offensive began against the interpretation of the conservative tradition that had been dominant in party publications for so much of the postwar period. Gilmour complained that if the inquisition went on much longer the Conservatives would have a gallery of heroes consisting of Lord Eldon and Judge Jeffreys.

The reassessment of the past had a serious purpose however. The argument of those supporting the new course inaugurated by Margaret Thatcher was that by the mid-1970s the party had lost its way. It no longer offered a distinctive alternative to Labour and was in danger of fighting and losing on ground staked out by its opponents. The call made by Thatcherites was for a major reassessment of the practice of the party since 1945; specifically its acquiescence in the policies and priorities of the postwar social-democratic state.

This kind of argument immediately encountered a major difficulty. The Conservatives had been in office for more than half of the time since 1945. This meant that if the party were to challenge the 'consensus' under which Britain had been governed since 1945 it had to criticise many of the policies and actions not just of the Heath government between 1970 and 1974, but also those of the Conservative government between 1951 and 1964. Many of the supporters of the new leadership were prepared to do this. Accusations of appeasement and surrender abounded. Postwar Conservative governments, it was said, had never put the clock back a single second. Collectivism had crept forward. They had acquiesced in the ratchet of socialism. Periods of Conservative government had merely administered the status quo, while each period of Labour government had advanced the collectivisation of Britain another notch.[17]

According to this scenario Britain was slipping steadily down the road to serfdom. Conservative governments had not actively connived in condemning Britain to a totalitarian future, but in failing to reverse the measures passed by Labour governments they had failed to arrest the progress of collectivism. They had also been partly responsible for the policies that had led to accelerating inflation, the growth in trade-union influence and the increasing burden of public spending.

What all sections of the New Right demanded was a Conservative Party that now sought to regain the ideological initiative and change the policy agenda by challenging the postwar consensus between the parties on domestic policies. They argued that the kind of collectivism practised under postwar social democracy was exhausted and discredited, and that the electoral risk to the Conservatives of deserting the hallowed 'middle ground' of politics was minimal. The middle ground no longer represented a genuine popular consensus, but was a construct of politicians and the progressive intellectual establishment, and as such was ripe for overthrow.

From the New Right, therefore, came numerous ideas as to how the Conservative Party could regain the political initiative firstly by developing a strategy for reversing decline based on a free economy and a strong state, secondly by winning the ideological struggle against social democracy and one-nation conservatism, and thirdly by building a strong electoral coalition. The New Right argued that the Conservatives could appeal to all those who were disillusioned with the recent performance of governments, eager for the re-asertion of political authority and open to new populist commonsense arguments about the economy and politics.

The challenge to the Thatcherites came from those Conservatives who identified themselves with the postwar tradition of progressive conservatism and saw no reason to abandon it. They were not a movement like the New Right, although they created a few organisations such as the Tory Reform Group. Their former institutional strength had lain in their control of the Conservative Party itself, particularly Conservative Central Office and the Conservative Research Department. This was now lost to them.

The tactic of these Conservatives against emergent Thatcherism was to deny its legitimacy on the grounds that if the party were to continue as a party of government, it must not become an ideological party but remain predominantly a party of realists, trimmers and pragmatists; a party that believed in governing in the light of circumstances rather than in accordance with any abstract principle or dogma. Since the aim of the party was to govern, adherence to an ideology, any ideology, was a serious handicap to carry and risked ceding the priceless asset of being perceived as the party of efficient and pragmatic government to the party's opponents.

A second argument was that the ideology of Thatcherism was the wrong ideology for the Conservative Party. The Thatcherite view of what conservatism was about challenged the carefully constructed interpretation of the Conservative tradition that had become more or less undisputed in the party after 1945, and that had been associated with the leadership style and philosophy of Churchill, Macmillan, and Heath.[18]

This interpretation emphasised the identity of the Conservatives as the party of one nation, the party of the 'middle way'. The middle way was between state socialism on one side and laissez-faire capitalism on the other. The role of the Conservative Party was to curb the tendency of their opponents to push their policies to extremes. Conservatism in this view meant governing a society rather than managing an economy, so what was essential was to pay proper attention to the interests and customs of the society to ensure that all legitimate interests achieved representation and that the continuity of the society was preserved.

This gave government an important role in the management of the economy. Peter Walker's views are representative of his wing of the party:

In a modern society the government must elaborate national goals, let industry know its target for the rate of growth, and make clear how productive capacity may be increased to make the objective feasible. Governments also have a duty to prevent the unpleasant by-products of growth such as damage to the environment, as well as very wide responsibilities in the fields of housing, education, and the social services.[19]

Walker argued that the problem facing the Conservatives was not to argue for the superiority of private enterprise in theoretical terms but to relate those arguments to the hopes and fears of ordinary people. How could private enterprise be made morally legitimate? Harold Macmillan's great insight, according to Walker, was to understand that 'unless capitalism could show sufficient social responsibility it could never win mass support'.[20]

Ian Gilmour in similar vein claimed that 'there is no ideal extent of government intervention. The position of government in industry, as Mr Macmillan once put it, is not a principle it is an expedient'.[21] The reason was that in Conservative statecraft, politics is always more important than economics. The choice of policy measures should not be a matter of economic theory or political principle, Gilmour argues, but should be guided by what is compatible with the continued existence of a free society with institutions than command respect and allegiance, a society free from excessive and avoidable social tensions and too much injustice.

Conservatives who were important in this tradition were those who had taken an interest in social reform and had sought remedies for some of the evils of nineteenth-century capitalism. The list includes Peel, Shaftesbury and Disraeli. The reputation of Disraeli as a practical reformer may have waned, but his one-nation rhetoric and his perception of the role a Conservative Party might occupy in an era of mass suffrage allowed him to be presented as the founder of a tradition that was carried on by Randolph Churchill with his call for Tory democracy, by Baldwin and Chamberlain, and finally by Churchill and his heirs, notably Macmillan, Butler and Heath.

The core of this tradition, when it was defined in the 1950s, was held to be the acceptance of state intervention where necessary to remedy evils and abuses and to create the basis for consent. It seeks to incorporate new interests into the governing process by making concessions to them in order to maintain the authority of government and the stability of the state. Policies are judged on whether or not they promote loyalty to the state. As Gilmour puts it:

> The preservation of freedom is a complex business. But if people are not to be seduced by other attractions, they must at least feel loyalty to the state. Their loyalty will not be deep unless they gain from the state protection and other benefits. Homilies to cherish competition and warnings against interference with market forces will not engender loyalty. People will not tolerantly sit back and wait for impersonal forces to overcome disaster. They expect and demand action, and if they do not get it they are likely to look elsewhere or take action themselves. If the state is not interested in them, why should they be interested in the state?[22]

Gilmour and other one-nation Conservatives in the 1970s warned against the new statecraft of the Thatcher leadership because of the damage they expected it to do to prospects of the party being reelected. Trevor Russel expressed a common view (and hope) in the Tory Reform Group when he wrote in 1978:

> Mrs. Thatcher's grip on the party may prove short-lived.... Some on the Tory Left, who dismiss her as an aberration, or a mistake, already regard the period of her leadership, which they expect to be brief, as an unfortunate although possibly necessary interlude.[23]

The longer the aberration lasted the harder it became to dismiss Thatcherism as an ideology alien to conservatism. It looked more and more like a new phase in the party's long development, a new Tory statecraft, that after 1981 was crowned by success. As the victories piled up and the Conservatives regained their old knack of winning and holding office (which first rivalled and then surpassed the success of the Conservatives after 1951), the more the grounds for argument about Thatcherism in the party shifted. As Sir John Harington once explained:

Treason doth never prosper: what's the reason? For if it
prosper none dares call it treason.

Three election victories made Thatcher no longer vulnerable to the charge that she betrayed conservatism and
threatened its survival by deserting the middle ground
of politics. She built her new electoral coalition and the
opposition fell to pieces. She also won the battle inside the
party. Many of her earlier critics fell silent or were marginalised, while others learnt to become trimmers in the new
Thatcherite ascendancy.

The success of Thatcherism in mastering the politics of
support baffled and dismayed many one-nation Conservatives. They had tried to brand it as a species of ideological or
doctrinal conservatism that was alien to the British Conservative tradition, because it subordinated questions of
state-craft, of how to win and hold power and preserve hegemony, to questions of ideology, of the correctness of policies
measured against abstract principles. But Thatcherism
proved to have its own ways of combining the two.

As a result Thatcherism never did subordinate statecraft
to ideology as its critics complained. It simply had a different view of statecraft. It rejected the idea that a successful
statecraft had to practise opportunism and be ready to surrender principles. This kind of statecraft has often been
associated with the British conservatives, and with the one-
nation tradition. Of all ruling groups they have been most
ready to pursue strategies of concession and flexibility in the
face of new demands and new interests.

A Conservative statecraft, however, need not be defensive,
a strategy of delay, – as Salisbury wrote, 'delay is life' – or be
geared to continual retreat. Henry Kissinger, in his analysis
of Metternich's politics, has pointed up the difference
between two styles of Conservative statecraft. Metternich
objected to the views of the Peelite Sir James Graham, who
had argued that the statesman's wisdom consisted of
recognising the proper moment for making concessions:

My conception of statesmanship differs completely. The
true merit of a statesman ... consists in governing so as

to avoid a situation in which concessions become necessary.[24]

Metternich has had his followers among the British Conservatives, but it is Sir James Graham's approach that has more often been ascendant. Thatcherism endorsed the Metternich view. Once the authority of the state is restored, no concessions and no compromises with the enemies of conservatism and freedom are necessary.

Thatcher did not convince one-nation Conservatives. Whatever the short-term success of Thatcherism in both the politics of support and the politics of power some Conservatives, such as Edward Heath and Ian Gilmour, still expected it to end badly, and when it did they thought themselves vindicated. They regarded Thatcher as a reckless politician who took needless and unacceptable risks. The centralisation of power, the war on so many established institutions, the polarisation of society between north and south, rich and poor and employed and unemployed, and the exacerbation of social tensions had depleted the legitimacy of the state to a dangerous degree. The Thatcher government held the initiative throughout the 1980s and became contemptuous of all sources of opposition, but at the cost of isolating conservatism from many of the associations and institutions of civil society.

The real problem for Conservatives of the Metternich persuasion is that the very strength of their rule and the success that attends it can blind them when the moment arrives for concessions and compromise. Sir Ian Gilmour uses the example of the situation created by the Taff Vale Case in 1901. If the Conservative government led by Balfour had at once legislated to change the law, it might have forestalled the much more radical reform that was enacted by the Liberal government after its sweeping election victory in 1906, and might therefore, Gilmour argues, have checked the later growth of trade-union influence. Conservatives can pay dearly for such mistakes.

Many of the opponents of Thatcherism survived to see Thatcher toppled and many aspects of Thatcherism discarded. But they have been unable to deny the historical significance of Thatcherism as a manifestation of conservatism. The success of Thatcher's leadership in restoring the Conservative Party to a position of dominance in British politics has ensured Thatcherism's place as an integral part of the Conservative tradition. Since this tradition has always placed such weight on statecraft rather than on ideology Thatcher will always be viewed as one of the most important leaders in the history of the party. She has reshaped the tradition and provided a powerful new myth on which future Conservatives will draw. But the nature of the statecraft she pursued will always be controversial and subject to different interpretations. These interpretations include the nature of the Conservative ideological tradition, the idea of the constitutional state and limited politics, the promotion of a governing class, the practise of high politics and the upholding of authority.

Libertarianism and collectivism

As a purely ideological phenomenon there is little difficulty in seeing Thatcherism as an authentic expression of one of the two major strands in the Conservative tradition. These two strands have been identified by many political historians but most recently and most persuasively by W. H. Greenleaf. He identifies libertarianism and collectivism as the two axes around which ideological debate has revolved in the Conservative Party in common with all other parties.[25] Greenleaf conceives these ideological strands as being much broader than the party system itself, and he has no difficulty in showing how in the British political tradition the balance between them has shifted, so that libertarianism has been dominant in one period and collectivism in another. The charge was often made by critics of Thatcherism that it represented a return to Victorian values and the principles of laissez-faire and Gladstonian finance. Statements by John Nott and Milton Friedman that Margaret Thatcher was really a nineteenth-century liberal were eagerly seized upon to demonstrate that she was not a true Conservative.

The picture is, however, much more complex than this. It is true that Margaret Thatcher and her supporters can be seen to be reasserting ideas that were dominant in the nineteenth century. But the libertarian tradition at that time spanned all parties, and has continued to have adherents right through the period of the relative dominance of collectivism in the twentieth century. What was at the core of the libertarian tradition was a strong anti-statism. The Manchester-School doctrine that if left alone any economic or social evil would cure itself was accompanied by strong beliefs in the advantages of free trade and sound finance, and in the importance of individual responsibility. In the 1880s and 1890s the Conservative Party was strongly identified with the belief that in matters concerning the economy and property the role of the state should be limited as much as possible. The role of government was to maintain law and order rather than to interfere with the morals and activities of the people. The party was strongly against intervention.

The growth of collectivist legislation and the power of the labour movement were fiercely resisted by many Conservatives. Many were active in organisations such as the Liberty and Property Defence League, the Constitutional Association, and later the Anti-Socialist Union.[26] The Liberty and Property Defence League was a major pressure group against collectivist legislation. It organised campaigns to preserve the open shop, limit picketing and prevent the growth of profit sharing. It also helped to break strikes.

What agitated Conservatives was that the extension of the suffrage in stages was leading to an inexorable growth in pressure for class legislation – legislation aimed at redistribution or even confiscation of income and wealth from the propertied groups to the propertyless. As one exasperated Conservative put it, the coming of democracy meant that the traditional checks and balances of the constitution were in danger of being replaced by continual cheques and no balances.

Anxieties about the economic consequences of democracy and the growth of state intervention in the economy did not have to wait for the 1970s to find expression within the Conservative Party. Such sentiments were party orthodoxy before 1914. They continued to be strong throughout the period when collectivist ideas had their greatest ascendancy. The defection of many Liberals to the conservatives after 1918 as the party best placed to resist the advance of Labour, further increased the dominance of libertarian ideas about the organisation of the economy and society.

Even after 1945, when the triumph of collectivism seemed assured with the electoral victory of the party most closely associated with collectivism, the libertarian strand of thought in the party was not entirely eclipsed. Waldron Smithers, Nigel Birch and Enoch Powell were prominent exponents of libertarian ideas within the party. The emergence from the 1950s onwards of a new movement of doctrinal anti-statism spearheaded by the Institute for Economic Affairs therefore connects with a long-standing tradition in the Conservative Party.

Any examination of the Conservative tradition will therefore find that it offers no one answer to the question – 'is Thatcherism conservatism?' There are no clear guidelines as to what beliefs a Conservative should hold about the role of government. The Conservative tradition legitimates both liberal and collectivist ideas. Margaret Thatcher and her supporters cannot be excommunicated from conservatism by identifying a core strand of doctrinal belief. There is no single core.

This argument has been used to suggest that Thatcherism is indeed a return to true conservatism. Some historians sympathetic to Thatcher's politics have argued that if there is an aberration in Conservative Party history it is the period between 1945 and 1975. Lord Blake for example believes that the Conservative tradition is based on four key traditions from which the party deviated between 1957–63 and 1972–4. These traditions are opposition to centralism, defence of the national interest, opposition to equality and the avoidance of internal splits. The party returned to distinctive Conservative principles in 1970–2 and since 1975. These distinctive principles are reductions in the role of the state measured by spending and the range of decision-making, the weakening of trade-union power and a renewed emphasis on individual self-reliance.[27]

The problem with this argument is that in the eyes of many Conservatives the Thatcher government deviated from the first and last of the four traditions. In many areas, far from diffusing power it centralised it, while internally the party remained deeply divided, particularly over Europe. Many one-nation Conservatives doubted that a stable hegemony could be rebuilt in Britain if the problems of polarisation, social division, poverty and unemployment were not tackled; many remained sceptical that the economic decline had been permanently reversed.

Hugh Thomas, for a time director of the Centre for Policy Studies, echoed some of Blake's ideas. Thomas claimed that Thatcherism represents a new libertarian impulse in British politics and signalled the reversal of the trend towards paternalistic collectivism identified by Dicey. Thatcherism's mission, he claimed, was to force the middle class to become independent and self-reliant again and to abandon collectivism. For this to become possible employment had to be drastically reduced in the public sector. Techniques of economic management, such as monetarism, were not important in themselves but were only tactics in a wider war to end government responsibility for problems such as unemployment and recreate the conditions in which a revival of the private sector became possible.[28]

In the hands of Blake and Thomas, Thatcherism becomes the quintessence of the Conservative tradition, and collectivism a bad dream the British people had to endure and from which Margaret Thatcher bade them wake. But it is too easy to veer from one extreme to the other. As Greenleaf points out, no party has been more responsible than the Conservatives for introducing and shaping the kind of collectivism that has been introduced in Britain. The debate between liberals and progressives has been a central part of the Conservative tradition throughout this century. Neither side can legitimately claim to be the sole representative of conservatism. At different times one approach rather than another has been in the ascendancy. The Conservative Party would be greatly impoverished for the future if one tendency were entirely to drive out the other. That would be a sign that the party really had become an ideological party.

Limited politics and the constitutional state

One of the most influential characterisations of the British Conservative tradition came from Michael Oakeshott.[29] He argues that there is a distinct Conservative disposition in politics, that does not need to be buttressed by speculative beliefs of the kind favoured by many European conservatives. Conservatives engage in political activity in order to resist the 'over-activity' of modern European civilisation and defend from misguided destruction the traditional institutions and ways of life and the social and political identities established through them.

The great evil for Oakeshott in modern politics is rationalism, and its avoidance the greatest task for the Conservative. Rationalism is the attempt to plan societies according to some abstract idea rather than forming judgements on the basis of experience and circumstances. What matters for the Conservative is not the content of political programmes but their form. Oakeshott commented acidly on Hayek's famous polemic *The Road to Serfdom*: 'a plan to resist all planning is better than its opposite, but it belongs to the same style of politics'.[30]

For Oakeshott it is rationalism rather than individualism that is the great disease of the modern world and it produces a distinct conception of the modern state – the state as an enterprise. Governing becomes the attempt to organise all resources in a single direction, eliminating conflict. Against this he counterposes the conception of the modern state as a civil association. Here government accepts the current condition of circumstances and does not attempt to interfere with individuals' desire to make their own choices and set their own goals. Such government rests on the current beliefs and practices of its subjects; it acts as an impartial umpire, and its manner of ruling is the making and enforcing of rules of conduct.

For Oakeshott the meaning of British conservatism has been its desire to maintain the state as a civil association, resisting plans to transform it into an enterprise. In a civil association the function of government is always limited and specific. When rules have to be modified the changes should always reflect, and never impose, a change in the activities and beliefs of those subject to them. Those Conservatives such as Gilmour who see Thatcherism as a rationalist enterprise importing an alien ideology into the party cite Oakeshott in their support. The desire to impose a blueprint on Britain, whether it is a liberal blueprint or a socialist blueprint is what the Conservative opposes. The ideal of a free economy and the attempts made to realise it through privatisation, engineering an enterprise culture, centralising powers in Whitehall in education, housing and transport, and the manner in which monetarism was implemented, suggested a government possessed of a single overriding purpose and seeking to remove all obstacles to its achievement. If Oakeshott was worried that the rationalist bug had bitten the Conservatives when he read Quintin Hogg's 1947 book *The Conservative Case*, how much more must the plans of the New-Right think-tanks of the 1970s and 1980s have alarmed him?

Many aspects of Thatcherism were rationalist in Oakeshott's sense. At times Thatcher and her supporters presented what she was trying to achieve as a grand enterprise – to restore the conditions for a market economy, reduce the role of public decision-making in the private sector and extend market criteria to as much as possible of the public sector. The Thatcher government did not hesitate to confront and refashion institutions and impose solutions against resistance. The practice of the Thatcher governments was very distant from Oakeshott's stress on the importance of building a consensus in which every legitimate interest had its rightful place.

But there is an Oakeshottian defence that could be mounted for the statecraft pursued by the Thatcherites, and it does throw rather a different light on the opposition between libertarianism and collectivism in the British Conservative tradition. It was the collectivist wing of the party that, until the advent of Margaret Thatcher, had most success in characterising the libertarian wing of the party as the diehards and reactionaries, and was successful in projecting its own views as the expression of the Conservative disposition in politics – uniting the concern for governing a society with the belief in the desirability and feasibility of extending state control into new areas.

One reading of Oakeshott, however, would suggest that most collectivist legislation represents a concession to rationalist politics and a move away from conceiving the state as a civil association in which the role of government is to hold the ring and remove obstacles to individuals expressing themselves freely. The Thatcher programme to restore a civil association might have been a rationalist enterprise, but it is being undertaken to remove the effects of a long period of collectivist legislation and the resistance of institutions entrenched under collectivism.

Rationalist politics tends naturally towards a strong interventionist state in which the sphere of political decision making is constantly expanding. If it were possible to recreate a civil association and a limited state then the opportunities for rationalist politics would be greatly reduced. If the Thatcherite programme did genuinely seek a limited state, it might be forgiven its rationalist tendency by an Oakeshottian, for its outcome would be the restoration of a situation in which Conservative statecraft could once more be practised, and conservatives would be freed from pretending to be collectivists or planners.

Such a defence of Thatcherite statecraft would suggest that the heart of the British Conservative tradition is not one-nation Conservatism – an acceptance of the state intervening in the economy to provide welfare and promote prosperity in order to maintain the legitimacy of the state – but libertarian anti-statism. The counterargument of one-nation Conservatives is that their endorsement of collectivist measures has been based not on rationalist blueprints for remodelling the whole of society, but on the need for measures to remedy specific grievances and shortcomings in current arrangements. Most Conservatives claim the authority of Oakeshott if they can. Nevertheless the basis of Oakeshott's understanding of the modern state does stigmatise enterprise politics as unconservative as well as all policies that lead away from or infringe a civil association. The accumulation of collectivist institutions, attitudes and policies could therefore be regarded as the legacy of rationalist politics, which a genuine Conservative would wish to strip away.

An assessment of Thatcherism using the criteria of Oakeshott's characterisation of Conservative statecraft reinforces the point that ideology and statecraft cannot be neatly separated in an analysis of British conservatism. Thatcherism cannot therefore be treated simply as a new form of doctrinal conservatism in opposition to the dominant pragmatic Conservative tradition. Matters are more complex. In reasserting the party's libertarian tradition Thatcher at the same time reasserted a traditional Conservative orientation to government.

Grave doubts remain, however, as to how far the actual statecraft of the Thatcher government realised that aim. Here there was a significant conflict between elements of the liberal and the conservative New Right. For the economic liberals the Thatcher government did not go nearly far enough in using the powers of the state to create the conditions for a free economy. For many Conservatives on the New Right, however, the chief aim of the Thatcher government should not have been the creation of the conditions for a free economy but the creation of the conditions for limited politics. Pursuit of the first objective can lead to never-ending interventions in social institutions. Pursuit of the second encourages conservatives to concentrate upon the proper task of government – the constitutional requirements for limited politics.[31]

Roger Scruton argued that in England conservatism has sought expression through the activity of a single party, 'a party dedicated to maintaining the structure and institutions of a society threatened by mercantile enthusiasm and social unrest'.[32] More recently this tradition was threatened because the party seemed prepared to join 'the competitive market of reform', endorsing such unConservative things as the code of economic internationalism and the free-market economy, which it once strenuously opposed:

It has begun to see itself as the defender of individual freedom against the encroachments of the state, concerned to return to the people their natural right of choice, and to inject into every corporate body the healing principle of democracy.[33]

Such a judgement viewed the Thatcher government as being as unlikely to restore limited politics and the constitutional state as the much reviled government of Edward Heath. They belonged to the same style of politics, just as economists often note the similarities of Keynesianism and monetarism as styles of economic management. Noel O'Sullivan has written of the crisis of identity for Conservatives that developed when the party abandoned its concern for limited politics. He judged that Thatcherism had not resolved the crisis, but intensified it by substituting for the middle way of the progressive Conservatives the free economy of the New Right.[34]

A governing class

A third perspective on Conservative statecraft stresses the importance of the existence of a stable governing class. Such a class is often formed when property ownership and ruling are fused. Land-owning aristocracies are the classic form of such a class, but recruitment from other groups is not excluded.

Members of such a governing class are expected to treat ruling as a highly skilled activity involving obligations as well as privileges. Plato's guardians are never far away in these conceptions, which helped shape the ethos of the nineteenth-century public schools in which the apprentice guardians of the British state were (temporarily) deprived of property and family, the better to inculcate into them an ethic of public service, patriotism and a shared sense of the patria they were being called on to defend.

The British governing class has had many admirers, although more recently an increasing number of critics. For its admirers, such as Joseph Schumpeter, the considerable stability and continuity enjoyed by Britain in comparison with other European states owed much to the capacity of Britain's rulers. The skill of the British ruling class in knowing the right time to make concessions, the best means to maintain and extend its support and divide its opponents made it seem indestructible in a way seldom managed by ruling classes elsewhere:

The unrivalled integrity of the English politician and the presence of a ruling class that is uniquely able and civilised make many things easy that would be impossible elsewhere. In particular this ruling group unites in the most workable proportions adherence to formal tradition with extreme adaptability to new principles, situations and persons. It wants to rule but it is quite ready to rule on behalf of changing interests. It manages industrial England as well as it managed agrarian England, protectionist England as well as free trade England. And it possesses an altogether unrivalled talent for appropriating not only the programmes of oppositions but also their brains.[35]

Gaetano Mosca, the analyst of political elites, struck a similar note:

In the course of the nineteenth century England adopted peacefully and without violent shocks almost all the basic civil and political reforms that France paid so heavily to achieve through the great Revolution. Undeniably, the great advantage of England lay in the greater energy, the greater practical wisdom, the better political training, that her ruling class possessed down to very end of the past century.[36]

British conservatism was perceived in this way because it was so successful, and because it appeared free from the doctrinal conservatism of so many European parties. This in part was the result of the liberal strand within the party's ideological tradition. Doctrinal conservatism had never become firmly implanted in Britain. The anti-Enlightenment tradition emphasised authority rather than individual liberty, attacked Protestantism and democracy and regarded individualism as a subversive force, the disease of the modern world. Some of these themes are to be found in some of the writings of the Salisbury Group and the Monday Club, but they have never been influential.[37]

Assessing the skill of a governing class is notoriously difficult. Survival is clearly one criterion. In the case of Britain, however, the most striking aspect of the governing class is how the Conservative Party not only established itself as the dominant section of that political class, and united the interests of all sections of property behind it, but went on to dominate the mass democracy as well. Since 1885 the Conservatives have emerged victorious from sixteen out of twenty-nine elections and were in government, either alone or in coalition, for seventy-four of the one hundred and eight years between 1885 and 1993.

This degree of dominance by one party is remarkable, especially given the fears expressed by Conservatives themselves at the beginning of the period about the effects of extending the suffrage. The small population still working on the land, and the predominantly urban and industrial character of Britain, made any foothold for a predominantly rural landowning party associated with the interests and values of pre-industrial England seem precarious.

The Conservatives had no grand design for democratic politics. They felt their way forward cautiously. They became aware, however, that in an electorate that was already after 1885 and still more so after 1918 and 1928 dominated by the votes of manual workers, they must find ways of winning a substantial section of working-class support. In electoral terms at least to be a popular party the Conservative Party had to be a working-class party.

Without the kind of solid non-industrial base that Conservative parties could rely on, the Conservative leadership was unusually conscious of the electoral problem it faced. The other major constraint on its behaviour was its identification with the institutions of the country – the monarchy, the peerage, the law, the army, the navy, the universities and the Church. Conservative leaders interpreted their role as defending the interests and privileges of the propertied and professional classes, upholding the institutions of the country in ways that could command majority support.

In a unitary state such as the United Kingdom all contenders for national power are forced to present themselves as national parties. This was particularly true for the Conservative Party since its class base was not nearly large enough to be a substitute for the nation itself. The Conservatives were always anxious therefore, to find bases for political alignment that did not emphasise class. In this sense they are a one-nation party and must continue to aspire to be a one-nation party, even when in practice they fall short of this. The content of their national appeal is not fixed, however, but constantly shifting.[38]

The Thatcher government appeared to threaten in two ways the traditional Tory conception of a governing class. Firstly it was very critical of many of the established institutions of the British state, particularly the civil service. It did not hesitate to have open rows with the leaders of many public institutions, including the Church, the universities and the BBC. All were once considered sound Conservative institutions whose defence against meddling radicals was one of the main purposes of the Conservative Party. During the Thatcher era they were more often viewed as institutions that nurtured an anti-enterprise culture and stood in the way of the creation of a free economy. The Thatcher government at times deliberately gave the impression of being against the establishment through which Conservative governments have normally ruled. This may partly reflect the decline of the old governing class itself, and the strengthening of the populist aspect of democratic politics. Peregrine Worsthorne, one of the most persistent advocates of the need for a permanent governing class, wrote in 1978:

There used to be a governing class, whose social position lent them such weight and substance that they could pass through the demeaning processes of democratic politics with their stature and authority intact. Sir Alec Douglas-Home was a splendid relic of those days. But the contemporary politician has no such inherited advantage. Lacking nobility by birth, he must manufacture his own prestige, create his own authority, forge his own claim to rule, in conditions which yearly become more hostile to any such achievement.[39]

A second reason is that under Thatcher the Conservatives finally abandoned the formulas of one-nation politics, that had served the party so well for so long – the Union, the Empire and social reform. The Empire is no more, even though all its old power to provide the Conservatives with a national cause was displayed in the Falklands conflict. Social reform, in the collectivist and paternalist sense in which social imperialists and middle-way Conservatives[40] interpreted it, was openly rejected by Thatcherites. The Union too was visibly crumbling.

The years of Thatcher's leadership marked the final end and exhaustion of the Conservatives' old Unionist formula. The Conservatives are no longer the party of the Union, striving to unite the country on the basis of the attachment of solid bodies of opinion in all regions and cities of the country to the crown and parliament. Ulster Unionism is permanently estranged from the British Conservative Party. Since the Heath government suspended Stormont and imposed power-sharing the Ulster Unionist MPs have refused to take the Conservative whip at Westminster. The signing of the Anglo–Irish agreement by the Thatcher government in 1985 further embittered relations. Scotland has drifted rapidly away from conservatism since the 1950s, and the conservatives have become less representative of Wales as well as the major industrial cities in the north of England.

The passing of Unionist politics has made the Conservatives look more than ever more the party of the shires and the suburbs, above all the party of southern England, and of an increasingly remote and alien central state. The Conservatives have so far survived the consequences of the breakdown of their old electoral alliance across all regions because the concentration of population and prosperity means that the Conservatives can win not a single seat in the north of England and Scotland and still have a majority in the House of Commons.

In aspiration Thatcherism was a one-nation strategy. It sought to transform the whole country so that the north would become like the south, dependency, poverty and unemployment would be overcome through a thriving enterprise economy, and all regions would vote Conservative. But the actual practice, as Bob Jessop and others described it, was a two-nation politics, that divided the nation and sought to confront and destroy the culture, communities and institutions of the minority.[41]

But, as was noted at the end of the previous chapter, the radicalism of the Thatcher government had limits. It blamed the old governing class for British decline, but its constitutional iconoclasm did not extend to the House of Lords, or parliament, or the law. It was visited on institutions in the second rank. The central icons of the British state were not touched.

High politics

There is another way of looking at Thatcherism, a way that sees a great continuity between the traditional statecraft of the old Conservative establishment and that of the Thatcher government. This is the concept of high politics, which has been analysed with great detail and insight by Jim Bulpitt.[42]

High politics assumes the existence of a tightly-knit governing class that chooses to reserve certain matters for itself and attempts to exclude the participation of others. The supreme practitioner of high politics was Lord Salisbury. He led the Conservatives in the early period of the enlarged franchise after 1885. He had bitterly opposed Disraeli over the extension of the franchise in 1867, but under his leadership the guidelines of Tory statecraft in the new conditions of mass democracy were laid down.[43]

Lord Salisbury's period as leader of the Conservatives has received a great deal of attention in recent years. For a long while Salisbury's reputation has been overshadowed by that of his more flamboyant predecessor. It was Disraeli that was seen as the creator of the modern Conservative tradition – the leadership of Salisbury and Balfour were frequently portrayed as a period of defensive reaction, which culminated in the Liberal landslide of 1906. Recent work on the Salisbury period has considerably changed that assessment. Defensive Salisbury certainly was. He saw the role of the Conservative statesman as trying to make sure that the established institutions would continue to give us 'shelter for our time'. He wanted to defend the existing state and delay the advance of democracy and collectivism for as long as possible. At the same time he fully accepted the need for the Conservatives to participate in the new electoral arena and try to secure a majority in defence of the established order.

The statecraft that emerged, argues Bulpitt, had three elements. Firstly the Conservative Party sought to win power at the centre, on its own whenever possible. Secondly the party developed a readiness to seek electoral support from any quarter. Thirdly the Conservatives in office sought to maintain the autonomy of the centre by insulating it from both domestic and external pressures. This meant in practice that the Conservatives tried to restrict the number and type of issues that were to count as 'high politics'. All other issues were delegated to subordinate bodies, where they constituted a sphere of 'low politics'.

One of the Conservatives' main aims, in which they were highly successful, was to resist the emergence of the kind of executive government that was growing up in other parts of Europe. The range of responsibilities of central government remained narrow. Much was left as the responsibility of local government. These structures were not directly controlled from the centre; instead the central government came to rely on various informal mechanisms for ensuring the collaboration of local authorities with the programme of the centre.

The centre concentrated on dealing successfully with the issues of high politics – in particular foreign and imperial affairs. In return for exclusive sway in this sphere the centre gave autonomy to local authority and other public bodies in their sphere. For the system to work well it was necessary that the citizenry should remain deferential and not seek participation or open government; that local administrators should be prepared to cooperate with the centre and administer their programmes within parameters laid down by the centre; and that the principal opposition party competing to win power at the centre was prepared to operate the same system.

According to this view of conservatism, what is most important in understanding the practice of the party is not the beliefs and doctrines held by leading Conservatives, but the overriding need to preserve the unity of the party and its ability to win power at the centre and maintain the centre in its traditional form. The formula developed by the Conservatives was to maintain the authority of the state by protecting the autonomy of the circles of top decision-makers from the pressures of democracy. This was attempted not only for those parts of the state outside the government, such as the judiciary and the armed forces, but also for the cabinet and the higher civil servants.

From this perspective the debate on whether Thatcherism is conservatism looks very different. In terms of this dimension of its statecraft Thatcherism is a return to traditional Tory principles. The Thatcherites argued that the steady growth of corporatist structures and arrangements in British government, and the great increase in the number and range of programmes for which British government by the 1970s had taken responsibility, meant that the authority of British government was being seriously compromised. This in turn was weakening conservatism both because the Conservative Party appeared less necessary as an agency of government in such a state and because the party was so strongly identified with the authority of the British state.

However it also involved the Thatcher government in a paradox. In seeking to restore the autonomy of the centre the Thatcher government was unable to rely on the cooperation of many parts of the state beyond Whitehall, particularly some local authorities and some autonomous public agencies. This led it increasingly to centralise power in Whitehall and to enlarge the sphere of high politics. The Thatcher government bequeathed to its successor a state machine with considerably extended powers, undermining many of the principles, such as local autonomy and the diffusion of power, that Conservatives had supported so strongly in the past against the centralist, collectivist doctrines of British socialism. It is a measure of the extent of the decline both of the British economy and of the old governing class that the Conservatives were willing to pursue policies with such radical implications for the way in which the British state is organised.

Authority

The most basic task of all for Conservatives is to uphold the authority of the state. Despite playing the party-political game, Conservatives have generally been anxious to ensure that the authority of the state is not compromised. Roger Scruton has argued that for Conservatives the state is always an end not a means to some other end, such as the achievement of maximum freedom in civil society. Individuals belong to the state, and its authority comes not from the mandate of citizens but from the exercise of established power.[44]

Conservatives have always understood this. The essential task of Thatcherism was therefore to propose ways in which the authority of the state could be restored and the Conservative nation rallied to support it. As J. H. Grainger notes, what Thatcherism set out to do was to mobilise the patria against its enemies both within and without: 'In dangerous times the Conservative Party is the appropriate party to sustain the country's institutions, to use the authority of the state'.[45]

The Conservatives have always viewed the British state as their state. There may be a Whig history of England, but there is also a Tory history, the history of the nation-state, its expansion within the British Isles and throughout the world. The success of the British state in avoiding both internal overthrow and external defeat for so many centuries has ensured that most of the national myths are Tory myths, and most of the rituals and institutions of the state are Tory rituals and institutions.

As R. W. Johnson and others have argued this makes the national culture a Tory culture.[46] The assumptions of racial and national superiority; the deferential attitudes towards authority, the secrecy surrounding the practice of high politics, the anti-egalitarian ethos and the status hierarchy are some of its characteristic features.

Despite its decline the British governing class remains a powerful and cohesive social bloc. Only very fleetingly has Labour looked like challenging its dominance. In this dominant Tory culture, as Johnson points out, the state and its institutions are synonymous with the nation itself. What is the meaning then of a Conservative Party pursuing an anti-statist programme? The Thatcherites argued that the era of collectivism, far from being an inevitable further stage in the nation's evolution, was a departure from its essential traditions. Some judicious rolling back of the state was justified to make the state strong again. The crises of state authority in the 1970s were blamed on the extended state of social democracy, which has weakened rather than strengthened the state by overburdening it with responsibilities it could not discharge. The real anxiety conservatives had about British socialism, Worsthorne argued, was that it produced ungovernability.[47]

A government that pursued a libertarian programme would be a profoundly unTory thing, but there was no danger of Margaret Thatcher's governments taking such a radical course. The issues taken up by the Conservatives under Thatcher – defence, public order, the rule of law, the power of trade unions, the Falkland islands – were all issues that helped to restore the image of British government as a strong defender of the state and its institutions. Reasserting the power and authority of the state were popular things to do, as Johnson points out. Confronting trade-union power, standing firm against the Common Market, going to war over the Falklands were all issues readily understood and communicable in the language of the national culture. It hardly needed a highly partisan and overwhelmingly Tory tabloid press to further emphasise it.

There are great advantages to a party that can appear strong and competent in government. This effect is most easily communicated in a British context where the responsibilities of the state are limited, where the governing class is free to define what is to count as high politics, where the authority of the state can be confidently reasserted.

The significance of the Thatcher era is that Margaret Thatcher and her allies attempted to reorganise the basis of Conservative hegemony in the British state. For fifty years an important part of that hegemony had been the social-democratic compromise endorsed by Conservative leaders from Baldwin to Heath. The labour movement, which had appeared so threatening in the early part of the century, was successfully neutralised through a reorganisation of the state that saw the establishment of collectivist welfare programmes and the protection of basic trade-union rights through the institutionalisation of collective bargaining. Thatcher judged that these concessions were no longer necessary and had become damaging to the state's authority, and that Conservative hegemony could be reestablished on a new basis. The free economy and the strong state is a doctrine and also a political project, which makes a bid for a new hegemony and announces a new phase of political and ideological struggle throughout society.

The advocacy of the free market is not in conflict with the state being strong. On the contrary it has been the attempt to restore the free market that has highlighted once more the authority of the state. Many conservatives came to believe that the period of collectivism had brought the old Tory state to the point of collapse. Thatcherism reinvigorated it and restored the confidence of the party of its basic appeal to the English. This was not Unionism. The Scots, the Welsh and the Irish were increasingly detached; but then so too were the former colonies of Great Britain. There could be no return to the dreams of Empire.

Despite its pretensions to making Britain great again, Thatcherism could in practice do little more than aspire to be the latest religion of little England; it is unlikely to be the last. But even while it worked to restore the authority of the state and reaffirm the traditional Tory culture, it had to act in highly unconservative ways. This paradox is constantly encountered in Thatcherism and is one reason why Conservatives have been so divided over how to interpret it. Its critics have noted that there has been a strong rationalist tendency within Thatcherism, and that in practising a Tory statecraft the Thatcher governments launched assaults and directed criticism against many of the institutions that Conservatives once took for granted and defended.

One of Thatcher's hallmarks was her willingness to acknowledge that a gulf had opened between the people and the institutions of the state. She always placed herself unequivocally with the people, and from that standpoint criticised the institutions of big government and even specific public bodies such as the BBC. Remoulding the state to make it once again a true expression of the Tory culture was an important objective in the Thatcherite project. As J. H. Grainger noted, Thatcher's success was due to her ability to combine passion and vulgarity, to develop a popular common sense that found a response in public opinion: 'Her ultimate appeal is not to classes or interests but to widespread, secular, individualist, conservative, moralising opinion'.[48] As a result, Grainger argues, she tapped a layer of Toryism running through the whole nation.

As statecraft Thatcherism was certainly no simple return to the practice of Lord Salisbury. Instead of conserving an order and resisting change wherever possible, the Thatcher governments attempted to stimulate change and reshape institutions. The Thatcherites were much closer in this respect to the Chamberlainites, who argued for a strong state to remedy the abuses of laissez-faire and make the economy more efficient and society more dynamic. The debate between collectivists and libertarians in the party in the early part of this century reappeared in the 1970s. Only this time it was the collectivists who wished to conserve existing institutions and urge caution in making reforms, and the libertarians who wished to reshape and remodel society. Margaret Thatcher sought to restore conditions that would make possible once again the statecraft of limited ends practised by Salisbury. But the means she used to create those conditions were more reminiscent of the statecraft of Chamberlain.

6

The struggle for hegemony

> Those half-formed spectres which once hovered on the
> edge of British politics ... have now been fully politicised
> and installed in the vanguard as a viable basis for hege-
> mony by the Conservatives. As the span of Labour's fra-
> gile base is eroded, this is the historical 'bloc' poised to
> inherit the next phase of the crisis. It is a conjuncture
> many would prefer to miss.
>
> Hall *et al.*, *Policing the Crisis* (1978), p. 316

The writing on the relationship of Thatcherism to the Conservative tradition and its character as Tory statecraft provides one angle of vision on Thatcherism as a political
project, its challenge to the social-democratic state and the
new basis for the hegemony it sought to establish. Another
came from Marxist writing on British politics, and in particular from those influenced by the Gramscian concept of
hegemony. The debate between Gramscian Marxists and
their critics became one of the central intellectual debates
of the 1980s.

The crisis of the regime

The interpretation of Thatcherism that was at the heart of
this debate was based on the concept of authoritarian populism, a term first used by Stuart Hall. But its origins lay further back in a series of debates on the British left about the
nature of the British crisis. These debates centred upon the

crisis of the British state, and in particular the problems of sustaining the British ancien régime, the impasse of British social democracy and the relative decline of the British economy.

The seminal writings for these debates were the series of essays published by Perry Anderson, Tom Nairn and other contributors to *New Left Review* in the 1960s and early 1970s.[1] These essays analysed the backwardness of the British state and the backwardness of British social democracy. They provided a socialist perspective on the British crisis and an important contribution to the extensive discussions taking place in the 1960s on the ways in which the British economy and British society needed modernising.

Anderson and Nairn argued that Britain was ripe for modernisation, but that to be successful modernisation would have to involve a thorough restructuring of both state and civil society. Changing a few government policies would not be sufficient. Britain's real problem was that it had a governing elite that was opposed to fundamental modernisation of the domestic economy and society, and it had a labour movement that had abandoned much of its radicalism for an assured but subordinate place within the British state.

These early analyses in *New Left Review* were influenced by concepts drawn from Gramsci. They were the first serious application of the concept of hegemony to the analysis of British politics. The failure of modernisation, according to Anderson and Nairn, was due firstly to the peculiar character of the English Revolution of the seventeenth century, which broke the back of royal absolutism and accelerated the formation of a capitalist mercantile and agrarian class, and secondly by the failure of the new industrial bourgeoisie in the nineteenth century to wrest hegemony from the representatives of this mercantile and agrarian class. Instead of a clearcut victory for the coalition of industrialists and radical democrats, a fusion took place between the forces of property, which allowed the landed aristocracy to retain predominant influence and resist the bourgeois radicalism that was so evident in many other countries. The bourgeois revolution in Britain was therefore incomplete. Britain was modernised, but much more slowly than some

other countries and many pre-modern institutions and practices remained.

In the 1960s the question appeared to be whether the
agent of modernisation could come from within the governing elite, or whether the Labour Party could assemble a coalition that would permit the modernisation to take place
under social-democratic auspices. For a brief period in the
mid-1960s this appeared possible, but the opportunity disappeared. The failure of the Labour Party to constitute itself as
a radical force allowed the initiative to pass to the right. The
late 1960s saw the first major upsurge of New-Right ideas
and New-Right activities. Enoch Powell was the first architect
of the new direction. Powell was marginalised within the
Conservative Party but his extraordinary success as a tribune
of the people revealed how fragile were the defences of
social democracy.[2]

Powell identified the main contours of the political project
that became Thatcherism. But his intervention was prema-
ture. Labour's modernisation programme was discredited by
its failures, but modernisation – the attempt to extend and
improve the Fordist regime of accumulation that had been
partially installed in Britain – remained the horizon of the
Conservative leadership's ambitions. The programme for
government developed by Heath was influenced by Powell
and by Labour's mistakes, but it remained firmly within the
parameters of postwar politics. It was when this programme
failed that Powell appeared to be vindicated, and many more
Conservatives began to question the viability of their continued attachment to the 1940s settlement. A space was created
that Thatcherism was to seize.

Heath's programme was analysed by Robin Blackburn in
New Left Review in 1971.[3] Blackburn noted that the Heath government was innovative in certain crucial respects. The old
political formula inaugurated by the Attlee government and
sustained by the Conservative governments between 1951 and
1964 had come under increasing strain during the Wilson
government and now appeared exhausted. Blackburn saw
Heath making changes in two critical areas – the policy to
make Britain part of the European Community and loosen
the ties with the United States; and domestic policies aimed at

remedying Britain's industrial backwardness through tougher market conditions, lower real wages and weaker trade unions.

When the market cure seemed slow in delivering results and encountered fierce opposition, the Heath government supplemented it with corporatist and interventionist measures. Before these had a chance to prove themselves the government was shipwrecked by the oil crisis and its renewed clash with the miners. It was the experience of policy switch and then electoral rejection that, as argued in Chapter 3, provided the launch pad for Thatcherism. Another corporatist and interventionist programme had been discredited. The Conservative government had compromised its principles by allowing the distinctive programme up on which it had been elected to be overridden.

From the Anderson/Nairn perspective the Heath government, like the Wilson government before it, was another failed attempt to find a means to modernise state and economy that could command consent from both capital and labour and win electoral endorsement. Their analysis of the deep inertia of the political structures of Britain's ancien régime and the paralysis of policy this induced appeared to be amply vindicated.

Terms like impasse, stalemate and deadlock abounded in analyses of British politics in the mid-1970s. To the apparent inability of the governing elite to modernise itself was added the mounting evidence of the seriousness of Britain's economic position. One influential study, published during the Heath government in 1972, was Andrew Glyn's and Bob Sutcliffe's book *Workers, British Capitalism and the Profits Squeeze*.[4] They argued that as a result of the industrial militancy of the British working class and the intensification of international competition, profits had been severely squeezed and the rate of profit had declined to levels that were potentially catastrophic for the survival of British capitalism.

To the evidence of low profitability was added evidence of low productivity and low investment. A weak economy placed enormous strains on the government's ability to contain inflation and to fund ever rising levels of public expenditure. These problems were exacerbated by the world recession that began in 1974. Governments had to cope with its impact against a background of major policy failures, serious industrial conflict and many signs of popular dissatisfaction with government.

This crisis of capitalism in the mid-1970s was also simultaneously a crisis of social democracy. Great opportunities seemed to be beckoning for the left but even greater ones were seized by the right. The discrediting of so many of the assumptions up on which postwar policy had been based allowed both the New Right and the new socialist left to argue that a quite new approach to the problems of British decline and modernisation had to be developed. Both rejected social democracy as it had developed in Britain.

The impasse of British politics in the 1970s was symbolised by the weak electoral mandates obtained by Labour in 1974 and the proliferation of new third forces and nationalist movements. Events suggested a major crisis of hegemony was unfolding. Elements of the right began to question democracy and endorse violence. The emergence of vigilante organisations, the speculation about military coups and the plotting of elements of the security services against the Labour government were signs of the deep disorientation and profound demoralisation that events in the early 1970s had created in sections of the British establishment.[5]

Authoritarian populism

This exceptional situation in British politics was analysed by David Purdy in two articles in *Marxism Today* in 1976.[6] The central question, Purdy argued, was whether the British ruling class could generate a new hegemonic project to overcome its new weakness and reknit its fractured system of power. Such a new hegemonic project would need at least three elements: a vision of the lines of future economic development, a means to make this vision effective and a means to make it popular.

Stuart Hall and others came to see Thatcherism as it emerged as just such a project. Following Gramsci, Hall defines hegemony as 'the ceaseless work required to construct a social authority throughout all levels of social activity'.[7] The starting point for the Thatcherite project was the discrediting of the social authority that had been established under the regime of social democracy.

The social-democratic regime developed not in the 1940s with the election of the Attlee government, but further back in the last great crisis of the state between 1880 and 1930.[8] Hall and Schwarz have argued that during this period there was a succession of crises of the state, and each was only partially resolved. The state in crisis was the liberal state of the nineteenth century:

> In the closing decades of the nineteenth century, the liberal state and its attendant modes for regulating civil society could no longer be reproduced by means of liberal policies, practices, and objectives.

One sign of this was the decline of the Liberal Party, marked by major internal splits in 1886 and 1916; another was the growth of collectivist legislation and the challenge this presented to the ideologies of individualism – the free individual in civil society as market agent, as the owner of property, as the patriarch in the domestic household – as well as to the idea of the state as a nightwatchman with very limited functions. The relevance and coherence of liberal ideas about the appropriate relationship between state and civil society and the relationship of public and private spheres were also being questioned.

Under the pressures of mass democracy at home and the increasing imperialist rivalries abroad, a major reconstruction of the state occurred. The radical solutions to the problems of the state, whether proposed by socialists, feminists or social imperialists, were rejected. But liberal constitutionalism was substantially modified to take account of the pressure coming from both above and below to introduce collectivist legislation. The market remained the most important regulator of social relationships, but it was suspended in some areas and in others the political conditions governing the manner of its employment were changed. The growth of organised labour and organised capital helped legitimate policies of continuous intervention by the state in areas that formerly had been ignored or left entirely to private initiative.

As a result of the upheavals of these years a compromise eventually emerged in the 1920s. The liberal state had been transformed in a passive revolution, a revolution in which the decisive pressure came from above. The new state was launched on a trajectory towards social democracy. It had embraced the notion of universal citizenship and the social rights that went with that; the coming of universal suffrage had established the Labour Party as the main representative of the working class and the alternative to the Conservatives; and the rejection of the ambitions of the social imperialists to create an integrated British imperial world state had made necessary a new agenda for coping with the problems of empire and a declining world position.

This analysis finds many echoes in other writers, such as Samuel Beer's concept of an 'age of collectivism' and Keith Middlemas' analysis of the rise of corporatism in Britain, which he too dates from the 1920s.[9] The ideologies of the new collectivism were supplied by social imperialists, by new liberals and by Fabians. The general intellectual climate became progressively dominated by them.

The advance of collectivism was neither smooth nor uncontested, but there was a general belief that collectivism did represent modernisation. In all parties those who considered themselves progressives became collectivists. The legitimacy and effectiveness of state policy came increasingly to be determined by its relationship to group and corporate interests. Parliament declined in importance and the direct relationship between government departments and the great producer interests increased.

Hall and Schwarz argue that just as the liberal state entered into a complex crisis and was reconstructed between 1880 and 1930, so the social-democratic state entered a similar crisis from the 1960s. The bias towards increasing collectivism and intervention was halted, the principal political party associated with social democracy, the Labour Party, began to decline and suffered one major split, and the influence of socialist and collectivist ideas began to wane. There are naturally many contrasts between the two periods as well as similarities. But one parallel is that the social-democratic state like the liberal state before it became discredited not only in the eyes of its opponents but in the eyes of many of its supporters. In seeking to cope with the problems of economic decline and the management of an advanced industrial society, social democracy tended to degenerate into what Nicos Poulantzas called 'authoritarian statism'.[10]

The concept of authoritarian statism has a crucial bearing on how Thatcherism itself has been explained. Faced with the need to modernise the economy and society, governments experimented with programmes designed to widen the basis of consent for measures of state intervention, such as prices and incomes policies and public-investment policies. In some countries such programmes were successful, but in others – Britain is a leading example – the policies failed to gain sufficient cooperation from either labour or capital. This brought a shift away from consent towards coercion. The state seized new powers to impose its policies; gradually the democratic aspects of political life began to be eroded and every base of independent countervailing power to the state came under threat.[11]

Poulantzas described this as authoritarian statism because the state was assuming ever more wide-ranging interventionist powers while both parliamentary and corporate mechanisms of representation for conferring legitimacy on the exercise of those powers were increasingly overridden. Greater powers came to be assumed by the permanent agencies of the state in many spheres, but especially in relation to the maintenance of public order, the handling of emergencies and the gathering of intelligence.

There was a clear trend towards authoritarian statism in Britain from the mid-1960s onwards, caused by the breakdown of the attempt to organise corporate consent for modernisation programmes as well as by rising levels of industrial and political unrest and the renewed conflict in Northern Ireland. But to make it a success governments needed to go much further than they were either prepared or able to contemplate. The result was that despite incurring increased unpopularity by measures to coerce various groups in civil society to fall in line with state policies, the policies themselves still failed to secure their objectives, and successive governments were defeated at the polls.

The apparent inability of either of the two main parties to organise consent for a programme of modernisation and to govern effectively opened the space for a new right-wing project to develop, the project of Thatcherism. From the start the Thatcherites sought to organise a bloc of interests around the themes of anti-statism, anti-collectivism and anti-socialism. It was this project that Stuart Hall calls authoritarian populism.[12] It was populist because it drew upon popular discontent with many aspects of the social-democratic state to win support for a radical-right programme. It was authoritarian because in the implementation of its programme it further increased the central power of the state and weakened opposition to it.

As a form of populism Thatcherism fed off a wide range of discourses that were already established in a number of arenas – discourses on law and order, on the family, on welfare, on education, on race, on economic management and on the trade unions. It was not narrowly targeted on a single set of issues. But it constantly sought to explain the ills of society from permissiveness to industrial militancy, in terms of the malign influence of state collectivism and the activities of bodies, such as trade unions, upon which collectivism conferred a privileged status.

One of the features that marked this project as an attempt to organise a new hegemony was the scale of the assault. The attack on social democracy was conceived as a struggle on all fronts and in all institutions. The New-Left project of a long march through the institutions became the Thatcherite practice. As Stuart Hall put it, the state was no longer conceived, as Lord Salisbury might have conceived it, as a passive status quo to be defended against attack, but as a strategic political field of force to be reconstructed.

One measure of the success of Thatcherism was the extent to which it disrupted the old commonsense of social democracy and established a new commonsense in its place. The market was reconstituted as a major ideological force, and crucial distinctions between the productive and unproductive, private and public, wealth creating and wealth consuming came to be the yardsticks for judging policy.

In seeking to reconstruct the state Thatcherism necessarily appeared a radical political force. It launched a fierce ideological and political assault on old landmarks and on the 1940s settlement, specifically on the priority to be accorded full employment, on the collectivist basis of the welfare state, on the principle of redistribution to limit inequality and on the value of partnership between the corporate interests. It sought to shift the terms of the political debate. The liberal New Right constantly presented themselves as the party of progress, and put forward their own utopia – an economy without unions, markets without rigidities, a minimal public sector and private provision of almost all goods and services.

Such an attempt to redraw the political terrain, change the scale of political values and redefine what was meant by the politically possible was naturally experienced as deeply threatening by parties and social groups still wedded to the old framework. To the extent that a new project of this kind makes headway, the opposition becomes disorganised and defensive. In Britain the Labour Party became deeply divided over how to respond to Thatcherism. Many in the party could not understand how Thatcherite policies could bring the Conservatives electoral success; at the same time there was fundamental disagreement over the achievements of recent Labour administrations and whether the party should defend social democracy as it had come to be understood in Britain, or launch a radical programme to transform it.

The split that occurred in the Labour Party in 1981 with the formation of the SDP came about from the same set of forces that created Thatcherism. The Labour Party finally split because the old formula for social democracy no longer commanded wide assent. A divided opposition was a highly favourable circumstance for the pursuit of the radical Thatcherite project, and the Conservatives missed few opportunities to weaken their opponents still further by carefully targeted legislation and propaganda.

Central to Stuart Hall's interpretation of Thatcherism was the idea that the labour movement was not outside the crisis of hegemony but part of it. The crisis was not a crisis of

British capitalism that the left could watch with folded arms, waiting its turn to take over power. Instead the crisis precipitated the reconstruction of the state and this necessarily involved the labour movement, both its industrial organisation and its modes of political representation. In the course of this reconstruction the left was threatened not only with exclusion from the possibility of power, but also with the reversal of the gains that had been won during the rise of the labour movement and that at one time had seemed inviolable.

The forward march of labour halted?

The second strand in the *Marxism Today* interpretation of Thatcherism was the analysis of the crisis in the labour movement, and the problem the Labour Party had encountered in forging a political strategy to defeat the Conservatives. It was advanced most forcefully by Eric Hobsbawm, starting with an article in 1978 – before the Labour government had lost office and the Thatcher government had been installed.[13] Hobsbawm's analysis was prosaic and was criticised for stating familiar facts. But it did focus attention on the precariousness of the left's political position. Even the bitterest critics of the Labour Party and its policies tended to assume that there was a latent majority for the left in Britain. The problem was how to mobilise it.

Hobsbawm was less reassuring. He argued that in the relatively short period in which Labour had been operating as a political party, it had enjoyed a period of steady and almost uninterrupted advance up to 1951, the year in which it achieved its highest percentage vote, even though it narrowly lost the election. Since 1951, however, the party had steadily lost support. Only the election in 1966 was a major exception to the trend. In the elections between 1955 and 1970 the Labour vote ranged between 43 per cent and 48 per cent. At the general elections in 1974 and 1979 it ranged between 37 per cent and 39 per cent. In I983 it fell below 30 per cent for the first time since 1922, recovering slightly in 1987 to 31 per cent.

Even Hobsbawm cannot have expected that his analysis would be so starkly confirmed. Labour's progress at one time seemed so inexorable and its social base so secure that the labour movement was sometimes pictured as a machine throbbing its way to socialism.[14] Demography, sociology and psephology all appeared to be on Labour's side. By identifying itself with collectivist legislation and the extension of the role of the state Labour was also identified as the party of progress and the party of the future. The Conservative political strategy during this period was one of containment.

Hobsbawm argued, however, that Labour's optimism that history was somehow on its side was not justified. Long-term changes had occurred that on balance were unfavourable to Labour. Hobsbawm singled out the decline of manual occupations, changes in the organisation of capitalism and increasing sectional and ethnic and lifestyle divisions in the working class. The labour movement as a result had been declining in numbers and importance, and had been handicapped by what Hobsbawm called the 'pure wage militancy' on display during 1970–4 and the absence of a political strategy to enlarge the appeal of radical and progressive ideas to counter the shrinking of the Labour party's core support in the electorate. He dismissed the increasing strength of the left in the Labour Party as likely to produce only internecine warfare and the pursuit of organisation politics. Meanwhile the vote and membership of the Labour Party continued to decline. All factions in the Labour Party seemed unaware of the increasing fragility of their support.

This was all written before the Winter of Discontent, before the three major election defeats and before the split in Labour's ranks over changes in the party's constitution. Reflecting on these events Hobsbawm argued the need for Labour to reconstitute itself as a people's party, to reforge an alliance between progressive professional and intellectual groups and the working class, and to shed its trade-union and class image.[15] From other writers came the call for Labour to be the party of radical democracy rather than of socialism in order to begin to tackle Thatcherism on its own ground – to create a new popular mass constituency for radical ideas.[16]

It was often argued that Labour had done best electorally – in 1945 and 1966 – when it had succeeded in creating a broad coalition of interests around a coherent reform programme. At such times Labour aspired to become the party agent of hegemony in the state, and for a time it succeeded. In the mid-1970s the crisis of hegemony meant that no political party was fulfilling this role. The vacuum was filled by the elaboration of the new Thatcherite project. Labour had no alternative to pitch against it.

In assessing any movement that aspires to be hegemonic Stuart Hall has suggested that there are three questions:

– Can it lead the key sectors?
– Can it win the strategic engagements?
– Can it stay in front when challenged?

On such a test the labour movement was clearly failing in all three in the 1980s.

Class politics

The most widespread alternative on the left to the interpretation of Thatcherism associated with *Marxism Today* became known as the thesis of class politics. Sometimes the issue was presented by counterposing the theory of hegemony to the theory of class. Theorists of hegemony were portrayed as being exclusively concerned with questions of ideology. Whatever may be true for individual writers, it represents a major impoverishment of the concept of hegemony, which as argued throughout this book involves ideology, politics and economics. The concept of hegemony makes little sense if it excludes the notion of an economic strategy and economic interests, which have always been fundamental to any kind of class analysis. Nevertheless the two terms, hegemony and class, have come to denote very different emphases in political analyses.

For proponents of the class-politics thesis the ideological aspects of Thatcherism were secondary to the political and economic crisis of British capitalism – the relative economic decline, the impact of the world recession, the weakening of the world power of the British state and the consequent disorientation of the ruling class and the crisis of legitimacy for state institutions and the political system. The succession of crises that engulfed the British state from the mid-1960s produced a marked polarisation of British politics and the revival of a socialist left in the Labour Party. The forward march of Labour may have halted for a time in the 1950s, but on this reading of recent history it resumed in earnest in the 1970s.[17]

The evidence cited for this interpretation was firstly the industrial militancy of 1968–74 which helped force two governments to climb down in their attempt to curb shop-floor union power; secondly the growing disillusion with the ideas of the revisionist generation inside the Labour Party following the failure of the Wilson government to carry through the modernisation programme that had owed so much in its formulation to these ideas; thirdly the rethinking of policy and strategy on the left in the 1970s, which produced the programme that later became known as the alternative economic strategy and which appeared to offer a clear direction for the party away from the existing orthodoxies of social democracy; fourthly the radicalisation of sections of groups outside the traditional organisations of the working class, such as women, the black communities and students, which created new policy agendas and a new injection of energy and commitment into the party; and fifthly the growth in influence of the left inside the Labour Party, which enabled it to dominate the NEC during the 1970s, shape the party's policies and after 1979 push through major constitutional changes.[18]

The changes in the Conservative Party's leadership and policies were the other side of the political polarisation brought about by the failures of social democracy. But the rise of Thatcherism was regarded by many theorists of class politics as a sign of weakness rather than confidence, a despairing last throw by the ruling class to hold on to power, but quite inadequate as a solution to the problems of British capitalism. It reverted to the kind of deflationary programme familiar from the past. Unemployment was increased to lower real wages, break working-class resistance to restructuring and reorganisation of production and restore the conditions for profitable accumulation.

This line was advanced with particular force by Tony Benn. He argued in the 1970s that the choice lay between three broad political economic strategies – the free-market policies of Thatcherism, the corporatism of the Labour right and Tory moderates, and Labour's alternative economic strategy. Only the latter, he believed, was capable of restoring prosperity and extending democracy. Both the free-market programme and the corporatist programme would lead to attacks on democracy.[19]

The class-politics perspective suggested that although Thatcherism might be hegemonic in aspiration, it lacked the means to become hegemonic because it could not overcome the resistance of the working class and could not win their consent. It was also claimed that the class interests represented by Thatcherism were narrow and did not embrace all fractions of capital, so that the base of support for its new regime was fragile.[20]

There was no single 'class-politics' interpretation of Thatcherism. A number of different variants were advanced. One that had brief currency in the 1970s was that Thatcherism represented a radicalisation of elements of the small business class who felt themselves squeezed between big capital and the trade unions. This idea appeared to be supported by evidence of mounting middle-class protest against particular aspects of government controls and interventionist policies. The proliferation of ratepayers' groups and organisations such as the Small Business Bureau and the Freedom Association, as well as the writings of able polemicists such as Patrick Hutber, gave some credence to it.[21] So too did the fact that the leaders of the New Right in the Conservative Party – first Powell and then Thatcher – both came from lower-middle-class backgrounds, and espoused a free market ideology which emphasised self-reliance, independence, small-scale enterprise and household economics.

The theory never developed, however, because there was so little evidence to sustain it.[22] Thatcherism was always a passive revolution from above. There was not even the limited mass mobilisation that Powellism briefly created in the late 1960s over immigration. Thatcher gained the leadership of the Conservative Party through the votes of her parliamentary colleagues and not in any unorthodox manner. In organisational terms Thatcher was a conventional leader of the Conservative Party and has done little to transform its internal structures. The point was well made by Bob Jessop and his colleagues, when they asked:

> Where are the Thatcherite new model unions, the Tebbit Labour Front, the Thatcherite Youth, the women's movement, Thatcherite sports leagues, rambling clubs etc? They do not exist and this highlights a certain vulnerability for the Thatcherite project.[23]

What their absence indicated was that Thatcherism could not be presented as some kind of fascist or even Poujadist movement within the Conservative Party. There was no internal purge of those opposed to Thatcher's leadership and little evidence of Thatcherite factions appearing in the constituencies. But the most important evidence was that the programme adopted by Thatcherism, while containing elements likely to appeal to small businessmen, was supported by and tailored to the needs of the dominant sections of British capital.

A much more influential interpretation of Thatcherism as class politics took this as its starting point. Thatcherism was a class response to the strength and militancy of the working class, but it was the response of the dominant fractions of the capitalist class rather than the mobilisation of lower-middle-class strata. It was a determined attempt to roll back postwar gains made by the working class in three main areas – welfare programmes, nationalisation and trade-union rights.[24]

In the early stages of the Thatcher government adherents of a class-politics perspective often regarded Thatcherism as doomed, a last bid to hold back the working class, maintain the unity of the Conservative Party and reverse Britain's economic decline. But the strategy was regarded as flawed because it was economically irrational. This argument rested on two claims. The first was that the interests of banking capital dominated the coalition of interests supporting Thatcher. The second was that monetarism was ideologically archaic and quite unsuited to the complex task of managing an advanced capitalist economy. This meant that Thatcherism was a reactionary spasm. Its policies conflicted with the 'objective interests' of the bourgeoisie. The bourgeoisie was defined as large-scale industrial capital, which appeared to bear the brunt of the recession in 1979–81. The optimistic conclusion drawn from this was that with capital divided and with the economy plunged into chaos by Thatcherite policies there was a real prospect of winning wide support for a socialist alternative.

This kind of perspective on Thatcherism was gradually abandoned during the 1980s. What it found difficult to explain was why, if the policies were so much against their 'objective interests', corporate capital protested so little. Apart from the brief flurry of CBI opposition in 1981, when the director general, Sir Terence Beckett, talked of a bare-knuckle fight with the government over the high level of interest rates, capital seemed remarkably content under the Thatcher yoke. All business organisations gave fulsome backing to the Conservatives in the 1983 and 1987 elections, and the flow of financial contributions to Conservative Party funds from business did not diminish significantly.[25]

A second objection to the thesis is that far from being archaic and a throwback to ideas from a much earlier stage in the development of capitalism, monetarism was a modern doctrine that expressed the logic of the growing financial and commercial integration of the world economy. Its existence as an international orthodoxy rather belied attempts to portray it as a home-grown British lunacy. It was doctrines of political economy based upon national economies, such as most variants of Keynesianism, that became outmoded and 'archaic' in the 1970s. Monetarism prescribed a new and viable programme of policy for national governments within the capitalist world economy.[26]

A third objection was to become the most telling of all. After the initial shake-out of labour and the wave of bankruptcies in 1979–81, the economy stabilised and a slow recovery began. The expectation that the Thatcherite programme would push the British economy into a downward spiral of ever increasing unemployment and declining production was not borne out. The avoidance of further collapse and the real advance of some sectors of the economy after 1981 made the Thatcherite experiment look very different in 1987 than it had in 1981. The possibility that it was preparing the way for the emergence of a new post-Fordist regime of accumulation began to be discussed.

Others argued that although Thatcherism might in some respects be considered economically irrational, because of the short-term damage it was doing to the economy and to particular sectors, it was nevertheless politically rational as a strategy for capital.[27] According to this view capital was prepared collectively to accept short-term costs in the form of bankruptcies and losses in order to secure a long-term, lasting improvement in the environment for business in the United Kingdom. The essential requirement for this was a government prepared to confront and permanently weaken the power of organised labour. The weapons employed included mass unemployment, trade-union legislation, the denationalisation of public enterprises and privatisation of public services, and the scrapping of corporatist bargaining structures. The crisis did not therefore come about by accident or because of mismanagement. The crisis was precipitated in order to effect a restructuring of the economy and a change in the balance of power between labour and capital. Mass unemployment in particular was used as a means to break the resistance of labour and introduce a range of changes designed to prevent labour regaining its former strong bargaining position within enterprises.

Many who analysed Thatcherism in this way as a planned class offensive also claimed that it was doomed to fail because it would be unable to break the resistance of organised labour. Much greater force would be needed. When the economy revived, it was predicted, so would industrial militancy. This prediction was not borne out by events. The economy did revive, but industrial militancy did not.

Apart from its confident predictions about the level of resistance to Thatcherism, however, this interpretation did have greater plausibility than some other variants of the class-politics thesis. The attack on the trade unions had been a central feature of the Thatcher government's programme ever since it was elected, and the government fought several major battles with unions. There was no repetition of the defeats suffered by the government between 1968–74. In most cases the government faced down industrial militancy and contributed to a climate of demoralisation and acquiescence on the shop floor.

The greatest of the industrial battles was with the miners in 1984–5. The events of that strike provided powerful support for the class thesis. The short-term economic irrationality of the strike was plain from the start. The cost of the strike to the country and the government was very high – approximately £2.5 billion. But the government was prepared to write off this cost for the long-term benefits it expected from a clearcut miners' defeat. This was not only the effects on the running of the coal industry, but the wider symbolic effects of defeating the group of workers who had successfully resisted the Heath government. To gain this prize the government made detailed preparations for a miners' strike, resisted all pressures to compromise and won a complete victory.[28] It was a key moment in the emergence of a new hegemony.

The thesis, however, is more difficult to sustain outside particular examples, because it assumes that the major objective of the Thatcher government was to crush the organised working class in the interests of reviving industrial capital in Britain. The recession of 1979–81 and the unemployment that resulted are sometimes seen as being deliberately engineered by the government for this purpose. But there is no evidence that the government expected the level of unemployment that resulted from its first two years in office. Some transitional unemployment was anticipated from the application of monetarist policies, but the world recession was unforeseen.

What is undeniable is that the government used the recession as an opportunity for more radical restructuring. But to argue that the Thatcher government had a clearly worked-out plan for destroying trade-union power, which it proceeded to implement when it was elected, overstates the degree of coherence of the government's objectives and overlooks the extent of muddle and improvisation in the making and implementing of policies that is apparent from the evidence reviewed in Chapter 4.

Finance and industry

A powerful objection to many of the cruder variants of the class-politics thesis was that their conception of the British social formation and their understanding of the forces represented by Thatcherism were misleading, because they suggested that the core of British capital was still industrial capital and that there was something abnormal in banking capital playing such a prominent role. British capital was still analysed as if it were primarily a national interest, and that it was self-evident that every national economy must have a strong national industrial bourgeoisie.

The most valuable class-politics interpretation of Thatcherism came from those who analysed the significance of the split between the industrial and financial sectors of the British economy.[29] What all these writers stressed is the rationality of Thatcherism as an economic strategy for the dominant sections of British capital. The manner of Britain's integration into the world economy over two centuries has made the bloc of commercial and financial interests dominant over industry in the determination of Britain's foreign economic policy. At times of crisis, when major choices have had to be made, the issue has generally been resolved in favour of Britain's traditional links with the world economy.

Thatcherism was no exception to this. As John Ross showed, while there were some heavy losers under Thatcher, such as heavy engineering and chemicals, a significant bloc of capital benefited.[30] Oil, food and construction, as well as banking and the protected sectors of defence and agriculture, all performed strongly throughout the recession. The Thatcher government presided over a further major shift away from manufacturing. Those sectors able to trade and produce internationally were consolidated as the leading sectors of the economy.

From this standpoint it makes no sense to regard Thatcherism as a misguided industrial strategy for reversing Britain's industrial decline. Most of traditional British industry as well as many of the Fordist industries that were the basis of postwar prosperity were written off. Thatcherism had no industrial strategy except to promote the complete integration of Britain into the world economy. Companies had to survive unaided in international competition if they were to have a future in the British economy. Some ministers in the Thatcher government doubted that many of the successful companies in the future would be industrial in the traditional sense.

Such a policy greatly benefited those sectors able to seize the new opportunities as well as the foreign capital that had entered the British economy. The policies of the Thatcher government proved most effective in destroying the structures of the (incomplete) Fordist regime of accumulation that had been established in Britain.[31] Mass unemployment and trade-union laws helped management in some industries to reorganise industrial relations towards the new model of flexible specialisation, with the workforce divided into core and periphery workers.[32] The evidence is mixed as to how far a general pattern emerged. The new pattern was associated particularly with transnational companies keen to use Britain as a base for assembly of industrial products for distribution to the European market.[33]

For some observers this policy represented the final defeat of the manufacturing interest, since the destruction of the manufacturing base that was involved prevented the possibility of any future revival. Manufacturing will continue to exist in Britain but only subordinate operations will be retained. The design and development of new industrial products will have passed largely elsewhere. Britain's new status as a secondary economic power would then be confirmed.

These arguments are powerful, if sometimes exaggerated. The questions they raise are: why has the manufacturing interest been so weak? Why was the Fordist regime of accumulation never consolidated? Why did Thatcherism receive so little opposition from manufacturing companies? The

most detailed explanation of the acquiescence of the manufacturing industry to the economic strategy of the Thatcher
government was given by Colin Leys.[34] He argued that there
were four factors involved. Firstly the mode of representation of capital has always been weak both politically and
bureaucratically. The main organisation, the CBI, has been a
forum for all sections of capital rather than a pressure group
for manufacturing. Thirty per cent of its members are not
industrial companies at all. The desire to present a consensus has made many of the policy stances taken by the CBI
extremely bland and non-controversial.

The second reason was that manufacturing itself is not a
single interest but is highly divided in terms of scale, the
degree of monopoly, and the splits between exporters and
domestic producers and national and multinational production. As Leys put it, the veto on opposition to Thatcherism
came:

> primarily from distributors and other commercial com-
> panies, from the larger, more monopolistic, multinational
> firms oriented to the domestic market, and from those
> which had the best chance of restructuring, relocating
> abroad, or contracting into greater productivity, or which
> were less affected by the squeeze.[35]

A third reason was the political crisis between 1974 and
1976. A permanent shift in the balance between labour and
capital was widely feared throughout industry. This explained, according to Leys, the very strong opposition that
was mounted to proposals such as the Bullock Report, which
would have extended industrial democracy, with strong
trade union representation throughout industry. The support given by business to Margaret Thatcher was because she
offered a strong stand against the encroachment of labour
and trade-union influence.

The fourth factor identified by Leys was that British
business had never learnt to think in terms of hegemony.
British businessmen participate little in politics and have
had little interest in macroeconomic questions. Only two of
twenty business leaders interviewed by Leys in 1983 saw the

direction of the state, the definition of national goals and strategies for achieving them as natural concerns for businessmen. Their policy concerns have been more immediate – particular tax rates, tariffs, controls and subsidies. The wider issues of economic strategy have been left to the policy communities in Whitehall.

Gender and race

The writing on authoritarian populism and the writing on class politics emphasised different aspects of the Thatcherite political project. Both were in turn criticised for their relative neglect of the issues of gender and race. This failure was most acute in the case of some writing from a class-politics perspective. Thatcherism was treated as a return to much more open forms of class struggle. Gender and race issues were part of the struggle being waged by capital to subordinate labour by dividing it. But the heart of the strategy was a class strategy, and class was the starting point for understanding it.

The thesis of authoritarian populism gave a much less privileged position to class. Gender and race were given equal importance for analysing the nature of social stratification and for interpreting politics. Such a focus was clearly laid out in *Policing the Crisis*.[36] The question raised by many feminist writers, and by writers on the politics of race, is whether this was carried through in the actual analyses of Thatcherism.[37]

From the feminist perspective the attempt to create a free economy was evaluated not principally as an economic strategy but as a much wider political and ideological project to reestablish hegemony. The drift towards a strong state was regarded as the most significant aspect of Thatcherism. The policies of the Thatcher governments greatly damaged the position of women and blacks, but even more importantly consent for these policies was mobilised partly through a concentrated ideological assault on the new rights secured by women and blacks during the 1960s and 1970s.

This highlights the point already made, that for the theorists of authoritarian politics what has to be analysed is the crisis of social democracy rather than the crisis of capitalism, because the latter is too often narrowly conceived in terms of the struggles between capital and labour over how to resolve problems of accumulation. A central component of the crisis of social democracy was the erosion of the bases of authority in the state and civil society that resulted in a widely perceived threat to social order.

From this angle the Thatcherite project was about reclaiming the nation and the family from the ideological and political forces unleashed in the 1960s that threatened to subvert both. Thatcherism appeared as the authentic voice of white, working-class patriarchal values, preaching the importance of a strong nation and a strong family for social cohesion.

One chosen target for attack was the permissive society, which became the terms in which gender and many race issues were discussed. In the permissive society that developed in the 1960s the public moral code was relaxed to the point where a much wider range of sexual behaviour was tolerated and many taboos were lifted. Activities previously secret become public. Homosexuality was legalised, which enabled gays and lesbians to campaign publicly against discrimination. Abortion was legalised, which allowed the opening of many clinics and much wider public awareness of issues of birth control. Divorce became easier, cohabitation more common and extended families more fragmented, which focused attention on the loosening of family ties and the growing number of single-parent families and handicapped and elderly people requiring state support.

The greater public freedom accorded sexual behaviour was blamed by many critics of the permissive society on a general questioning of authority and the undermining of moral community represented by the traditional family. Evidence of indiscipline, whether in the classroom, on the football terraces or in urban ghettos, was seized on to suggest a general malaise and a collapse of the firm structure of authority that an ordered society required. The backlash against permissiveness was interpreted as a crucial part of the New-Right project. Such 'moral-majority' politics sought consent for wider New-Right programmes and politicians by addressing the fears of all those citizens who considered their way of life to be under threat.[38]

Thatcherism was as a result a deeply divisive political project, since the unity it sought to build could not be a unity of the whole nation. The nation that was to be restored would render illegitimate the idea of a plural society in terms of both gender and race. The white nation and the patriarchal family as an ideological project marginalised and excluded many of the groups that began to assert their rights to full citizenship in the 1960s and 1970s.

The conservative New Right persistently sought to identify social democracy as the breeding ground for the permissive society, as part of a wider assault on the modernisation projects of Labour revisionists and Tory progressives in the 1960s. As Bea Campbell argued, the modernisation proposed by the Conservative Party under both Macmillan and Heath involved no cultural modernisation.[39] It tended to assume the bedrock of the 'English way of life' – the culture of respectability and patriarchy. Many leading Tories were progressive in their views on social policy; strong grass-roots demands for the return of hanging and flogging, much in evidence at party conferences, were successfully resisted throughout the 1950s and 1960s.

However the failure of the modernisation projects opened the way for an increasingly powerful assault on the permissiveness that had accompanied the attempts at modernisation, whether it was the permissiveness towards immigration control in the 1950s or the permissiveness towards sexual behaviour in the 1960s. Both were treated as major threats to the English way of life – the traditional English identity of moderation at home and imperialism abroad, which was already suffering from the precipitate decline in Britain's world status.

The rejection of progressive 'Keynesian' conservatism was therefore also accompanied by a rejection of progressive social conservatism and a marked hardening of the party's attitudes on questions of immigration, law and order and the family. From a feminist perspective the Thatcherite project was very successful in exploiting gender and race issues to win popular support for its wider programme.

Yet important though these populist themes may have been they did not easily translate into positive government policies. The plural society survived the first eight years of the Thatcher governments. The Conservatives introduced still stiffer immigration laws and a British Nationality Act, but no moves were made to repatriate immigrants already in the UK, as voices on the right were urging, nor was any attempt made to repeal existing race-relations legislation.

Similarly, despite occasional outbursts from ministers, little was done positively to reinforce the family. Social engineering on the scale required to refashion social relationships to conform with the Conservative ideal was too much to contemplate. The proposals of the Cabinet Committee on Family Policy in 1982–3 were leaked in 1983.[40] What was striking about most of the proposals, such as teaching children how to manage pocket money, was that they were little more than the expression of pious hopes. Few serious policy recommendations flowed from them.

Thatcherism as a political project sought to reassert the importance of a strong nation and the patriarchal family. Both were significant in the construction of its electoral bloc, and helped to justify government indifference to the increased burden that the recession and government cuts in welfare services and welfare benefits had inflicted on women and the black community. The 'feminization of poverty' became as marked a feature of the Thatcher years as it has been in Reagan's America.

The public stance of the Thatcher government towards women's rights remained ambiguous. It continued to support the principle of equal pay for women in careers. Jobs for women were less hard hit by the recession than jobs for men, and the economy during the Thatcher years became more dependent than ever on women workers. The new industrial relations systems of post-Fordism, with their emphasis on flexible specialisation, were particularly suited to the employment of women workers since they could be more easily recruited and laid off, and because their expectations of pay and conditions of service tended to be lower than men's. As an economic strategy Thatcherism needed more women workers. What it did not want, however, was commitment to the kind of public services and policies that would enable women to combine work and family and encourage the shifting of child care and housework burdens between the genders.[41]

Despite its rhetoric the Thatcher government tended to lack clear policy ideas as to how the nation might be made more racially and culturally homogenous and how sexual behaviour could be altered and traditional families recreated. The dilemmas of moral conservatism were exposed by the AIDS crisis, which at one level appeared to confirm everything the New Right had ever said about the permissive society, but which still obliged the government to develop a public health programme whose basis was an acceptance of the facts of sexual behaviour in Britain as they were, not as the moralists of the New Right might like them to be.

Yet as the AIDS crisis demonstrated, and as crises of race relations had also revealed in the past, there is an enormous potential for active government policies that make particular minorities scapegoats for major social problems. The Thatcher government did not move far in that direction. But Thatcherism helped create a political climate in which such movement is no longer inconceivable. The weakening of the social-democratic idea of universal rights of citizenship was a major step in this direction.

The state and public policy

A different line of criticism of the thesis of authoritarian populism came from those who emphasised the dimension of state policy-making. It drew upon much detailed work that has been done by analysts of particular Thatcherite policies. It emphasised the continuity of policy and the gap between rhetoric and achievement.

Many political journalists, notably Peter Riddell, have criticised views of Thatcherism that have attributed to it great coherence and novelty.[42] Riddell is responsible for one of the best-known judgements on the Thatcher revolution. 'If there was a Thatcher experiment', he wrote, 'it was launched by Denis Healey'.[43] In his book on the Thatcher government he showed how in every policy area the changes are not as great as might be supposed from reading ministers' speeches. The social-democratic consensus, he argued in the first edition of his book, was still intact.

This view was endorsed by many political scientists. Richard Rose analysed the 'moving consensus' that guided policy formation, and argued that political parties, despite their adversary rhetoric, had little impact on policy outcomes. The constraints on policy-makers were so tight that there was little scope for radical innovations that made big differences to the way the country was governed.[44]

This echoed a long-established view of politics and politicians. Christopher Hollis once wrote that 'politics as politicians well know is largely a matter of giving names to what is happening anyway and persuading people to vote for it'.[45] This implies a very sharp disjunction between the politics of support and the politics of power. The means used to construct an electoral majority may have little relevance to the policy agenda in government, although politicians have an obvious interest in pretending otherwise.

As Chapter 4 showed, there is considerable evidence to support this view when the policy record of the Thatcher government is looked at critically and in detail. The analysis of economic policy under the Thatcher governments by writers such as Grahame Thompson, Jim Tomlinson, Paul Mosley and Maurice Mullard also reveal the enormous part played by inertia, rules-of-thumb, crisis management, political pressures and unexpected events in shaping the actual course of policy.[46] Thompson argued for example that New-Right ideas have only had a limited and uneven impact on policy formation under the Thatcher governments. They may have served an important function in providing ideological support, but in the actual process of policy formation and implementation they tended to be eclipsed by the instruments of policy that were available and by the constraints that inhibited any actual changes. Continuities with the policies of previous administrations still appear stronger than any radical changes that have occurred.

One of the greatest changes in stabilisation policy was the introduction of the Medium-Term Financial Strategy. This was certainly an innovation, but the real foundations of monetarism had been laid long before. As Thompson notes, the use of the PSBR as a central indicator of the confidence of the private-sector financial markets in government policies was an important feature of the Thatcher governments, but its use as such an indicator dates from 1973–4. Similarly the use of cash limits and monetary targets began in 1975. The MTFS, if it had remained inviolate, would have been a significant innovation, but it was gradually diluted after 1982, particularly under Nigel Lawson, until the range of monetary measures was so wide and the discretion allowed the chancellor in selecting his monetary and fiscal policy so great that by 1987 there was little that was distinctively monetarist about the government's policy.

These doubts about the radicalism and coherence of Thatcherism in practice form the main theme of the critical review of the thesis of authoritarian populism by Bob Jessop, Kevin Bonnett, Simon Bromley and Tom Ling.[47] They argued that there was a tendency for the thesis to concentrate too much on the ideological aspects of Thatcherism and to fail to analyse it either in the political and institutional context in which it developed, or to assess it as an economic strategy. The different levels of analysis of Thatcherism as a hegemonic project were conflated, and this led to suggestions not just that Thatcherism was hegemonic in aspiration but that it had already achieved hegemony. They disputed this claim on four main grounds.

Firstly there was little firm evidence that Thatcherism had created a new national–popular consensus. The electoral success of Thatcherism owed as much to shrewd calculation of political interests, such as the sale of council houses, as it did to any widespread acceptance of New-Right ideas. Certain aspects of postwar social democracy, such as nationalisation, might be unpopular, but they were already highly unpopular in the 1950s. What was more serious for the success of the Thatcherite project was the difficulty encountered by the Conservatives of shifting popular attitudes towards collective provision of welfare in areas such as health. In the elections of both 1983 and 1987 the Conservatives were as a result forced on to the defensive, and were obliged to claim that the

National Health Service would be safe in their hands. The Conservatives achieved solid electoral success but with a relatively low percentage of the total vote. Their success was due to the divisions among their opponents, and to their own skill in maintaining a bloc of support sufficiently concentrated to assure them of a parliamentary majority. The electoral map of Britain was now so peculiar and the patterns of voting so diverse in different regions that the national government might not need a national–popular consensus to support it. Power at the centre could be attained by the Conservatives without being a national party.

A second criticism was that the thesis of authoritarian populism attributed too much dominance to social democracy in the period preceding the rise of Thatcherism. The Thatcherites drew a picture of Britain suffering almost continuously under the collectivist yoke from 1945 until liberation in 1979. The thesis of authoritarian populism also treated Thatcherism predominantly as a response to the failures of the governments that had tried to operate within the constraints of social democracy. But social democracy was less developed in Britain than in many other countries. The 1940s settlement was not only about domestic policy; of equal importance was the consensus on foreign policy and foreign economic policy – the Atlantic Alliance, the acceptance of an open international trading order, and the various attempts to rebuild the international business of the City of London and the dominant sectors of British industry, as well as seeking to maintain wherever possible British influence and power through overseas military spending and diplomatic activity.

Britain never was dominated by the left; indeed it was never properly modernised. The origins of the accommodation between capital and labour that was first worked out in the 1920s led to many important concessions and extensions of public responsibilities but hardly touched either the structure of the state or the manner of Britain's integration into the world economy and the world state system. The 1940s settlement has often been described as producing a social-democratic consensus between the parties; the extent of genuine consensus is easily exaggerated, and the extent to which the consensus reflected Conservative priorities easily ignored. Thatcherism's radicalism was limited to attacking aspects of the consensus on the priorities of domestic policy. It sought to reinforce crucial aspects of the bipartisan consensus on external policy.

A third problem is that, whatever the radical objectives of the Thatcherites, they encountered serious problems in realising them. This was in part due to what Jessop has labelled the 'dual crisis of the state'.[48] The state requires some means to secure consent for its policies, but the two principal modes of achieving this – either through the mobilisation of public opinion through the party system and parliament, or the orchestration of group interests through corporatist bargaining structures – have both for different reasons become less and less effective. This has led to the growing autonomy of the state elite in making decisions.

Under the Thatcher governments this process was accelerated. The corporatist structures developed by previous governments were swept away, but there was no major restoration of the primacy of party and parliament. Instead other channels, such as the media, were increasingly relied upon to provide the consent for policies that was obtainable from no other source. At the same time the Thatcher government, in a bid to achieve some of its objectives, found itself embroiled in a major restructuring of the state – in such areas as the relationship between central and local government – but without a very clear set of principles to guide it.

The fourth problem is that the thesis of authoritarian populism was good at analysing some of the key ideological shifts that changed the relationship of forces between the ruling class, the working class and the state. But it tended to neglect the relations within the bloc of dominant interests itself and their relationship to the state. From this standpoint authoritarian populism registered one very important ideological and political shift in Britain, but it tended to downplay or ignore others. Among these others were the constraints imposed by the requirements of economic restructuring on a world level. The great contradiction of Thatcherism was that in the circumstances of modern capitalism it is very difficult for the state to withdraw either economically or politically. Despite the anti-statist rhetoric the

Thatcher government proved remarkably interventionist and dirigiste. The state had to be considerably strengthened in order for the Thatcher government to press ahead with freeing the economy.

The outcome was, not surprisingly, highly confused. There was no comprehensive Thatcherite project that triumphantly seized hold of the social formation and refashioned all the institutions of state and civil society. Instead there was an economic strategy aimed primarily at liquidating specific sources of weakness of British capital on the world market, eliminating the unfit and freeing the companies able to compete internationally from restrictions and extra burdens at home.

At one level this economic strategy was the reassertion of the old commercial and financial logic of British external policy. But it offered little prospect of recovery of all parts of the national economy, as previous modernisation plans had done. It was not a programme for extending the Fordist regime of accumulation. It sought rather to destroy central parts of that regime, particularly the industrial structure and the organisation of industrial relations, and to search pragmatically to establish a new regime of accumulation in Britain based on full integration into the world market, flexible specialisation and the encouragement of new enterprise through deregulation, privatisation, denationalisation and tax cuts.

Jessop argued that this economic strategy was not formulated as a coherent plan before the Thatcher government took office, but became more coherent as the government experimented with various policies for handling the recession and promoting recovery. One important outcome of these policies was what Jessop describes as a two-nations strategy.[49] The destruction of aspects of the Fordist regime of accumulation and the confrontation with political and social groups seeking to resist or obstruct it produced a sharp divide between institutions, regions and categories of the population. The metaphor for this old and new Britain became the North and the South, and has required the formulation of different policies.

The rewarding and encouragement of the prosperous and expanding southern economy had to be accompanied by programmes for managing what threatened to become a new permanent underclass on the margins of prosperity and employment, concentrated in the inner cities, and requiring both increasing income support and surveillance.[50] This tolerance for a two-nations outcome to its policies and the evidence of growing regional and social divisions was what caused most unease among one-nation Conservatives.

Stuart Hall made a sharp rejoinder to these criticisms of the thesis of authoritarian populism.[51] He argued that the thesis had never been intended to be a comprehensive explanation of Thatcherism. From the start it had deliberately concentrated on ideological factors without ever suggesting that they were the only important ones. He also claimed quite fairly that he had never stated that Thatcherism was in fact hegemonic, only that its project was hegemonic. He agreed that the difficulties encountered by the Thatcher government in establishing a viable new regime of accumulation meant that while Thatcherism had become dominant it had not achieved hegemony. True hegemony requires the economic dominance of a successful regime of accumulation to be combined with the winning of political, moral and intellectual leadership in civil society.

As Stuart Hall readily conceded, an interpretation of Thatcherism in terms of authoritarian populism alone would be inadequate, however valid that perspective might be in pointing to a crucial dimension of the Thatcherite project. What was required was a much broader political analysis that could make sense of this highly confusing and contradictory phenomenon by allowing all the different aspects of it to be given their appropriate weight.

What the debate on authoritarian populism brought out was not only the different dimensions of Thatcherism that needed to be considered in analysing its progress, but also the great differences that exist between the politics of support and the politics of power. Thatcherism was initially a project developed when the Conservatives were in opposition. Quite different problems were encountered after the Conservatives entered government. The experience of the Thatcher government substantially changed the way in which Thatcherism was interpreted.

7
The legacies of Thatcherism

> The comfortable illusions that accompanied our gradual decline have been shattered. The nation has woken up to the reality of the need to earn its place in the world.
>
> Margaret Thatcher, Speech to the Institute of Directors, 1983

> [The Conservative] party ... is still harking back to a golden age that never was, and is now invented.
>
> John Major, 23 July 1993

Throughout this book Thatcherism has been analysed as a political project of the Conservative leadership, which sought to organise a new hegemony in British politics. As explained in the Introduction hegemony has several dimensions: electoral hegemony, ideological hegemony, state hegemony and economic hegemony. It involves a politics of support and a politics of power. The struggle to gather support, build new coalitions of interests and win the battle of ideas for a radical change of direction and the dismantling of old structures and old priorities has to be carried through in a programme for government if it is to be durable. A statecraft that is confined to the winning of office will leave few permanent marks.

Hegemony is often misrepresented as meaning simply ideological leadership, but properly understood it involves the successful interweaving of economic and political as well as ideological leadership. Gramsci emphasised this point:

the fact of hegemony presupposes that account be taken of the interests and the tendencies of the groups over which hegemony is to be exercised, and that a certain compromise equilibrium should be formed – in other words, that the leading group should make sacrifices of an economic–corporate kind. But there is also no doubt that such sacrifices and such a compromise cannot touch the essential; for though hegemony is ethical–political, it must also be economic, must necessarily be based on the decisive function exercised by the leading group in the decisive nucleus of economic activity.[1]

Thatcherism was an ambitious, often contradictory, attempt to create conditions for a new hegemony across all four dimensions of hegemony. The Thatcherites were more adept at staking out new ground and repudiating the old consensus than at making sacrifices or seeking the compromises necessary to build a new one. If there was one idea running through the whole project as it unfolded it was that to win hegemony Conservatives no longer needed to make the kind of concessions to the demands of the labour movement that they had once believed necessary.

Looked at in this way two of the central mysteries about Thatcherism – its relationship to Conservatism and the gulf between its ambitions and its achievements – can be unravelled. The kind of task the Thatcherites defined for themselves was an unusual one in the history of conservatism. British Conservatives have generally been defenders of the existing state against those seeking to reform or overthrow it. Attempting to dismantle and discredit the institutions, structures and policies that once carried the full authority of the state is not normally characteristic of Conservative politics. The crusading style and the ideological certainties evident among Thatcherites seem alien to traditional conservatism. But understood as statecraft aimed at determining the Conservative Party interest and restoring the freedom of action and authority of the party in government, Thatcherism is placed firmly in the most central Conservative tradition of all.

Similarly the gulf between ambition and achievement is explicable given the scale of the task that was being attempted. The Thatcher government willed the ends but had no way of organising effective means to implement the policies that might achieve them. Since it was committed to overturning many aspects of the 1940s settlement it was obliged to confront and attempt to reconstruct many of the institutions not just of the state and the public sector, but of civil society as well. Many of the institutions that had been important buttresses of the old order were obstacles to the creation of the new. Establishing a fresh basis for a stable hegemony required their reconstruction, or in some cases their destruction.

It is hardly surprising if, after four years in opposition and eleven years in government, neither a new political settlement from which a consensus might develop nor a remodelled society and economy were close to being achieved. The last period (the 1880s) when hegemony broke down led to several decades of political turbulence and conflict. It is unlikely too that the policy agenda that was dominant under the Thatcher government will be more than the first phase in the development of a new political compromise. The construction of a new and stable hegemony is rarely the work of a single party.

Nevertheless the Thatcherites were the first group to grapple with the problem of turning their criticisms of postwar social democracy into practical programmes and policies. The success they achieved did not amount to the 'Thatcher revolution' that is sometimes spoken of. But the Thatcher years were important in demolishing old assumptions, challenging institutions and policies, and clearing the ground for future initiatives and changes.

The success or failure of the Thatcherite project has to be assessed as both a politics of support and as a politics of power, aimed at creating a hegemony for the Conservatives based on their ability to win votes and the battle of ideas, as well as to successfully manage the economy and the state. It sought to reestablish the political fortunes of the Conservative Party and to make economic liberalism once again the dominant public philosophy; and it also pursued an economic strategy to reverse the relative decline of the British economy. To achieved these ends the Thatcherites came to see that they required a strategy for reorganising the state and civil society.

Some of the most influential interpretations of Thatcherism, developed in the 1980s, rejected theories of hegemony in favour of single-factor explanations, such as statecraft or policy implementation.[2] The theory of Thatcherism as Tory statecraft explained many of the policy decisions and priorities of the Thatcher government as guided by calculations of the Conservative Party's political interests, discounting the importance of ideology or economic interests. The theory of policy implementation focused attention on the policy-making process and the gap between political rhetoric and the actual policies pursued by the government.

Both these explanations are based on important insights into politics. Statecraft theories draw attention to the party element in politics. It provides a plausible explanation of the numerous attempts by the Thatcher government to weaken the Labour Party and the labour movement. Political parties must first win elections and outmanoeuvre their political opponents if they are to survive. The detail of political competition within and between parties, the rise and fall of ministers, and the calculation of party advantage and disadvantage absorbs the attention and interest of politicians often much more than the formulation and implementation of policy. In Britain no programme for government, however coherent and planned, can ever hope to advance if it is not closely intertwined with party interest.

Policy implementation theories emphasise the constraints of the policy-making process. They analyse how institutions and circumstances tend to determine how policies are actually formulated and the extent to which they are implemented. This view sees politicians acting out roles and performing actions in which their own ideologies and political preferences play a small part. The politicians exaggerate their own importance. Their role is simply to smooth the path of the changes that are necessary and inevitable. This view punctures the idea that politics is just a matter of will, and that the successful implementation of a radical programme depends solely on having a leadership determined and capable enough to see it through.

Statecraft and policy implementation are key approaches for understanding Thatcherism, however they are not rival interpretations but components of the broader theory of hegemony. The theory of hegemony can be caricatured as the claim that Thatcherism was a precise ideological doctrine that was embodied in a detailed set of policies that the Thatcher government set out to implement in every field of policy. But, properly understood, what the theory of hegemony allows is consideration of the many different structures and agencies in their proper historical context that are necessary for understanding a complex and contradictory political phenomenon such as Thatcherism. The theory of hegemony does not assume that hegemony can be achieved by acts of will or that it is predetermined by the nature of the social structure. It explores precisely the interaction between agency and structure that defines the space in which politics takes place.

The politics of support

The main objectives of the new leadership in 1975 was to restore the Conservatives to their leading position in the British state. The party had to be united behind its new leader in the drive to win ascendancy in parliament and in ideological argument, to win back lost voters and recruit new ones, and to regain the confidence of all the interests that looked naturally to the Conservative Party.

The victory in 1979 marked the successful completion of this first stage. But that was only the beginning. The requirements of the politics of support in opposition and in government are very different. The real test of the new leadership was how it coped with the pressures of government. Could it govern in such a way as to keep the support of its voters, its party members, its MPs, its press and business allies, as well as the goodwill of non-aligned opinion? Could it win acceptance for its policies and justify them in ways that commanded agreement? Could it push through policies in the face of disagreement and resistance? Could it maintain a strategic line despite the pressures of events that could unite the cabinet and the party? Questions like these provide the criteria for assessing the success of the Thatcher project as a politics of support.

Electoral hegemony: managing the party

Thatcher liked to project an image of herself as an exceptionally dominant leader and powerful prime minister. Her personal style was an essential ingredient of Thatcherism, but she was more successful in establishing a personal regime than in creating the conditions for either a Thatcherite leadership or a Thatcherite party after her departure.

She possessed considerable structural advantages as Conservative leader, including control of appointments in Conservative Central Office from the party chairman down, the selection of the shadow cabinet, and the right to determine what is and is not party policy. Such powers automatically give Conservative leaders a degree of influence in their party that other political leaders in Britain have to win.[3] Nevertheless, following her unexpected victory against Heath, Thatcher's position was at first a weak one, and it took her a long time to consolidate her power in the party, gradually promoting her allies and banishing her more troublesome opponents. But she remained cautious throughout her tenure of the leadership, and proved either unable or unwilling to assemble a corps of Thatcherite leaders. She fell out with political friends, such as Norman Tebbit and John Biffen, and though she removed many of her cabinet critics, such as Francis Pym, James Prior and Ian Gilmour, she came to rely on others, such as Kenneth Baker, Kenneth Clarke, Douglas Hurd and Chris Patten, who did not share her ideological convictions. It is a measure of her failure that after the 1992 general election John Major's cabinet only contained three committed Thatcherites.

One reason for this was that, to the despair of some of her ideological allies, Thatcher often behaved like a traditional Conservative, pursuing a Tory statecraft, which put party unity and vote-winning ahead of ideological objectives. Because of the media focus on her the government as a whole often appeared more committed to the Thatcherite project than it really was. 'A brilliant tyrant surrounded by mediocrities' was said to have been Lord Stockton's judgement. After a number of disappointments Thatcher picked out one of the mediocrities, John Major, to succeed her, believing him to be 'one of us', but she was soon complaining that she had been cruelly deceived. As Major increasingly aligned himself with the pragmatic centre of the party, Thatcher became openly disloyal to him, particularly over his European policy, even voting against a three-line whip in the House of Lords on the Maastricht Treaty in July 1993, and criticising him in her memoirs.

During Thatcher's leadership some Conservatives, notably the former leader, Edward Heath, felt that their party had been stolen from them. After 1990 it was the turn of the Thatcherites to feel that. One of Thatcher's lasting legacies was a more faction-ridden and ideological party, with some deep divisions over policy. The Conservative Party was still recognisably a party of government rather than a party of doctrine, but less securely so. The emergence of a deep animosity among the Thatcherites and their press allies towards John Major and certain members of his cabinet, and the long-drawn-out parliamentary struggle over the Maastricht Treaty in 1992–3 showed how faction-ridden the Conservative Party had become.[4] A key failure of the Thatcher project was that continuity in its direction was not assured. The Thatcherites never forgave the manner in which Thatcher was ousted in 1990, and were never reconciled to the new leadership, even though initially it had Thatcher's blessing.

One reason for the Thatcherites feeling so betrayed was that John Major used his position as leader to mobilise support from the bulk of the party for the policies of the government, just as Thatcher had done. What that exposed was the shallow base that existed for ideological Thatcherism within the Conservative Party. In the parliamentary party the strong personal loyalty to Thatcher as leader had not been based upon endorsement of the objectives of radical Thatcherism. The Conservative Party never became a Thatcherite party. It remained the Conservative Party led by Margaret Thatcher.[5]

The same was true of the Conservative Party in the country. The Conservatives' enthusiasm for imposing democratic practices on trade unions never extended to their own party organisation. The annual conference remains a rally rather than a policy-making body, and the officers of the party are still appointed not elected. The party·ethic of loyalty and unity that generally inhibits opposition and dissent is still strong. Such features made the party seem very Thatcherite, especially during the adulatory standing ovations given to Margaret Thatcher herself. She was probably more in touch with the opinions and instincts of the party rank and file than any previous Conservative leader. She showed none of the disdain many previous leaders have felt for the passions and prejudices of the delegates. She shared them and expressed them. Her stance on crime and punishment, particularly her support for hanging, on defence, on trade-union power, on permissiveness and the family, and on immigration aligned her with the views of Conservative conferences. Her populism was first of all a populism of the Tory grass roots. Previous leaders manipulated the sentiments of their supporters but never identified with them in the way that Thatcher did.

But this close relationship between Thatcher and her party did not mean that the Conservative Party had become Thatcherite in the sense of embracing Thatcherite ideology. In Thatcher the party had found a leader to express its dominant emotions and concerns, but despite this advantage the New Right struggled to gain a secure organisational foothold. One of its few successes in the Thatcher decade was winning control of the Federation of Conservative Students, but the publicity given to the behaviour and views of some of its members obliged Norman Tebbit, as party chairman, to close down the organisation in 1986.

Under Thatcher organised ideological groups in the party, chiefly but not exclusively from the right, flourished. But although these were important in feeding ideas to the leadership and fighting ideological battles, they made little impact on how the party was run. The influence of the New Right on the selection and deselection of MPs was small. Open critics of the prime minister survived unscathed, and there was no obvious pattern in the selection of new MPs.

New-Right groups never achieved a position where they could influence constituency selection conferences.

Electoral hegemony: winning votes

None of this mattered so long as Thatcher remained leader and the party remained electorally successful. The forward momentum of the Thatcherite project was assured by the three consecutive general-election victories under Thatcher, and the achievements of the Thatcher decade seemed secure following a fourth under John Major in 1992. The contrast with the party's situation in 1974 was sharp. The party had moved from a position where it had been threatened with marginalisation to one where all the talk was of the creation of a new, dominant party system.

Significant elections allow a redrawing of boundaries and a reshaping of our understanding of the past. After the 1992 election result the period between 1940 and 1979 assumed a distinct shape. It was the period when Labour achieved its greatest success, a period when it was almost on equal terms with the Conservatives. Including the period of the war-time coalition government, each party was in government for twenty-two years between 1940 and 1979. This was the only time in the modern era when Britain has had a true two-party system, in the sense of a system in which there were two major parties with a reasonable opportunity of forming a government after each election.

In the 1920s and 1930s there was a dominant party system, in which the Conservatives were the normal party of government and the opposition to them was split. The vote of the Labour Party was increasing in this period but it never went above 40 per cent. Labour was able to form two governments, in 1924 and 1929, but both were minority governments, and neither lasted long – the first less than a year, the second just over two years. In contrast the Conservatives rarely fell below 40 per cent and in their best years went much higher. In 1924 they won 48.3 per cent of the vote; in 1931, 55.2 per cent; in 1935, 53.7 per cent. The percentage margin over Labour in those three elections was 15.3 per cent, 24.6 per cent and 15.8 per cent respectively (see Table 1).

Table 1

Election Year	Conservative		Labour		Lib/All/LDP	
	%	Seats	%	Seats	%	Seats
1945	39.8	213	48.3	393	9.1	12
1950	43.5	299	46.1	315	9.1	9
1951	48.0	321	48.8	295	2.5	6
1955	49.7	345	46.4	277	2.7	6
1959	49.4	365	43.8	258	5.9	6
1964	43.4	304	44.1	317	11.2	9
1966	41.9	253	47.9	363	8.5	12
1970	46.4	330	43.0	288	7.5	6
1974	37.8	297	37.1	301	19.3	14
1974	35.8	277	39.2	319	18.3	13
1979	43.9	339	37.0	269	13.8	11
1983	42.4	397	27.6	209	25.4	23
1987	42.3	376	30.8	229	22.6	22
1992	41.9	336	34.4	271	17.8	20

Since 1979 a large gap has once again opened up between the two parties. In absolute terms the Conservatives' share of the vote did not match the levels they achieved in the 1920s and 1930s, but in relative terms they once again had a significant lead. In 1979, 6.9 per cent; in 1983, 14.8 per cent; in 1987, 11.5 per cent; in 1992, 7.5 per cent. In 1983 Labour recovered from its slump, but its absolute share of the vote in 1992 was still below its 1979 level.

These changes suggest that in electoral terms a watershed was crossed in the 1980s. After its failure at the 1992 election Labour had·not won more than 40 per cent of the vote at any general election since 1970. At all seven elections from 1945 to 1970 Labour took over 40 per cent of the vote and in several it took close to 50 per cent. The period also contained the only two occasions so far when Labour has won a parliamentary majority of more than ten seats – 1945 and 1966. Looking at British political history since the decisive widening of the franchise in 1885, the Conservatives have been the leading force. Between 1945 and 1979 Labour was at least on equal terms with the Conservatives. From 1979 this was no longer so. One of the greatest successes of the Thatcherite project was its restoration of the Conservative Party to its former position.

1979 is often seen as the key watershed election in the Thatcher era, but the Conservative victory in 1992 showed that 1983 was even more important. The result in 1979 could have been reversed, and for a time it looked as though it would be. No government in the previous twenty years had been reelected after serving a full term. The government had changed hands every five years on average – in 1964, 1970, 1974 and 1979. The depths of unpopularity to which the Thatcher government quickly plunged made it likely that this would be its fate also. Three factors changed this: the split in the Labour Party in 1981 that led to the formation of the Social Democratic Party (SDP) and the formation of the Alliance, an electoral pact between the SDP and the Liberals; the Falklands War, which might have been a disaster but was turned, not least by Thatcher herself, into a triumph; and the recovery of the economy from the deep recession of 1980–1, which brought back prosperity to key parts of the Conservative electorate, particularly in the south east.

These three factors allowed the Conservatives to hold their vote steady in the 1983 election, while the opposition parties fought for second place. The electoral system rewarded the Conservatives with a huge parliamentary majority of 144. But the real significance of 1983 was not the number of seats won by the Conservatives but their percentage lead over the other parties. Both have diminished since 1983, but both still exist.

1983 now looks like the election that realigned British politics and solidified a political and electoral structure that gave a permanent advantage to the Conservatives, making Conservative victories a more likely outcome of general elections than Labour ones. Labour victories may still occur, in part because the party benefits under the present electoral system from the regional concentration of its vote and the small size of the electorate in many of its constituencies. But in other respects the balance of the system has shifted against the party. Labour's base of support is too small relative to the

Conservatives' to make it an equal contest. Ivor Crewe has pointed out that the number of Labour identifiers in the electorate declined sharply during the 1980s.[6] Conservative identifiers outnumbered Labour identifiers by 45 per cent to 33 per cent. The range of the normal vote for each party is 28–40 per cent for Labour, 37–45 per cent for the Conservatives and 14–26 per cent for the Liberal Democrats. The overlap between the bottom of the Conservative range and the top of the Labour range means that Conservative victories have become much more likely than Labour victories. To this extent the two-party system that existed for forty years has been superseded by a dominant-party system.[7]

During the Thatcher period the concentration of Conservative support was more striking than its spread. The historic decline of the old Unionist Party continued in the big cities and some of the regions, especially Scotland and Northern Ireland. This process was not arrested under Thatcher; on the contrary it accelerated. Some of the regional differences in voting behaviour became very marked. The collapse of the Conservative position in Scotland was the most extraordinary example of this. In 1955 the Conservatives had 50 per cent of the Scottish vote and approximately 50 per cent of the seats. In 1987, despite a hundred seat majority in Westminster, the Conservatives only won 22 per cent of the Scottish vote and ten seats.

What the Conservatives learned, however, and particularly during Thatcher's leadership, was that it was no longer necessary or possible to project themselves as the party of the Union in order to win elections. Unionism declined with the Empire. Conservatism has had to find a new identity. The Conservative nation now is no longer the nation of Empire and Union. The appeal is directed much more towards England, and towards certain regions of England, the old metropolitan heartland of the Empire.

This is not a new trend. The divide between North and South in the UK has been steadily becoming more marked throughout the postwar period. But it seemed to have reached a new stage in the elections of 1983 and 1987, when Labour hardly won a seat in the south outside London, and the Conservatives did poorly in many northern areas, particularly Scotland.[8] This north–south divide was associated with differential regional prosperity and regional levels of unemployment. Under the impact of the global recessions since the 1970s and the economic and occupational restructuring they have prompted, many societies have become more segmented, leading to fears about the rise of a one-thirds/two-thirds society[9] – the poor, the unskilled and the unemployed forming a minority facing a majority of citizens with jobs, reasonable security and rising real incomes.

The Conservatives' electoral strategy throughout the post-war period had sought to enlarge the base of Conservative support by identifying prosperity and all forms of property ownership with Conservative voting. Thatcher did not invent this strategy but she pushed it still further, particularly through the sale of one million council houses and the promotion of wider share ownership through the nationalised-industry sell-offs. The creation of a mass of private-property interests willing to support market solutions for problems of public policy and antagonistic to state intervention and direction was a key objective of Conservative statecraft.

Defining the Conservative nation as a nation of property owners and consumers tended to exclude much more of the actual nation than some previous versions of conservatism. The Thatcherites always vigorously denied that they were opposed to the one-nation philosophy of Toryism. Thatcher wanted to see one nation as much as any Tory ever had, but it was to be a nation in which everyone had become a property owner and a consumer. It was no longer to be a nation composed of many different interests and classes, united through a common citizenship and a common loyalty to an ideal of nationhood.

Traces of this older Tory ideal lingered. The Falklands War saw its triumphant return. But the thrust of Thatcherism as an electoral strategy was away from this and towards the consolidation of a bloc of interests rather than the creation of a union of citizens. This necessarily limited Thatcherism's appeal and made it in practice very divisive, since entire sectors, institutions, categories and regions, such as the 'north', were stigmatised as problems and deemed to be in need of reform.

Thatcherites did not abandon the ideal of one nation, but argued that if that ideal was to be made reality the existing nation must first be reformed and purged of alien elements and practices. Only then could it be truly united. In practice therefore Thatcherism constantly split the nation into two.[10] The world was divided into allies and enemies, those with us and those against us. In Thatcher's new Britain legitimacy was withdrawn from voluntary associations such as trade unions, public institutions such as the BBC, the universities, the state education system, nationalised industries and local government until they had reformed themselves or had been reformed from outside.

This strategy moved away from ideas of the mixed economy and a balance between sectors and interests. It identified the national interest very firmly with the private sector and down-graded all public-sector activities except in privileged spheres such as the police and the military. This took advantage of the sectoral split that emerged between public and private sectors, particularly since the 1970s. The Conservatives sought to align themselves with the private sector both in terms of employment and consumption. This tactic was most evident in the case of council houses. In health and education the Conservatives had to be much more cautious because the private sector has always been so small, but the long-term aim of building up the same kind of lobby for private health and private education that exists for housing was clear enough.[11]

Ideological hegemony: policy agendas

The success of the Conservatives in establishing a clear electoral hegemony in the 1980s was reinforced by the trend towards a new consensus on policy. One of the most significant legacies of the Thatcher era on British politics was the way in which it changed the priorities of policy in several areas and the agenda of policy debate. The influence and relevance of this agenda was one of the explanations of Labour's shift on so many issues, from the sale of council houses to privatisation, from industrial-relations legislation to taxation, from defence to the European Community. After the polarisation in policies that opened up between the parties during the 1970s and early 1980s, the policy gap narrowed sharply, until by the 1992 general election the differences were marginal. Although the Conservatives had made some adjustments, abandoning a few of the more radical proposals of their third term, in particular the poll tax, most of the movement was from Labour. The Labour leadership, in order to make the party electable again, abandoned its alternative economic strategy and its unilateralist defence policy, emphasising instead the party's traditional role as the defender of collectivist public-sector welfare programmes. The manifesto upon which Labour fought the 1992 election had few radical proposals of any kind.

Winning electoral contests is only part of the struggle to influence policy agendas. Victorious politicians claim mandates for particular policies and programmes, but the link between voting and the endorsement of specific proposals is extremely loose. Electoral attitudes can shift very rapidly and unpredictably, and in practice the setting of policy agendas owes more to the policy debates among the political elite than to the preferences of the electorate.

Conservative ideological hegemony at the end of the 1980s was more marked, however, at the elite than at the popular level. The *British Social Attitudes Surveys* showed that remarkably large majorities remained opposed to many of the policy shifts in welfare and social policy most sought by the Thatcher government. The *1985 Survey* for example found the Conservative Party was at that time viewed as more extreme than Labour; there was strong support for price controls (66 per cent) and import controls (67 per cent); even wage controls had 42 per cent support (with 53 per cent opposed); on state ownership the argument had shifted from whether there should be more or less nationalisation to the merits of privatisation. But the survey still found a majority against privatisation among all groups except those identified as Conservative partisans. Even more striking results were found for welfare. Only 5 per cent of the sample supported reductions in services, even when linked to tax cuts; health and education were easily the most favoured areas for increased public spending. On attitudes to unemployment benefit and the gap between high and low incomes, only Conservative partisans thought the former too high and the latter justifiable. On the evidence of the surveys at least, eleven years of Thatcher government did not produce a Thatcherite consensus in the electorate.[12] The driving force for changing the policy agenda had to come from elsewhere. Winning support within the political elite was essential in translating electoral endorsement into shifts in policy priorities.

Crucial to the success that was achieved was the degree of support the government received from the media, in particular the newspapers. Since it is the newspapers that provide so much of the material and help fix the parameters for debates and news reporting on television, the active support given to the Thatcher government by the great majority of the national press was very important in sustaining the momentum of Thatcherism and projecting its policies as the only right and possible ones.[13]

Under the Thatcher government the British press was more one-sided in its partisanship than at any time in the history of British mass democracy. It made the relative objectivity and pluralism of the television output stand out in comparison, which explained why the Thatcher government became embroiled in arguments with the BBC over the 'bias' of its coverage. Strong efforts were made by the Conservative chairman, Norman Tebbit, during 1986 and 1987 to influence the editorial and news criteria of the BBC. He stopped short of dictation, but the message was clear enough.

The government looked for full support from the business organisations in its bid to reshape the policy agenda, and in general, after a shaky start, it received it. Apart from the brief outburst in 1980 from the director-general of the CBI against the policies of high interest rates and an overvalued exchange rate, which were doing so much damage to industry, both the CBI and still more the Institute of Directors threw full support behind the changes the government was attempting to engineer in the belief that the reforms would put the companies that survived on a stronger footing. Apart from a few rumbles of discontent from some of the regional offices of the CBI, and the contribution from senior industrialists to the 1985 House of Lords report on the state of the economy, the manufacturing sector failed to make a significant protest about the contraction that was being forced upon it.[14]

The uniting of the political representatives of capital behind its programme was of great importance to the construction of the new agenda. It lent enormous weight to the idea that there was no alternative. The credibility of the programmes put forward by the opposition parties and by critics of the government appeared to founder because no section of British capital was prepared to support an alternative programme. The partisanship of British business increased as the recovery got under way, and by the 1987 election the CBI was openly dismissive of the economic proposals of the Labour Party. A sure sign of business approval for the Conservatives was the continuing high level of business contributions to the party. The firms and sectors that were most prominent tended to be those that had gained most from the liberalisation of the economy over which the Thatcher government had presided.[15]

Support from the trade unions was never very likely for the Thatcher government since reform of union law was one of the government's major priorities, and because the government was determined to freeze the unions out of the policy-making process. The destruction of the old labour movement was a key political objective for the government but this meant a certain ambivalence in government attitudes since it could not decide whether the objective should be to encourage a union-free economy or an economy with new model unions, such as the electricians (EEPTU) and the breakaway Union of Democratic Mineworkers (UDM) in Nottinghamshire, that would provide positive support for the changes the government was seeking. The continuing high levels of unionisation, despite the falls in total union membership due to the recession, suggested that if the Thatcher reforms were to become permanent these new model unions needed to be encouraged so that they might participate in reaching a new political settlement.

Securing key support from the institutions and organised interests of the private sector was a major goal of the Thatcher government. It enabled it to pursue more easily its confrontations with the political representatives of the old labour movement in the unions and the town halls, and with the representatives of public-sector professionals in health and education and housing. In general it made little progress in winning over these groups so sought increasingly to weaken them by cutting their funding, reducing their autonomy, redefining responsibilities and forcing them to find sponsorship and clients directly from the private sector to support their activities.

In its eleven years the Thatcher government succeeded in shifting the terms of the policy debate, but few of the changes reflected a genuine consensus either within the electorate or the policy-making elite. Major interests and groups remained fundamentally opposed and there were only halting signs of the kind of intellectual revolution wanted by the government to underpin the new policies.

Its greatest success in building a new ideological hegemony was the implicit and sometimes explicit endorsement of the new political agenda by the opposition parties. A major shift in policy becomes permanent when the opposition parties adopt it as their own. Conservative ministers sometimes seemed unable to decide whether they preferred the Labour Party to reform or to be replaced by a new party. In either case what they sought was the withering away not just of socialism, but of collectivism. By the latter was understood political and intellectual support for public-sector and interventionist solutions to problems of public policy in preference to market ones.

Some success was registered. The split in the Labour Party and the emergence of a strong centre alliance in 1981 turned out not to be the long-awaited realignment of the British left, but it did remake British politics. The SDP failed to become the nucleus of a new majority party on the left, and after it too split over merger with the Liberals it dwindled away, until most of the remaining members joined the Conservatives. But its significance was still considerable. David Owen went further than any other opposition politician in endorsing major aspects of the Thatcherite policy agenda. He promoted the use of the concept of 'the social market economy'[16] and the need for efficiency and competition of the private sector, although he stopped short of endorsing the application of Thatcherite principles in the sphere of social policy.

Labour rebuilt itself under Neil Kinnock's leadership and by the 1992 election had changed its policies and was on the way towards changing its internal organisation in ways that met all the SDP demands of 1981.[17] The Liberal Democrats, who emerged from the ruins of the Alliance after 1987 as the dominant third force in British politics, also began to abandon their former support for the old collectivist consensus.

The opposition parties were forced by the new electoral hegemony, established by the Conservatives in the 1980s, to accept that the Thatcher years had permanently changed the agenda of British politics. Changes that had become irreversible by 1992 included the sale of council houses and the spread of share ownership; the denationalisation of public-sector industries; the abolition of exchange controls and the international integration of financial markets and production; the permanent contraction of manufacturing employment; and the reorganisation of work and industrial relations. What Labour in particular was forced to recognise was that there could be no return to national economic management and welfare programmes based on the Fordism of the postwar boom. If Labour was ever to succeed again it had to rethink the requirements for a successful economic strategy.[18]

Thatcherism perceived the weakness of social democracy in Britain and the national labour tradition, and it struck several blows at it. Thatcher made no secret of her wish to see socialism destroyed as an effective political force in Britain and a two-party system organised in which both parties fully accepted the legitimacy of capitalism and markets. A large part of reversing the decline of Britain meant destroying the political and industrial strength of the British labour movement, eradicating the industries, communities, organisations, and institutions associated with it. The attack on unions, local authorities, nationalised industries, public-sector employment, council housing and state education were part of a wider attack upon the labour movement.

The intention, and to some extent the effect, was to marginalise the Labour Party and the labour movement, associating it with declining regions, communities and industries while successfully identifying the Conservatives with sectors of growth, expansion and prosperity. The sense of a new policy agenda was created as much by this as by the new policies themselves. The Conservatives projected themselves as the party of the future, the party of the new politics, the party of modernisation. The collapse of communism in Eastern Europe and the Soviet Union at the end of 1989 seemed to underline that no alternative form of social and political organisation other than liberal capitalism was feasible.

The Thatcher record assessed

The Conservatives managed to achieve a considerable degree of electoral and ideological hegemony, but sceptics were still able to point out that the transformation was less than many of the Thatcherites wanted. Thatcherism failed to leave behind either a Thatcherite electorate or a Thatcherite party, and its ideological hegemony was far from complete.

The achievement is still more qualified in the realm of economic hegemony and state hegemony, the realms of economic strategy and policy implementation. The record of the Thatcher government, like that of all governments, often lacked symmetry, coherence and purpose. What coherence it did achieve was often imposed by events and decisions outside the control of the Thatcher government. The period from 1979 to 1990 did not see the unfolding of a New-Right masterplan, hatched in opposition, for overturning social democracy in Britain. The government reacted pragmatically, its course shaped more by the pressure of events than by its ideology or strategy.

Nevertheless the Thatcher government was still unusual for the way in which its leader and some of its principal figures remained committed to a distinctive ideology, and for the extent to which it did attempt in some areas to formulate and carry through a strategy. Both ideology and strategy were an influence on the way in which the government behaved. They helped the government renew its radical momentum and differentiated it markedly from almost all its predecessors. It was never content simply to administer and react to events, even if for much of the time that was precisely what it had to do.

In its own estimation the Thatcher government was a radical government that sought to reverse British decline. In her foreword to the 1979 manifesto Margaret Thatcher claimed that the balance had been tilted too far in favour of the state at the expense of individual freedom. The 1979 election, she wrote, was the last chance to reverse that process. It was the most crucial election since the war. She found a feeling of helplessness in the country – 'that we were once a great nation that has somehow fallen behind and that it is too late now to turn things round'.

The Thatcher government believed it knew how to turn the country round. It set itself five main tasks:

1. To restore the health of economic and social life.
2. To restore incentives.
3. To uphold Parliament and the rule of law.
4. To support family life.
5. To strengthen Britain's defences.

The first two of these tasks involved the creation of a free economy – a strategy for economic management and accumulation that marked a break with the strategy associated with the Keynesian techniques and corporatist structures of Fordism. The second involved the creation of a strong state, to provide the institutions that would support and nourish the free economy. How far were these goals realised by the Thatcher government? More specifically, to what extent did the policies of the Thatcher government realise the objectives of the 1979 manifesto?

Making the economy free

The economic policy of the Thatcher government should be assessed from two aspects: its conduct of economic management and its strategy for growth. The radicalism of the first has been much disputed. The change to a monetarist policy regime had already occurred before the government took office. Monetarism served important ideological and political needs, but it was less important as a guide to policy. Monetary targeting proved impractical and had been abandoned by 1985. Some economists have argued that the reduction in inflation owed more to the severe fiscal deflation that the government imposed on the economy.[19] Keynesian techniques continued to be used, only now the objective was to restore financial stability rather than preserve high levels of employment and growth. This was a major political shift, consolidating the change under the previous Labour government. But in terms of economic management it was a much smaller shift; economic management remained discretionary and interventionist.

The management of the economy tended to become more discretionary and flexible as time went on. But certain key Thatcherite policy objectives remained. The control of inflation continued to head the list, followed by a reduction in taxation and public spending as a proportion of GDP. In the early years of the Thatcher government the trend in both taxation and public spending was up. Aided however by the recovery after 1982 the objectives were reaffirmed and cuts in the rate of income tax were delivered in 1986 and 1987 and 1988.

What was also delivered, however, were increases in public spending in real terms. Since the economy was growing faster, increased public spending was still compatible with the objective of reducing its share in national income. Nevertheless it meant that at best its fall would be very slow. The tax cuts were also very gradual. By 1987 income tax had been reduced from 33p in the pound to 27p. But after the first reduction to 30p in the 1979 budget, which also reduced the top rate from 83p to 60p, the next cut had to wait until 1986. The biggest change came in the 1988 budget when Nigel Lawson reduced the basic rate to 25p and the top rate to 40p. In the early years financial stabilisation took priority over more ambitious supply-side proposals for boosting growth by encouraging enterprise.

The same picture is apparent if the public-spending programmes are looked at in detail. Few programmes were terminated altogether and few radical solutions were applied.[20] Such solutions were canvassed within the government. The CPRS options to avert a major public-expenditure crisis were leaked in 1983. They included privatising the NHS and introducing student loans. They were instantly disavowed by the government.

The government's preferred strategy in relation to public expenditure was to force increases in efficiency by reducing cash limits and promoting privatisation and deregulation. This threw most institutions in the public sector into turmoil and created deep demoralisation and a permanent atmosphere of financial crisis and retrenchment. The government, however, was very slow to take responsibility for reorganising the sectors directly, introducing the techniques of the new public management, preferring at first to use central financial pressures.

The deepening conflict that this strategy produced between central and local government and the inability of central government to achieve either control over local spending or the kind of local policies it wanted, brought a marked shift towards centralisation of power, finance and functions away from the town halls. The most radical proposals, however, were put forward in the 1987 manifesto. These included the poll tax (community charge) to replace domestic rates, the establishment of a uniform business rate, the opportunity for schools and council estates to opt out of local-authority control and the intention to transfer responsibility for inner-city regeneration, as well as much of further and higher education to national agencies such as the Manpower Services Commission (later the Training Agency).

Despite its unwillingness to take radical measures in public spending by closing down major institutions and programmes, the Government's hostility to many forms of public spending was unmistakeable and it was determined to squeeze budgets regardless of the consequences for the organisation and quality of the services that had to be funded from them. The government had no means of measuring these consequences.

This was clearly unsatisfactory in many areas and gradual recognition of this fact led not to a restoration of the

budgets that had been cut but increasing central intervention to reorganise and restructure institutions and programmes. This produced some important changes in the
way the public sector was organised, but the overall size of
the public sector had not been reduced by 1990. The limited reductions in some areas were more than balanced by
increases in others, either through choice, as with defence,
or through necessity, as with social security.

The failure to make deep cuts in public spending meant
increasing reliance by the Treasury on windfall revenues
to control and reduce public borrowing. The two major
sources of revenues tapped in this way were the proceeds of
petroleum revenue tax on the North-Sea producers and
the proceeds of denationalisation. This enabled public-
spending levels to be maintained, and even increased in
1986–7, while at the same time making tax cuts affordable.
Without the cushion of asset sales and oil revenues public
spending would have had to be cut much more sharply or
taxes or borrowing increased.[21] When the economy again
began moving into recession in 1989, public borrowing
began to rise steeply. With the approach of another general
election the government refused to cut public spending or
raise taxes. The result was that the public-sector deficit rose
sharply to levels not seen since the mid-1970s, and the share
of public expenditure in GDP rose back to the levels
inherited in 1979.

Denationalisation became a central feature of the
Thatcher government's programme, although it had hardly
been mentioned in the 1979 manifesto. It emerged very
strongly as a central theme after an initial period in which
the government's policies towards nationalised industries
were highly contradictory. The government did not seem
able to decide whether it wanted nationalised industries to
be run like private-sector companies, subject to the same
constraints but allowed the same managerial autonomy, or
whether it wished to use them as milch cows for the Treasury or as laboratories for experiments with industrial
restructuring. Profitable nationalised industries such as gas
and electricity were repeatedly forced to raise their prices
substantially and to contribute their excess profits to the

Exchequer. Those making losses were given tough financial targets and tough new managements.

Ministers gradually became convinced, however, that the political opportunity existed for permanently removing many industries from the nationalised sector. The objective of eliminating losses in the nationalised sector remained, but it was rather overtaken by the urge to sell-off any assets that could be made attractive to the markets. The success of state restructuring of some of the nationalised industries prepared the ground for denationalisation, because if companies could be made viable commercial entities they became potential targets for denationalisation. This made the most profitable nationalised industries, such as British Telecom and British Gas, rather than the least profitable, such as British Rail and the National Coal Board, the most tempting targets.

A major transfer of assets between the public and private sectors took place, mostly during the second and third phases of the Thatcher government – 1982–7 and 1987–90. In several cases the need to make the sale as attractive as possible to investors prevented industries being broken up and competition being increased. Few economists thought the sales likely to make much difference to economic efficiency, any more than the original nationalisations in the 1940s had done. But like those nationalisations, the denationalisations of the 1980s were a symbol of the changing political climate and the shift away from collectivist solutions in public policy. The wider share ownership made possible by the sales became a central part of popular capitalism.

The denationalisations were preceded by the dismantling of corporatist institutions such as the National Enterprise Board and the Price Commission (even the role of the National Economic Development Council was substantially downgraded; its abolition came later under the Major government). This was part of the government's drive to reduce the influence of trade unions in the policy-making process and to avoid committing itself to the formulation of an industrial strategy.

In its first two years the government presided over a major manufacturing recession. Manufacturing employment in Britain fell by 28 per cent between 1979 and 1986, a loss of two million jobs. Manufacturing output fell 14 per cent between 1979 and 1981, and did not regain its 1979 level until 1987. Trade in manufactures swung from a £5 billion surplus in 1978 to a £5.4 billion deficit in 1986. Faced by this decline the government proposed few specific measures to help industry other than exhorting firms to reorganise themselves and become more competitive. To aid this process the government introduced some measures of deregulation; some obstacles to the free working of labour markets were removed; enterprise zones and freeports were established; and foreign inward investment was encouraged.[22]

In general the restructuring of industry was allowed to take its own course. The government appeared indifferent to the fate of manufacturing industry. Several ministers argued that the only test of whether an economic activity should survive or not was whether it was profitable. The expansion of the service industries was seen as the potential replacement for manufacturing. No strategic priority was given to the need to maintain a strong manufacturing sector.[23] This was reflected in the low importance given to investment in education and infrastructure. The budgets for universities and science were cut, and a huge backlog of spending on infrastructure projects – roads, sewers, communications – was allowed to build up. The government made it clear that major new infrastructure projects, such as the Channel Tunnel, would have to be financed with private money.[24]

In its policy towards the private sector the government's stated free-market position was not entirely borne out by its actions. There remained major protected sectors in the British economy – defence, agriculture and parts of the public sector and their suppliers, such as the nuclear industry. These were not subject to the competitive pressures that devastated so many other parts of the private sector because their markets remained guaranteed by government spending programmes. Significant areas of investment and employment were thus maintained through government policies. Fifty-two per cent of all government-supported research and development expenditure in 1986 went to the defence industries.

There were also brief flurries of more interventionist policies associated with particular ministers and departments.

Some limited support was given for the British information-technology industry through Kenneth Baker and Geoffrey Pattie. Michael Heseltine favoured using urban development corporations to deal with inner-city problems when he was secretary of state for the environment and was keen to use government defence spending to sustain a strong arms industry, if necessary in cooperation with the Europeans. Lord Young launched numerous schemes to encourage enterprise. This was the origin of the Westland affair. Successive ministers of energy gave full backing to the expansion of the nuclear industry, even though it was difficult to justify on economic grounds.

These remained exceptions however, and no attempt was made to formulate a national industrial strategy. Maintaining the openness of the British economy and forcing companies to be competitive on world markets were the watchwords of government policy. Under this policy domestic manufacturing contracted, while the financial businesses of the City – deregulated in the Big Bang – boomed, as did many leading industrial companies whose operations were now international.

Along with manufacturing the position of trade unions suffered an eclipse. The dismantling of corporatism deprived unions of public platforms and public visibility. Mass unemployment brought a substantial drop in union membership (1.8 million or 14 per cent between 1980 and 1983). Union membership as a proportion of those still employed decreased by 5 per cent. The climate of industrial relations was changed in many industries. The legislation passed in 1980, 1982 and 1984 placed important new constraints on trade-union activity in relation to strikes, picketing and the closed shop, and exposed unions once more to court action and financial penalties. In several cases the new laws assisted in the defeat of strikes.[25]

The government would have nothing to do with an incomes policy for the private sector, but successfully imposed pay curbs in the public, and tried to dismantle or weaken collective-bargaining arrangements. Public-sector strikes over pay or job losses or conditions of service were confronted and defeated. The big set-piece strikes, culminating in the miners' strike in 1984–5, were important for demonstrating that a Conservative government could once more assert its authority over the trade unions. Repeated successes against the trade unions encouraged the government to give support to the idea of a new industrial-relations structure in which unions would either be absent altogether or would be company unions willing to accept no-strike agreements and fully committed to the success of their companies. The developing split among the unions, the establishment of the Union of Democratic Mineworkers in Nottinghamshire, so crucial to the government's success in the miners' strike, the growth of 'the new realism' associated with unions such as the electricians' and the engineers' (AUEW), were all seen as aiding the breakup of the traditional labour movement and increasing the flexibility of the labour market.[26]

While it welcomed such trends as these, however, the government still trod cautiously in this field. It rejected proposals to scrap all trade-union immunities granted since the 1906 Act. It abolished wage councils and minimum-wage legislation and weakened the closed shop, helping to increase the pool of casual part-time workers. Strikes dwindled to very low levels. But trade-union organisation remained strong. Examples of union-free industries and no-strike agreements remained rare, and earnings of unionised workers in permanent employment continued to rise faster than output and inflation. The Thatcher government presided over a significant shift in the balance of power between labour and capital, but trade-union organisation remained formidable. A union-free economy did not look attainable.

The pursuit of the Thatcherite economic strategy assumed the fullest possible integration of the British economy into the world economy. The financial and industrial sectors, which benefited most from the increased freedom given by the policy, were already operating internationally, and this bias was reinforced.

Making the state strong

Restoring the health of economic and social life in Britain and restoring incentives, as promised by the 1979 manifesto, meant rolling back the state in many areas. But this could only be successful and a free economy established if the state was simultaneously strengthened in other areas. The manifesto was very clear about which these areas were – defence, parliament and the rule of law, and the family.

If the economic strategy were to be viable, then there had to be a defence and foreign policy, which would guarantee the continued prosperity and openness of the Western capitalist economy. The Thatcher government sought to ensure this by concentrating on strengthening the Anglo–American relationship. The European connection was given lower priority. This policy was entirely predictable but not without its critics. United States hegemony appeared weaker than at any time since 1945, and there seemed no way of rebuilding it. The political and defence advantages of a strong Atlantic Alliance were allowed to obscure the serious economic imbalance in the world economy that economic management during the Reagan presidency did so much to create.

The priority given to strengthening the West's defences against the USSR – deploying cruise and Pershing, modernising the British nuclear deterrent by purchasing Trident – overshadowed the relationship with the European Community. But despite the prime minister's dislike for the EC the growing integration of the British economy with Europe and the signs of increasing American economic and financial weakness made growing collaboration with Europe necessary in defence as well as economic policy.[27] The British attachment to formal sovereignty, however, still acted as a brake on further cooperation. The most obvious example was the British reluctance to join the European Monetary System until 1990.

The need to strengthen Britain's defences was seen almost entirely in relation to the Soviet threat. But the Thatcher government also had to deal with problems that stemmed from Britain's long imperial past. One of these, the Falklands War, allowed a dramatic demonstration of the strong state in action. But the entire episode belonged to Britain's past rather than its future. Only two years before the Thatcher government had attempted to negotiate with the Argentineans the transfer of sovereignty through a lease-back arrangement. The despatch of the task force depended on American and NATO support, and might have been logistically impossible if the plans in the 1981 defence review to reduce the surface fleet had already been implemented.

What the Falklands War demonstrated was that Britain no longer had sufficient strength to maintain defence commitments in Europe and the Eastern Atlantic as well as a capacity to intervene throughout the world.[28] The special circumstances of the conflict were unlikely to be repeated anywhere else. Victory in the war did not encourage the revival of imperial ambitions elsewhere. Agreement to transfer Hong Kong back to China in 1997 was rapidly concluded in December 1984.

The second major area where the state had to be strong was upholding parliament and the rule of law. These appeared very traditional, conservative demands. But in the context of the welfare programmes and the corporatist modes of representation that had been established under previous governments, they implied a new constitutional doctrine and potentially major upheavals in how the state was organised.

In formal terms the constitution changed little under the Thatcher government. In opposition the Conservatives had developed no plans for reforming the constitution to make permanent the changes they wished to see in the relationship between state and economy. Major constitutional reforms such as proportional representation, devolution of power to the regions or a bill of rights found no favour.[29] The government maintained the traditional balance between parliament and the executive. A new select-committee system was introduced, but no major new powers were granted to the committees.

The government's constitutional conservatism was quite at odds with the radical constitutional implications of what it was seeking to achieve in many of its policies. The government believed it had a mandate to undo many of the policies and institutions that had grown up in the collectivist era. But New Right analysis indicated that it was the way democracy worked that had created the pressure for collectivism and interference in the market order. If the constitution was not changed, how could the Conservatives guarantee that their reforms would not be swept away by a new collectivist government after some future election? Upholding parliament meant upholding the system of elective dictatorship that had produced the mass of collectivist legislation in the twentieth century and had provided no safeguards against interventionist government.

The dilemma for the government was that if it wished its reforms to become permanent it either had to believe that it could hold power indefinitely or it had to reform the constitution so as to make collectivist legislation much harder to introduce in the future. The rather narrow limits of the government's radicalism and its vision were revealed by its reluctance to examine the ways in which the constitution operated and might be changed. The advantages under the existing constitution of being the incumbent government inhibited reform.

This pattern was repeated in other areas. The government did eventually move to introduce a radical reform of the civil service – the Next Steps programme – but it came very late. The civil service was suspected of being inefficient and likely to obstruct or delay the radical policy changes desired by the government. Yet the government at first did little more than attempt to create a new climate in which civil servants had to work, through some minor administrative changes and appointments of personnel. Many of the prime minister's advisers argued that a radical reform of the civil service was desirable. John Hoskyns, head of the Downing Street Policy Unit from 1979–82, favoured the creation of an American-style central administration, with many of the top posts being filled by outsiders employed on short contracts and given particular briefs. Each minister would be allowed to appoint some twenty external advisers to civil-service posts in each department. To rely on the existing civil service to carry through radical policies, he argued, was to invite frustration and failure.[30]

This advice was never followed. Instead the Thatcher Government relied on a variety of initiatives to make civil-service departments more efficient. These included the seconding of Derek Raynor from Marks and Spencer to advise on the management of personnel, money and tasks within the civil service, and the MINIS scheme implemented by Michael Heseltine, first in the Department of the Environment and later in the Ministry of Defence. Substantial savings were identified.

The size of the civil service was cut[31] and a drive launched to make civil servants more productive. The prime minister used her powers of appointment to promote those civil servants who appeared ready to question Whitehall orthodoxies and had the drive and ability to carry through Conservative policies. Several senior appointments were made in this way, sometimes overturning normal seniority.[32] But these were minor changes compared with the major change that was introduced right at the end of the Thatcher government. The Next Steps programme envisaged the hiving off of most of the work of the Whitehall departments to independent agencies, so separating the role of policy advice and policy implementation. The civil servants in the new agencies would be subject to performance targets and specific incentives and penalties.

The cabinet functioned much as before. There were fewer cabinet meetings and fewer cabinet committees than under previous administrations. The cabinet committee system continued to be used as a convenient means of obtaining the decisions wanted by the prime minister before presenting them to full cabinet for ratification.[33] Like her predecessors Margaret Thatcher soon proved adept at choosing the members of cabinet committees in order to produce the right results. Few decisions appear to have been taken in cabinet.

None of this was new in British government but such was Thatcher's dominance of her government by 1983 that there was some speculation that a prime minister's department was being created, which might in time lead to a major constitutional downgrading of the cabinet in relation to the prime minister's office. It later became clear that there was no such intention, in part because the power of the prime minister in relation to the cabinet was already so great that no need was seen to formalise the position.

Only minor changes took place. The Central Policy Review Staff (CPRS), which had served the whole cabinet, was abolished in 1983 but the prime minister's policy unit survived. This began to play an increasingly important role in providing alternative policy advice to the prime minister and helped enhance the impression that Downing Street was intent on providing a strategic direction of government policy.[34] This impression was strengthened by the use of special advisers such as Charles Powell for foreign policy and Alan Walters for economic policy, who came to wield great influence, to the annoyance of the Foreign Office and the Treasury and their ministers. Yet what was distinctive about Margaret Thatcher as prime minister was not the new powers she seized for the premiership but her style of conducting it.[35] The permanent effects of her tenure on the premiership as an institution were small. The policy objectives may at times have been radical but the institutional means for carrying them out remained conventional.

Upholding parliament in Conservative eyes meant making the executive power of the state the supreme authority once again. The influence producer interests had acquired through corporatist structures was to be diminished. But the government had no clear idea of how it was to achieve its policy objective of disengaging government from intervention in the economy, when so much of that intervention was managed not by central government but by the quangos and agencies of sub-central government.

Attempting to resolve this problem piecemeal led the government to become increasingly centralist as time went on. It failed repeatedly to get the cooperation of other bodies, particularly representative bodies, in achieving its objectives. It then turned to finding ways to impose central control that often involved the creation of new state agencies to supplant the old.

This pattern was seen most clearly in relation to local government. The problems with local authorities arose through the desire of central government to control their spending. The government succeeded in pushing down the central government's contribution to local-authority budgets from 63 per cent to 49 per cent. As the conflict developed so it became clear to central government that in many areas the old collaborative relationship between central and local government had broken down. Increasingly the government tried to bypass local authorities. The cumulative steps taken to dispossess local authorities of responsibilities and finance amounted to a major shift in the balance of the constitution between central and local government.

The 1987 manifesto envisaged further major changes. The logic of government policy pointed to eventual abolition of local government altogether, removing education and other major services entirely from local control. The government disclaimed any such radical ambition but it seemed reluctant to try to define the appropriate powers and responsibilities for local government in the future.

The same attitude and impatience was manifest in government policy towards many other institutions. In seeking to promote the best possible conditions for profitable private enterprise, as it conceived them, the government tried to ensure that all institutions over which it had financial leverage should cooperate in helping to achieve them. When financial controls failed the government resorted to more direct controls.

Upholding parliament came to mean trying to subordinate all institutions in civil society to the pursuit of the national goals approved by parliament. The Thatcher government came into collision with many established institutions in civil society, such as the trade unions, the media, the Churches and the universities. The conflict was particularly intense in the case of the unions. In its legislation the government was not content with placing restrictions on lawful trade-union activity; it also forced changes in union rule books on such matters as the holding of ballots before strikes and the election of union officers. This was extremely unusual interference in the affairs of voluntary associations. It did not always prove successful. The attempt to get union members to vote down political funds backfired at the first attempt. Large majorities in every union voted to retain their funds.

The government also clashed with the media, principally with the television companies. This came to a head in the second phase of the Thatcher government, when overt attempts were made to change the editorial policy of the BBC following the reporting of the American bombing of Libya in 1986. Specific journalists, presenters and pro- grammes were targeted for attack. The Peacock Commission was set up to advise the government on the future of broad- casting, and recommended substantial deregulation and the breaking up of the monopoly of the BBC and ITV.

Clashes also developed with other major civil institutions – notably the universities, the schools and the Churches. The government cut education budgets severely in its first few years in office and moved increasingly to impose central control on education – by seeking to determine the content of the curriculum and weaken the influence of the teaching profession, by allowing schools to opt out of local-authority control, by ending academic tenure and placing higher edu- cation under new funding bodies that could ensure that uni- versities and polytechnics would meet national needs as defined by the government.

The rule of law was always interpreted rather narrowly by Conservatives to mean internal security. Strengthening the police and restoring public order were major campaign themes in 1979. Substantial increases were made in police pay, manpower and equipment. Several acts were passed to give the police greater powers and enforce tougher sen- tences. The Criminal Justice Act of 1982 introduced a new framework of custodial sentences for offenders under 21. The Police and Criminal Evidence Act, 1984, gave the police new powers in respect of stop and search, entry, search and seiz- ure, arrest and detention and the interrogation and identifi- cation of suspects. The Public Order Act, 1986, gave the police new powers to control demonstrations and crowds.

The Conservative government encouraged a trend towards tougher sentences, while promoting a better-paid, better- equipped and better-coordinated police force. Coordination between police forces, as in the miners' strike of 1984–5, was organised through the National Reporting Centre, which looked like the organisational base for a future national police force. This trend was strengthened by the attempts by some local police authorities to make their police forces more accountable. In this as in so many areas, however, the government, while encouraging chief constables to assert their independence, was reluctant to take the final step and formally organise the police as a national force.

The increasing use by the police of firearms and riot equipment was directed at coping with the rise in violent crime and with the picket-line violence and inner-city riots that erupted in the 1980s. Policing took on a more repressive character as those opposed to the Thatcher government came to be stigmatised as the 'enemies within' and likened to Argentineans and terrorists. Repression was particularly severe in the inner cities and was directed mainly against the black community. The breakdown of relations between the police and black communities was a major factor leading to the riots. By 1987 the police were equipped with massive force, sufficient to restore public order whenever it was threatened, and there were fewer restraints on its use.

The Thatcher government also took 'upholding the rule of law' to mean protecting the secrecy of government, and particularly the operations of the intelligence services. Its period of office was notable for a number of spy scandals, beginning with the belated unmasking of Anthony Blunt in 1980. It became involved in a number of attempts to prevent information about the operations of the British secret service and British government itself from reaching the public. The Official Secrets Act was invoked several times in an attempt to suppress embarrassing information and punish those who were seeking to reveal it. Clive Ponting and Sarah Tisdall were prosecuted and the government went to enormous lengths to stop the publication of Peter Wright's memoirs, and to prevent details appearing about the Zircon spy satellite project.

The Thatcher government reinforced the traditional secrecy of British government while refusing to investigate any of the charges surfacing about the unconstitutional activities of the security services. The obsession with security and secrets was revealed in the GCHQ affair, when the government banned trade unions at its intelligence-gathering centre in Cheltenham because of the alleged risk to national security.

The greatest prize of a law-and-order government – the restoration of capital punishment – eluded Thatcher. The most she could deliver was two free votes in the House of Commons in 1979 and 1983. On each occasion the move to restore hanging was defeated by a large majority. The cabinet and the parliamentary party remained divided on the issue. Thatcher was able to include in the 1979 manifesto a pledge that parliament should have a free vote on whether or not to restore hanging, but further than that she was not able to go.

The government launched many law-and-order campaigns, targeting groups such as young offenders and football hooligans for special attention, the latter acquiring particular prominence following the Heysel stadium riot in 1985. This led to stringent controls, such as membership schemes and football clubs being forced to ban alcohol at matches. Like previous governments, however, the Thatcher government had no ideas of how to turn the rising tide of disorder and crime, and chose for the most part to extract the maximum political advantage by promoting itself as the law-and-order party.

The third area where the 1979 manifesto proclaimed a need for a strong state was in support of family life. From the outset the Thatcherite project involved not merely an economic revival but a moral revival. The difficulty was finding ways of promoting it. The most crucial sphere for many Conservatives was the family. But although the government set up a cabinet committee in 1983 to produce a family policy, the practical results were highly limited. Serious measures to prevent women taking jobs outside the home were ruled out by the increasing importance of women in the labour market. The impact of the recession and many of the cuts in social benefits discriminated most heavily against women, but the government did not attempt to reinforce this with active policies. It retained the Equal Opportunities Commission and made no direct attempt to challenge the principles upon which it worked.

The assumption that the family should be the foundation of social policy and that only nuclear two-parent families were real families influenced much Conservative thinking about social policy. The stripping of functions in social policy from the state, such as care of the elderly, and returning them to the family was a trend made necessary by budget cuts rather than specific legislation. But it was a trend approved by Conservatives and nothing was done to arrest it. Supporting the family also meant supporting its traditional way of life. This included protecting families from being 'swamped' by alien cultures. This phrase was used by Margaret Thatcher on television in January 1978 in one of her most successful political interventions before becoming prime minister.[36] Her government had few ideas on how to convert it into a policy. Immigration controls were tightened further in the British Nationality Act of 1981. But compulsory repatriation was ruled out and the government made no moves to repeal the Race Relations Acts. It continued to adhere to the bipartisan consensus on equal opportunity and rights for all citizens.

The mounting burdens imposed on black people arose more from the consequences of the recession and the strengthening of internal repression than from deliberate government policy targeted at the black communities. Nevertheless the association of blacks with rising crime figures and inner-city riots did ensure a growing polarisation between the state and black communities. The government commissioned the Scarman Report after the Brixton riots but refused to accept any link between unemployment and the alienation of black youth. It proposed action on few of the report's recommendations.

Reforming education also became central to the government's conception of supporting family life. Teaching of appropriate skills and values was seen as vital in fostering social discipline and cohesion. The reconstruction of education that began to take shape in the Education Reform Bill of 1987 was an essential part of the government's wider plans for encouraging an enterprise culture and popular capitalism. Neither concept was at all well defined in policy terms when the government was elected in 1979, but they became increasingly important to justify many of the government's policies and to characterise the long-term objectives of its programme and the kind of society it wanted to see emerge.

The government argued that the anti-enterprise and permissive culture that had been fostered by social-democratic institutions since 1945 had become one of the chief obstacles to reversing decline. The economic and moral regeneration of Britain therefore required putting pressure on every institution to make it supportive of enterprise and capitalism.[37] This was seen as particularly important in the case of the media and education.

Popular capitalism (which had been in fashion once before in the 1950s)[38] became the term applied to a variety of policies aimed at widening property ownership and consumer choice. The denationalisation measures originally undertaken principally to raise revenue came to be seen as a way of extending share ownership. By offering the shares of companies such as British Telecom and British Gas at levels substantially below their real market value, large numbers of new investors could be tempted to buy shares in order to make quick capital gains. The number of individual shareholders was increased markedly by such means (from three million in 1979 to nine million in 1987), but the overall proportion of shares held by individual shareholders continued to decline. The government attempted to bolster the growth of shareholding by specific tax concessions. It also raised the thresholds on capital-gains tax and capital-transfer tax while reducing the upper tax bands on higher incomes and investment income.

A key measure to expand property ownership was the extension of the right of council-house tenants to buy their houses at substantial discounts. This was one of the most successful and symbolic of all the government's policies. The government sought means to extend it into education, pensions and health. The principle, so simple in the case of council houses, proved much harder to operationalise in other areas. In education vouchers were considered but discarded. By 1987 the favoured route for increasing choice in education was to allow parents and governing bodies of schools to decide to take schools out of local-authority control.

Economic hegemony

Instrumental theories of class suppose that the policies of the Thatcher government can be shown to benefit the capitalist class and to have been directly inspired by that class. The evidence for that is tenuous and ignores the way in which the modern state is structured. Political organisations such as the Conservative party have a great deal of autonomy within their own sphere to determine objectives and policies. There are no mechanisms of representation by which a general capitalist interest could be expressed, other than through the political sphere and the institutions of the state.

Thatcherism cannot be reduced to the economic interests that supported it, but the question of who gained and who lost from the policies, regardless of what may have been intended or planned, remains a crucial one to ask. The principal loser was the organised labour movement, but in the process many sections of capital also suffered heavily. The Thatcher government's policies ended the prospects of any restructuring based on the traditional manufacturing sectors and regions. Many of these were liquidated in the slump, their workforces made unemployed and the basis of union strength in those industries destroyed.

The sharp contraction of manufacturing in the 1980–1 slump led some to suggest that the policy represented the interests of the City. It is true that many of the policies, such as the ending of exchange controls, sound finance, the willingness to see sterling and interest rates rise during the first phase, the abandonment of industrial strategy and intervention, the denationalisation of public enterprises, the widening of share ownership and the lowering of taxes on capital and investment, were all favourably received by the City. But important though the City is in the British economy as a source of employment and export earnings, it is not large enough, coherent enough, or politically organised enough, to determine government policy.[39]

The explanation of the Thatcher government's policy stance and its effects on manufacturing was not that the government set out to favour the interests of the City, but that, by reasserting the traditional international orientation of British economic policy, the government gave priority to the maintenance of the openness of the British economy over the protection of domestic industry. Given the long relative decline of so much of this industry, in a sharp recession such a policy was bound to lead to the liquidation of many companies.

The economic strategy of the Thatcher government identified the national interest and the general interest of capital with furthering the integration of the British economy into the world economy and, apart from the few protected sectors such as defence and agriculture, and to a lesser extent nationalised industries, it obliged all other sectors to prove themselves internationally competitive or go to the wall. This policy favoured those industrial sectors that were already dominated by transnational companies – particularly those in construction, oil and food – as well as the financial and commercial companies based in the City.

The shakeout that these policies provoked cemented the alliance between British transnationals and the City and made the prospect of a national industrial strategy, which had flickered occasionally in the previous seventy-five years, very remote indeed.[40] The future of the British economy was tied not to a major revival of domestic manufacturing but to the development of (i) rentier incomes from the UK's rapidly growing portfolio of foreign investments[41] (ii) internationally tradable services, and (iii) the encouragement of inward investment by foreign transnationals establishing plants to assemble products, designed and engineered elsewhere, for sale in European markets. The British economic space lost any coherence it still possessed as a national economic space during the Thatcher decade.[42]

This strategy was both credible and coherent, and although sections of British capital complained bitterly about the harsh effects on them, criticism was muted and no effective alternative was canvassed. Despite the efforts of a few ministers the government gave little support to developing manufacturing and research capability in new technologies, and it reduced spending on science and scientific research.

In the last hundred years British governments have presided over the decline of the traditional manufacturing base, based on cotton, coal, iron and steel, shipbuilding and engineering. In the last twenty years they have presided over the decline of the mass-production industries of Fordism – the manufacturers of consumer durables, many of which first became established in Britain in the 1920s and 1930s and expanded in the 1950s and 1960s. The failure of the attempts to modernise these industries and make them internationally competitive was one of the major sources of the crisis in the 1970s. The Thatcher government abandoned the attempt made by earlier governments to get the old regime of accumulation to work. This was prompted partly on political grounds – the political costs of earlier modernisation strategies appeared too high and had threatened to marginalise the Conservative Party. Another reason, however, was the exhaustion of Fordist methods of production in so many sectors. New methods of industrial organisation were going to be required to establish the conditions for a new phase of rapid accumulation.

To adjust to the new conditions for global accumulation and to find a way of reversing decline, the Thatcher government moved pragmatically. It promoted those activities in which British companies had already shown they could be internationally competitive; it sought to increase incentives and reduce spending; it tried to weaken trade unions; and it attempted to disengage government as much as possible from involvement in the economy and widen the sphere for market criteria and private-sector competition in the allocation of resources.

As an economic strategy it returned to one of the constants in British development – the priority given to commerce and finance and therefore to policies that maintained the openness of the British economy, even when this was at the expense of domestic production. At times of crisis it has generally been this market perspective that has triumphed. Those sectors of the British economy that have grown strong under this policy find their position further reinforced and their political importance enhanced.

In the short-term the strategy worked. After a turbulent first two years between 1979 and 1981, when total shipwreck of the government seemed a possibility, the economy did stabilise and begin to grow again. By the 1987 election the government was able to boast of record productivity, record output, falling unemployment and low inflation. There was no doubt that the decline had been halted. What was unclear was whether or not it had been reversed. The answer was not long in coming. The severity of the recession between 1990 and 1993 and the large fiscal and trade deficits that accompanied it revealed that the improvements of the 1980s, although real, had not transformed the position of the economy as the Conservatives had claimed. The realisation of this fact damaged the Conservatives' reputation for competence and put at risk their hegemony in other spheres.

State hegemony

Supporters of the Thatcherite economic strategy can still be found who argue that it would have worked if the government had not become divided over the best means of pursuing it. If a free-market programme is to succeed in the future, however, then it will require a much greater degree of state reorganisation than anything attempted by the Thatcher government. The Thatcherite economic strategy aroused many doubts. But its ability to effect the necessary reforms in the state and civil society aroused even more.

The decline of Britain's postwar manufacturing sector was accompanied by the weakening of many of the social-democratic institutions made legitimate by the 1940s settlement. The failure of Britain to develop a viable Fordism undermined social democracy and exposed its limitations in Britain as a formula for strong and effective government. The 1940s settlement no longer provided a credible or desirable framework for government for a growing number of politicians on both the left and the right.

The Thatcher leadership united the Conservative Party around the claims that the country had become overtaxed, overgoverned and undisciplined. The traditional distance between the organs of government and the special interests had been eroded. Government had been invaded by pressure groups and too many decisions had been politicised. Government needed to disentangle itself and reassert its authority and independence. This meant reducing the number and the range of government responsibilities. In economic policy it meant asserting that the government only had responsibility for inflation and the money supply and none for unemployment and growth; it meant abandoning prices and incomes policies and most national tripartite arrangements in which the unions bargained directly with government. It meant promulgating new financial disciplines for public agencies, particularly local authorities, in an attempt to force them to operate within a set of financial constraints determined centrally. It meant launching a major programme of privatisation, giving up many government controls over how enterprises in various sectors operated. Government functions were to be simplified and government spending reduced.

Diagnosing a crisis of hegemony and then remedying it through political action are very different things. The Thatcherites accepted that there was a deep and complex crisis of state authority, but the remedies they recommended pointed in several directions at once. They were not easily reconciled. The Thatcherite project demanded a sweeping transformation of institutions, attitudes and personnel. Yet what was involved in detail in such a radical restructuring and whether it was within the capacity of the Conservative Party to deliver was little discussed. Among the intellectuals of the New Right the radical nature of the Thatcherite project was well understood, but relatively few of them became Conservative ministers.

Thatcherism was such a contradictory phenomenon in government because of the basic practical and theoretical uncertainty about the kind and degree of state restructuring that it sought. Creating a 'free economy' commanded wide support in the Conservative Party when it was interpreted to mean lower taxes, lower public expenditure, less nationalisation, weaker trade unions, less government regulation and control, and more inequality. But a free economy was also understood by some to mean a state strong enough to intervene actively in all institutions of civil society to impose, nurture and stimulate the business values, attitudes and practices necessary to relaunch Britain as a successful capitalist economy. This would have made the Conservative Party for the first time a bourgeois modernising party with no qualms about radical restructuring of all institutions in state and civil society in the interests of increasing economic efficiency. Such programmes have been proposed before, but foundered because their advocates were never prepared to reshape the British political, intellectual and business establishment, entrenched in the public schools, the universities, the professions, the civil service and the City.

The Thatcherite project to restore state authority by promoting a free economy would have been feasible if the institutions of civil society had been fundamentally sound, the public sector small and the economy thriving. Since they were not the government was drawn into numerous interventions and conflicts to try to transform attitudes and behaviour. Reestablishing the authority of the state required increasing intervention to force the compliance of other agencies and interests with the wishes and plans of the government. The seriousness of the condition of the British economy and the complexity of the public sector meant that a strategy of disengagement from accumulated responsibilities and commitments had to involve major efforts to reorganise activities and institutions in the public sector and in civil society.

The problem for the Thatcher government was that its own diagnosis of the crisis of state authority constantly impelled it towards intervention – whether in the internal affairs of trade unions, the spending priorities of local authorities, the curricula of schools and universities or the patterns of family behaviour. At the same time the government was very cautious in creating the kind of state machinery that could make such intervention effective.

Many of the capitalist modernisers among the Thatcherites, such as Sir John Hoskyns, grew impatient at the slow pace of advance. He argued forcibly as a result of his experience in the Downing Street Policy Unit that decline would not be reversed until major changes in the structure of government had been brought about, particularly the organisation and recruitment of the civil service. In 1986 Hoskyns set out his own radical manifesto for the next parliament. Imaginative thinking, he declared, was needed now, in advance of declining North Sea oil revenues. The measures included the immediate scrapping of rent and minimum-wage controls; abolishing the letter-post monopoly and denationalising the coal industry; outlawing strikes in all private and public monopoly services; introducing tax relief on fees for private health and private education; allowing parents an absolute right to choose to which state school to send their children, and allowing successful schools to expand to meet demand; and abolishing the rate-support grant by transferring education spending to central government.[43]

In order for such a radical set of measures to have a chance of success, the reforms of British government that Hoskyns also proposed would first have had to be carried through, and an executive government created that was capable of formulating, implementing and monitoring a coordinated programme of policies. Hoskyns and many like him believed that the Thatcher government's radicalism was constantly frustrated by the inadequacy of the civil service and the present organisation of government. The changes that were made (reviewed in Chapter 4) did not add up to radical overhaul of the state machine. Despite its misgivings about civil servants and its determination to reduce their numbers and contain their pay, the Thatcher government still relied on the traditional civil service to carry through its programme.

The Thatcher government was most successful when it faced major challenges to its authority and was able to win a trial of strength against an identifiable opponent. It triumphed over the IRA hunger strikers, the Argentinean military junta, the miners and the rebel local authorities. Here the strong state had a clear and obvious meaning. But such an approach was of little use in dealing with long-term problems such as the control of public expenditure or the refashioning of education.

The government's main success in reorganising state and civil society was in industrial relations. It achieved a large reduction in trade-union influence and visibility, and reversed the trend towards greater corporate representation. It put greater reliance on parliament as the source of government authority and the main intermediary between government and civil society.

This change increased considerably the power of the executive. The party system and the powers of patronage, allied to a strong prime minister, allowed the Thatcher government to dominate parliament in a way it could never have dominated the corporate interests. But the modern parliament is a fragile base upon which to exercise state authority. The interventionist actions of the Thatcher government exposed the absence of constitutional safeguards on the exercise of government power in Britain. Commanding only 43 per cent of the popular vote the Thatcher government still embarked on deeply unpopular and divisive policies. Parliamentary government became more arbitrary and less consensual. The drift towards a more authoritarian style of rule was marked.

But despite the initiatives the government took to reestablish its authority, they were still judged by Sir John Hoskyns and others to fall far short of what was required. To deal with short-term crises and problems the government steadily took more powers and centralised more functions in its hands. But this did not necessarily increase its effectiveness. One analysis of the government's handling of the state system beyond Whitehall concluded that although the government had formally more power, its ability to implement the policies it wanted across the whole public sector had diminished.[44]

The institutional and cultural transformation required to make the free economy a reality, and a plausible accumulation strategy for the 1990s, faltered because the Thatcher government for so long rejected the need, except in a piecemeal and reactive fashion, to create the kind of state machinery that might carry through such a programme. Such a state would have to be a strong state indeed, not tied down by any liberal or democratic scruples or institutional constraints. Only in respect of trade unions and public order has the state under Thatcher moved in this direction, and then only partially.

The result was a restructuring of the state that went some way to achieving a free economy but was unable to reverse the decline. What was discovered was another way of managing the decline and its consequences. The economy was to be an open economy integrated into the world economy, with transformed industrial relations, deregulated markets and a considerable enlargement of the private sector. But it was also to be an economy with sharp disparities between regions, and between the majority of workers in secure employment and a minority composed of the poor, the unemployed and those in low-paid and casual employment. As the labour market became more segmented, the inequalities of income and wealth more marked, and the decay of the inner cities and public services more evident, so the pressures grew towards a 'two-nation' politics – on the one side were policies that increased repression, subsidy, and dependence for the minority of the poor and disadvantaged, while on the other side were policies that maintained the physical security and economic prosperity of the majority.

The strong state needed for this economy to remain free was a state able to conduct effective surveillance and policing of the unemployed and the poor, able to confront and defeat any union challenge, and able to contain any upsurge of terrorism or public disorder. But it was not capable of becoming the kind of strong state needed to break out of the cycle of decline.

Conclusion

Thatcher left many legacies. She bequeathed a measure of electoral and ideological hegemony to her successor, but the economic hegemony the Thatcherites thought was in their grasp in 1987 melted away in bitter recrimination as the fragility of the Thatcherite boom of the 1980s was painfully exposed in the long recession of 1990–3; while the state hegemony the Thatcher government tried to establish was far from complete by the time Thatcher left office.

There are a number of possible scenarios for the future. In the Thatcherite scenario the Major years are only an interregnum. They will give way if not to a restoration of Thatcher herself, at least to the rise to the leadership of a true believer such as Michael Portillo. Then a Conservative

Party dedicated once more to the grand principles of national independence, economic freedom and the promotion of the vigorous virtues[45] can take up where Thatcher left off, and continue her project and safeguard her legacy. The main problem for this scenario is that without Thatcher the Thatcherites are a relatively small faction within the party. To win the leadership Portillo would have to reach out to a much wider constituency. The Thatcher mantle by itself is unlikely to deliver him the crown.

A second scenario is the routinisation of charisma under John Major and Kenneth Clarke, an unheroic and unadventurous period after the storms and drama of the Thatcher era. The Conservative government is now run by the kind of pragmatists that were familiar in the 1950s and 1960s. Despite the buffeting the government received after its election victory in 1992 it has many resources and may pull through. The long recession punctured one of the central myths of Thatcherism – that the economy had been turned round – and together with the battle over the ratification of the Maastricht Treaty freed the government from any obligation to maintain its ideological correctness. The Conservative Party's new leaders will be judged primarily by their success in managing the economy. If they are fortunate enough to preside over an extended period of growth, the strength of the underlying electoral position of the Conservatives may reassert itself, however great the loss of support in 1992 and 1993, and the Thatcherites may struggle to maintain their influence.

A third scenario however is less favourable to the Conservatives. The Conservatives have enjoyed a remarkable period of political success, due in part to the divisions of their opponents. After 1992, however, it was the Conservatives who increasingly appeared divided, while the opposition parties were growing in effectiveness. The combination of deep and bitter divisions within the Conservative Party, both personal and ideological, with the loss of any clear sense of purpose or direction in the government, raised the possibility in 1993 that the Conservatives might be about to throw away the position of strength they had built up since 1975. If this is so the Conservatives might yet suffer an historic defeat, made more serious by the fact that the opposition parties, if they ever secure a Commons majority, might enact constitutional changes that could remove many of the advantages the Conservatives have enjoyed for a hundred years. Thatcherism set out to be the great liquidator of social-democratic Britain. Yet despite its aura of economic modernisation the Thatcher regime also became a redoubt for old causes – the Empire, the Atlantic Alliance, the old constitutional state. It would be an irony if the disintegration of the Thatcherite project in the new era, marked by the ending of the Cold War and the special relationship, also led to the weakening of the British Conservatives to the point where the chance to organise hegemony in Britain passed to others.

Notes and references

Introduction

1. In this edition I use the term economic strategy rather than accumulation strategy, since economic strategy refers to the policies pursued by government agencies while accumulation strategy refers to the actual pattern of accumulation that becomes established with or without government involvement.
2. Martin Jacques, 'Breaking out of the Impasse', *Marxism Today*, 23:10 (October 1979), pp. 6–15.

Chapter 1: A Crisis of Hegemony

1. Analysis of the world system has been greatly influenced by the work of Immanuel Wallerstein. See *The World System* (New York: Academic Press, 1974).
2. For analysis of the long boom see E. A. Brett, *The World Economy since the War* (London: Macmillan, 1985).
3. See P. Armstrong, A. Glyn, and J. Harrison, *Capitalism since World War II* (London: Fontana, 1984).
4. The concept of Fordism has been developed particularly by the French regulation school. See M. Aglietta, *A Theory of Capitalist Regulation* (London: NLB, 1979); M. Aglietta 'World Capitalism in the 1980s', *New Left Review*, 136 (1982), pp. 5–41; Alain Lipietz 'Towards Global Fordism', *New Left Review*, 133 (1982), pp. 33–47.
5. The course of the 1973–4 crisis is described by Ernest Mandel, *The Second Slump* (London: Verso, 1978).
6. See the analyses by Ajit Singh and Alec Cairncross in F. Blackaby (ed.) *De-industrialisation* (London: Heinemann, 1979).
7. See Scott Lash and John Urry, *The End of Organised Capitalism* (Cambridge: Polity, 1987).

8. The existence of a new division of labour is controversial. See the discussion by Rhys Jenkins, 'Divisions over the international division of labour', *Capital and Class*, 22 (1984), pp. 28–58.

9. For analyses of the development of the postwar global political and economic order, the international monetary system, and the imbalances and conflicts of the 1980s, see E. A. Brett, *International Money and Capitalist Crisis* (London: Heinemann, 1983); R. Parboni, *The Dollar and its Rivals* (London: Verso, 1981); and Kees van der Pijl, *The Making of an Atlantic Ruling Class* (London: Verso, 1984).

10. One of the most influential characterisations of collectivism came from A. V. Dicey, *Lectures on the Relation between Law and Public Opinion in England during the Nineteenth Century* (London: Macmillan, 1905). See also Keith Middlemas, *Politics in Industrial Society* (London: Andre Deutsch, 1979) and W. H. Greenleaf, *The British Political Tradition*, vol I *The Rise of Collectivism* (London: Methuen, 1983).

11. See A. Prezworski, *Capitalism and Social Democracy* (Cambridge University Press, 1985); R. Miliband, *Capitalist Democracy in Britain* (Oxford University Press, 1982).

12. See Daniel Bell, *The Cultural Contradictions of Capitalism* (London: Heinemann, 1976); John Urry, *The Anatomy of Capitalist Societies* (London: Macmillan, 1981).

13. This is discussed by David Coates, *The Context of British Politics* (London: Hutchinson, 1984).

14. See David Edgar, 'The Free and the Good', in Ruth Levitas (ed.) *The Ideology of the New Right* (Cambridge: Polity, 1986), pp. 80–106; Stuart Hall *et al.*, *Policing the Crisis* (London: Macmillan, 1978).

15. See Bill Jordan, *The State* (Oxford: Blackwell, 1985).

16. See Nevil Johnson, *In Search of the Constitution* (London: Methuen, 1977).

17. On corporatism see Alan Cawson, *Corporatism and Welfare* (London: Heinemann, 1982).

18. See A. H. Birch, 'Overload, ungovernability, and delegitimation: the theories and the British case', *British Journal of Political Science*, 14:2 (1984), pp. 135–60.

19. See A. Crosland, *The Future of Socialism* (London: Jonathan Cape, 1956).

20. See R. C. O. Matthews, 'Why has Britain had full employment since the war?', *Economic Journal*, 78 (Sept. 1968).

21. See Milton Friedman, *Inflation and Unemployment* (London: IEA, 1977); Tim Congdon, *Monetarism* (London: Centre for Policy Studies, 1976).

22. For a guide and critique of the British constitution see Ferdinand Mount, *The British Constitution Now* (London: Heinemann, 1992); C. Graham and T. Prosser (eds), *Waiving the Rules* (London: Open University Press, 1988).

23. See Jonathan Clark, 'The History of Britain: A Composite State in a Europe of Patries?', in Clark (ed.), *Ideas and Politics in Modern Britain* (London: Macmillan, 1990), pp. 32–49.

24. See Andrew Gamble, *Britain in Decline* (London: Macmillan, 1990).

Chapter 2: The New Right

1. There is a rich literature on the New Right. See especially Ruth Levitas (ed.) *The Ideology of the New Right* (Cambridge: Polity, 1987); Gillian Peele *Revival and Reaction: the Right in Contemporary America* (Oxford: Clarendon, 1984); Norman Barry, *The New Right* (London: Croom Helm, 1987); Desmond King, *The New Right* (London: Macmillan, 1987); and David Green, The New Right (London: Wheatsheaf, 1987). For an intriguing insider's map of the New Right see Maurice Cowling, 'The Sources of the New Right: Irony, Geniality, and Malice', *Encounter*, November 1989, pp. 3–13.

2. For typical writing on this theme see Robert Moss, *The Collapse of Democracy* (London: Temple Smith, 1975).

3. For an initial exploration of this idea see 'The Free Economy and the Strong State', in R. Miliband and J. Saville (eds), *Socialist Register 1979* (London: Merlin, 1979), pp. 1–25.

4. An example is the very good study of what is termed here the liberal New Right by Nick Bosanquet, *After the New Right* (London: HEB, 1983).

5. See the excellent analysis in Peele, *Revival and Reaction*.

6. David Edgar provides a powerful treatment of the new politics of race and gender in 'The Free and the Good', in Levitas (ed.) *The Ideology of the New Right*, pp. 55–79.

7. Sam Brittan is one example. See among his many writings *Capitalism and the Permissive Society* (London: Macmillan, 1973).

8. One of the best analyses of the internal tensions in New Right thinking can be found in Patrick Dunleavy and Brendan O'Leary, *Theories of the State* (London: Macmillan, 1987), ch. 3.

9. Moss, *The Collapse of Democracy*, p. 46.

10. See the illuminating discussion by Andrew Belsey, 'The New Right, Social Order, and Civil Liberties', in Levitas (ed.) *The Ideology of the New Right*, pp. 167–97.

11. See Roger Scruton, *The Meaning of Conservatism* (London: Penguin, 1980).

12. See Ferdinand Mount, *The Subversive Family* (London: Johathan Cape, 1982).

13. I have explored the different components of the liberal New Right further in 'The Political Economy of Freedom', in Levitas (ed.) *The Ideology of the New Right*, pp. 25–54.

14. For a succinct summary see Alec Chrystal, *Controversies in Macroeconomics* (London: Philip Allan, 1979).

15. For one of the best analyses of the international economic order see E. A. Brett, *International Money and Capitalist Crisis* (London: HEB, 1983).

16. See Milton Friedman, *Inflation and Unemployment* (London: IEA, 1977), and Bosanquet, *After the New Right*.

17. See M. Kalecki, 'Political Aspects of Full Employment', *Political Quarterly*, 14 (1943), pp. 322–31.

18. For the main themes of Hayek's writings see Norman Barry, *Hayek's Social and Economic Philosophy* (London: Macmillan, 1979).
19. See W. Rees-Mogg, *The Reigning Illusion* (London: Hamish Hamilton, 1974).
20. See F. A. Hayek, *Denationalisation of Money* (London: IEA, 1978).
21. This was put forward in a paper by Kevin Dowd, *The State and the Monetary System* (Fraser Institute, 1988).
22. Hayek, *Denationalisation of Money.*
23. See the discussion by Bosanquet in *After the New Right*. A representative supply-side text is B. Bartlett and T. P. Roth (eds), *The Supply Side Solution* (London: Macmillan, 1983).
24. See the criticism by George Gilder, one of the leading American supply-siders in the preface to the English edition of *Wealth and Poverty* (London: Buchan and Enright, 1982).
25. For the interwar debates on the feasibility of socialism see F. A. Hayek (ed.) *Collectivist Economic Planning* (London: Routledge, 1935).
26. See the Omega Project of the Adam Smith Institute. It is described and analysed by Ruth Levitas in 'Competition and Compliance: the utopias of the New Right', in Levitas (ed.), *The Ideology of the New Right.*
27. For contrasting estimates see Bosanquet, *After the New Right* and Barry, *The New Right.*
28. Robert Nozick is best known for his book *Anarchy State and Utopia* (Oxford: Basil Blackwell, 1974).
29. Hayek's theory of how knowledge is dispersed in social institutions is one of his most important contributions to social analysis. See 'The Use of Knowledge in Society', in *Individualism and Economic Order* (London: Routledge and Kegan Paul, 1949).
30. Milton Friedman, 'The line we dare not cross', *Encounter* (November 1976).
31. For an analysis of the public-choice school see Bosanquet, *After the New Right*, ch. 4. and J. Buchanan *et al.*, *The Economics of Politics* (London: IEA, 1978).
32. Nozick, *Anarchy, State and Utopia.* Nozick's positions are criticised in several of the contributions to J. Paul (ed.) *Reading Nozick* (Oxford: Basil Blackwell, 1982).
33. See Hayek, especially *Law, Legislation, and Liberty, vol II : The Mirage of Social Justice* (London: Routledge, 1976).
34. For the extreme Austrian position see Murray Rothbard, *Power and Market* (Kansas: Sheed, Andrews and McMeel, 1977).
35. The analysis of the new class has been developed particularly by the American neo-conservatives, such as Irving Kristol. See I. Kristol, *Two Cheers for Capitalism* (New York: Basic Books, 1978) and Peele, *Revival and Reaction.*
36. Representative examples of conservative New-Right writing are Roger Scruton, *The Meaning of Conservatism*; Maurice Cowling (ed.) *Conservative Essays* (London: Cassell, 1978); and Rhodes Boyson, *Centre Forward* (London: Temple Smith, 1978).

37. The impact of the Cold War on postwar politics is emphasised by Phil Armstrong, Andrew Glyn and John Harrison, *Capitalism since World War II* (London: Fontana, 1984).

38. Those who moved right in the 1950s included former Trotskyists such as Irving Kristol, and former communists such as Alfred Sherman. There was later a further wave among those repudiating social democracy. See for example Patrick Cormack, *Right Turn: Eight Men who changed their minds* (London: Leo Cooper, 1978). The eight included Max Beloff, Lord Chalfont, Paul Johnson, Reg Prentice and Hugh Thomas.

39. The origins and course of the new Cold War are traced by Fred Halliday, *The Making of the Second Cold War* (London: Verso, 1983).

40. Moss, *The Collapse of Democracy*, is a good guide to subversion. See also the publications of the *Freedom Association* and Brian Crozier's Institute for the Study of Conflict. The flavour and tone of this literature can be sampled in Brian Crozier, *Socialism: Dream and Reality* (London: Sherwood, 1987).

41. F. A. Hayek, *The Road to Serfdom* (London: Routledge, 1944).

42. Colin Leys, in *Politics in Britain* (London: HEB, 1983), ch. 15, analyses right-wing scenarios of political collapse.

43. The ideas and politics of the American New Right has been analysed by Mike Davis in 'The Political Economy of Late-Imperial America', *New Left Review*, 143 (1984), pp. 6–38; and 'Reaganomics' Magical Mystery Tour', *New Left Review*, 149 (1985), pp. 45–66.

44. Irving Kristol, *Two Cheers for Capitalism*.

45. Gilder, *Wealth and Poverty*.

46. See Scruton's criticisms of Nozick in *The Meaning of Conservatism*.

47. A rich source of this writing is the *Salisbury Review*, published quarterly. On New-Right attitudes on the family and morality, see Martin Durham, *Sex and Politics* (London: Macmillan, 1991)

Chapter 3: From Butler to Thatcher

1. Ian Gilmour, *Inside Right* (London: Hutchinson, 1977).

2. See Rhodes Boyson, *Centre Forward* (London: Temple Smith, 1978); and Andrew Gamble, *The Conservative Nation* (London: RKP, 1974), ch. 5.

3. See J. D. Hoffman, *The Conservative Party in Opposition* (London: MacGibbon and Kee, 1964); Gamble, *The Conservative Nation*, ch. 3.

4. Gamble, *The Conservative Nation*, ch. 4.

5. The Institute of Economic Affairs was founded in 1957.

6. See also Macmillan's shrewd analysis of the result of the 1959 election in his memoirs, *Pointing the Way* (London: Macmillan, 1972), p. 15.

7. R. T. McKenzie and A. Silver, *Angels in Marble* (London: Heinemann, 1963).

8. See the excellent analysis of why British Fordism was relatively unsuccessful in Henk Overbeek, *Global Capitalism and National Decline* (London: Unwin Hyman, 1989).

9. For the debate on modernisation see Andrew Gamble, *Britain in Decline* (London: Macmillan, 1985).

10. Gamble, *Britain in Decline*, ch. 4.

11. Gamble, *The Conservative Nation*, ch. 5.

12. See T. E. Utley, *Enoch Powell* (London: Kimber, 1968); and D. Schoen, *Enoch Powell and the Powellites* (London: Macmillan, 1977).

13. See Enoch Powell, *Freedom and Reality* (Kingswood: Elliott Rightway Books, 1969), ch. 9.

14. See Schoen, *Enoch Powell and the Powellites*, ch. 2.

15. Schoen provides the most detailed examination.

16. Enoch Powell, *Income Tax at 4/3 in the £* (ed. A. Lejeune) (London: Stacey, 1970).

17. Nicholas Wapshott and George Brock in their study *Thatcher* (London: Futura, 1983) note the similarities between Thatcher's 1968 CPC lecture, 'What's Wrong with Politics', and the ideas Powell was expressing. She was known to admire Powell's book of speeches *Freedom and Reality*, she attended meetings at which he spoke and she was the only member of the shadow cabinet to wish him well in the 1970 election.

18. For writing on the Heath government see M. Holmes, *Political Pressure and Economic Policy: British Government 1970–74* (London: Butterworth, 1982); Douglas Hurd, *An End to Promises* (London: Collins, 1979).

19. See Robin Blackburn, 'The Heath Government: a new course for British capitalism', *New Left Review*, 70 (1971), pp. 3–26.

20. The idea of a U-turn was critically examined by Michael Moran in *The Price for Conservatism* (Political Studies Association, 1978). See also Andrew Gamble and Stuart Walkland, *The British Party System and Economic Policy 1945–83* (Oxford: Clarendon Press, 1984).

21. See Hurd, *An end to Promises*, and Holmes, *Political Pressure and Economic Policy*.

22. Two published collections of Sir Keith Joseph's speeches are *Reversing the Trend* (London: Barry Rose, 1975) and *Stranded on the Middle Ground* (London: Centre for Policy Studies, 1976). See also Morrison Halcrow, *Keith Joseph* (London: Macmillan, 1989).

23. Accounts of the 1975 leadership election are contained in Wapshott and Brock, *Thatcher*; Robert Behrens, *The Conservative Party from Heath to Thatcher* (London: Saxon House, 1980); and Patrick Cosgrave, *Margaret Thatcher* (London: Hutchinson, 1978).

24. The office of leader is very difficult to capture, but since 1965 it has been subject to election. This is not the case for other offices in the party.

25. Lord Stockton, *The Times*, 9 October 1975.

26. Quoted by Behrens, *The Conservative Party from Heath to Thatcher*, p. 3.

27. Lord Stockton, *The Times*, 9 October 1975.

28. Ian Gilmour, speech at Amersham, 1974.

29. Julian Critchley, *Westminster Blues* (London: Futura, 1985), p. 32.

30. J. Ramsden, *The Making of Conservative Party Policy* (London: Longman, 1980), ch. 10; Behrens, *The Conservative Party from Heath to Thatcher*, and Z. Layton-Henry (ed.), *Conservative Party Politics* (London: Macmillan, 1980).
31. Cosgrave, *Margaret Thatcher*.
32. Margaret Thatcher, 'Britain Awake', in *Let Our Children Grow Tall* (London: CPS, 1977), p. 43.
33. Ibid., p. 44.
34. Ibid., p. 46.
35. Ibid., p. 46.
36. Ibid., p. 47.
37. For Thatcher's style as opposition leader see Martin Burch, 'Approaches to leadership in Opposition', in Z. Layton-Henry *Conservative Party Politics*, pp. 159–187.
38. See David Coates, *Labour in Power* (London: Longmans, 1980).
39. The Lib/Lab pact was negotiated in March 1977 and preserved the minority Labour government from defeat in Parliament for a further two years.
40. See W. Keegan, *Mrs. Thatcher's Economic Experiment* (London: Allen Lane, 1984), Part I.
41. See Coates, *Labour in Power*, and M. Holmes, *The Labour Government 1974–79* (London: Macmillan, 1985).
42. Trevor Russel, *The Tory Party* (Harmondsworth: Penguin, 1978), p. 78.
43. 'Appomattox or Civil War', *Economist*, 27 May 1978.
44. See Bill Schwarz, 'Let them eat coal: the Conservative party and the strike', in H. Beynon (ed.) *Digging Deeper* (London: Verso, 1985).
45. The others were Airey Neave, George Gardiner and John Biffen.
46. See J. Rogaly, *Grunwick* (Harmondsworth: Penguin, 1978).
47. See Steve Ludlam, 'The Gnomes of Washington: Four Myths of the 1976 IMF Crisis', *Political Studies*, 40:4 (1992), pp. 713–27.
48. Keith Joseph, 'Solving the Union problem is the Key to Economic Recovery' (London: CPS, 1979).

Chapter 4: The Thatcher Government 1979–90

1. Walsall and Workington were won by the Conservatives in November 1976, Stechford in March 1977 and Ashfield in April 1977.
2. On the devolution bills see Coates, *Labour in Power*.
3. See Richard Rose, *Do Parties Make a Difference?* (London: Macmillan, 1984).
4. See William Keegan, *Mrs. Thatcher's Economic Experiment*; Colin Thain, 'The Medium Term Financial Strategy', paper presented to the Political Studies Association Conference April 1985; and Grahame Thompson, *The Conservatives' Economic Policy* (London: Croom Helm, 1986) ch. 2.
5. For contrasting assessments of the 1981 budget see Keegan, *Mrs. Thatcher's Economic Experiment*, and Alan Walters, *Britain's Economic*

Renaissance (Oxford: Clarendon Press, 1986). Patrick Cosgrave judged it to be the 'true strategic beginning of the introduction of Thatcherism into government'.

6. Prior's caution over trade-union reform and the conflict this created is described by Patrick Cosgrave in *Thatcher: The First Term* (London: Bodley Head, 1985).

7. See Chapter 3, note 43.

8. Her attitude was like Baldwin's in 1925. Cosgrave reports her as saying of the government's climbdown, 'It gives us time to get ready', *Thatcher: The First Term*, p. 131.

9. A transfer fee of £1.8 million for MacGregor's services was negotiated with his employers, Lazard Freres.

10. See John Burton, *The Job Support Machine* (London: CPS, 1979) and Jock Bruce-Gardyne, *Mrs. Thatcher's First Administration* (London: Macmillan, 1984).

11. Michael Heseltine, secretary of state for the Environment, took a very different line.

12. See Ian Bradley, *Breaking the Mould* (Oxford: Martin Robertson, 1981); D. Kogan and M. Kogan, *The Battle for the Labour Party* (London: Fontana, 1982); and Patrick Seyd, *The Rise and Fall of the Labour Left* (London: Macmillan, 1987).

13. The internal splits in the cabinet are detailed by Patrick Cosgrave, *Thatcher: The First Term*; Peter Riddell, *The Thatcher Government* (Oxford: Basil Blackwell, 1985); Martin Holmes, *The First Thatcher Government 1979–1983* (London: Wheatsheaf, 1985); and Dennis Kavanagh, *Thatcherism and British Politics* (Oxford: Clarendon Press, 1987); Ian Gilmour, *Dancing with Dogma* (London: Simon and Schuster, 1992). There is also rich additional information emerging from the biographies of ministers such as James Prior and Nigel Lawson plus, of course, Margaret Thatcher's *The Downing Street Years* (London: Harper Collins, 1993).

14. This is argued strongly by Grahame Thompson, *The Conservatives' Economic Policy*; William Keegan, *Mrs. Thatcher's Economic Experiment*; and Nick Gardner, *Decade of Discontent* (Oxford: Basil Blackwell, 1987); and David Smith, *The Rise and Fall of Monetarism* (Harmondsworth: Penguin, 1986).

15. For a full account see Cento Veljanovski, *Selling the State* (London: Weidenfeld, 1987).

16. See Mike Goldsmith, 'The Conservatives and Local Government, 1979 and after', in D. Bell (ed.) *The Conservative Government 1979–84* (London: Croom Helm, 1985); and Patrick Dunleavy and Rod Rhodes, 'Government beyond Whitehall', in Henry Drucker *et al.* (eds), *Developments in British Politics 2* (London: Macmillan, 1986), ch. 5.

17. See Huw Beynon, *Digging Deeper*; and Martin Adeney and John Lloyd *The Miners' Strike: loss without limit* (London: RKP, 1986).

18. See Michael Moran, 'Industrial Relations', in Drucker, *Developments in British Politics 2*, ch. 12, and Tony Lane, 'The Tories and the Trade

Unions', in Stuart Hall and Martin Jacques, *The Politics of Thatcherism* (London: Lawrence and Wishart, 1983), pp. 169–87.

19. The Labour Research Department estimated that in June 1986 the official government figure of 3 229 400 would have been 3 865 000 on the same basis as the 1979 count. In addition MSC programmes increased the numbers on special training and community schemes from 250 000 in 1979 to 737 000 in 1986; of these an estimated 561 000 would otherwise be registered as unemployed. See Labour Research, *A State of Collapse: The UK Economy under the Tories* (London, 1987), pp. 24–5.

20. See Anthony Barnett, 'Iron Britannia', *New Left Review*, 134 (1982), pp. 5–96; and Hall and Jacques, *The Politics of Thatcherism*, Part III (chapters by Eric Hobsbawm, Robert Gray and Tom Nairn).

21. See Peter Jenkins, *Mrs. Thatcher's Revolution* (London: Jonathan Cape, 1987), ch. 9.

22. See Peter Hennessy, *Cabinet* (Oxford: Basil Blackwell, 1986), ch. 3.

23. Cecil Parkinson resigned from the cabinet in 1983 following publicity of his affair with Sara Keays; Jeffrey Archer resigned as deputy chairman of the Conservative Party in 1986 following press allegations about an association with a prostitute; Harvey Proctor resigned as an MP in 1987 after pleading guilty to involvement with homosexual prostitutes; and Keith Best resigned as an MP in 1987 after being found guilty of making multiple applications for British Telecom shares.

24. See Paul Whiteley, 'Economic Policy', in Dunleavy *et al.* (eds), *Developments in British Politics 3* (London: Macmillan, 1990).

25. David Baker, Andrew Gamble, and Steve Ludlam, '1846...1906...1996? Conservative Splits and European Integration', *Political Quarterly*, 46:4 (1993).

26. Michael Spicer, *A Treaty Too Far* (London: Fourth Estate, 1992).

27. Lawson's own account is given in *The View From No. 11* (London: Bantam, 1992)

28. The best account of the Thatcher Years and her downfall is Hugo Young, *One of Us* (London: Macmillan, 1991).

29. Keith Dowding, 'Government at the Centre', in Dunleavy *et al.* (eds), *Developments in British Politics 4* (London: Macmillan, 1993).

30. Geoff Whitty, 'The Politics of the 1988 Education Reform Act', and Albert Weale, 'Social Policy', in Dunleavy *et al.* (eds), *Developments in British Politics 3* (London: Macmillan, 1990).

31. Gerry Stoker, 'Government Beyond Whitehall', in Dunleavy *et al.* (eds), *Development in British Politics 3* (London: Macmillan, 1990).

Chapter 5: The Pursuit of Power

1. William Keegan, *Mrs. Thatcher's Economic Experiment.*

2. Rhodes Boyson, *Centre Forward*, and Patrick Cosgrave, *Margaret Thatcher: A Tory and her Party* (London: Hutchinson, 1978).

3. T. E. Utley, 'The Significance of Mrs. Thatcher', in Maurice Cowling (ed.), *Conservative Essays* (London: Cassell, 1978), p. 44.
4. For a study of Salisbury's political thought see M. Pinto-Duschinsky, *The Political Thought of Lord Salisbury* (London: Constable, 1967).
5. Anthony Trollope, *The Bertrams*, quoted by W. L. Burn in 'The Conservative tradition and its reformulation', in M. Ginsburg (ed.), *Law and Opinion in the Twentieth Century* (London: Stevens, 1959), p. 43.
6. Quoted in Bernard Semmel *Imperialism and Social Reform* (London: Allen and Unwin, 1960), p. 100.
7. F. A. Hayek, 'Why I am not a Conservative', postscript to *The Constitution of Liberty* (London: RKP, 1960).
8. Ian Gilmour, *Inside Right* (London: Hutchinson, 1977), p. 115.
9. S. Huntington, 'Conservatism as an Ideology', *American Political Science Review*, 51:2 (1957), pp. 454–73. See also R. Eccleshall, 'Conservatism', in R. Eccleshall *et al.* (eds), *Political Ideologies* (London: Hutchinson, 1984).
10. See for example Henry Kissinger, 'The Conservative Dilemma: Reflections on the political thought of Metternich', *American Political Science Review*, 48:4 (1954), pp. 1017–30.
11. H. Glickman, 'The Toryness of English Conservatism', *Journal of British Studies*, 1:1 (1961), pp. 111–43.
12. Gilmour, *Inside Right*, Part III, ch. 2; see also Robert Blake, *The Conservative Party from Peel to Thatcher* (London: Fontana, 1985).
13. Cosgrave, *Margaret Thatcher*, p. 36.
14. Iain Macleod, *Spectator*, 17 January 1964. See also the attacks on the Tory Party's rightward drift by Humphrey Berkeley, *Crossing the Floor* (London: Allen and Unwin, 1972).
15. Trevor Russel, *The Tory Party* (Harmondsworth: Penguin, 1978).
16. Details of these organisations are given in 'Right Thinking People', *Labour Research*, 73:2 (1984), pp. 37–42, and updated in *Labour Research*, 76:10 (1987), pp. 7–11.
17. Keith Joseph, 'The Quest for Common Ground', in *Stranded on the Middle Ground* (London: CPS, 1976).
18. See Gilmour, *Inside Right*, and *Britain Can Work* (Oxford: Martin Robertson, 1983); Andrew Gamble, *The Conservative Nation*, especially chs 2 and 3. For a typical statement of one-nation conservatism see Sir Geoffrey Butler, *The Tory Tradition* (London: CPC, 1957).
19. Peter Walker, *The Ascent of Britain* (London: Sidgwick and Jackson, 1977), p. 29.
20. Ibid., p. 18.
21. Gilmour, *Inside Right*, p. 236.
22. Ibid., p. 118.
23. Russel, *The Tory Party*, p. 167.
24. Quoted by Kissinger in 'The Conservative Dilemma', p. 1020.
25. This distinction between libertarianism and collectivism is drawn by W. H. Greenleaf in his study *The British Political Tradition, vol. I The rise of Collectivism*, and vol. II *The Ideological Heritage* (London: Methuen, 1983). Greenleaf prefers 'libertarianism' to 'liberalism' because of

the associations the latter has acquired. His concept of libertarianism corresponds to the conception of the liberal New Right developed in Chapter 2.

26. See N. Soldon, 'Laissez-faire as dogma: the Liberty and Property Defence League 1882–1914', in K. Brown (ed.), *Essays in Anti-Labour History* (London: Macmillan, 1974).

27. Robert Blake, *Conservatism in an Age of Revolution* (London: Churchill Press, 1976), and *The Conservative Party from Peel to Thatcher*, ch. 11 and postscript.

28. Hugh Thomas, *History, Capitalism, and Freedom* (London: CPS, 1979).

29. Michael Oakeshott, *Rationalism in Politics* (London: Methuen, 1962) and *On Human Conduct* (Oxford: Clarendon Press, 1975). The most extended Oakeshottian interpretation of Thatcherism is Shirley Letwin, *The Anatomy of Thatcherism* (London: Fontana, 1992).

30. Oakeshott, *Rationalism in Politics*, p. 21.

31. Noel O'Sullivan, *Conservatism* (London: Dent, 1976). A famous expression of this approach can be found in Maurice Cowling (ed.), *Conservative Essays*.

32. Roger Scruton, *The Meaning of Conservatism* (London: Penguin, 1980), p. 15.

33. Ibid., pp. 15–16.

34. Noel O'Sullivan, *Conservatism*.

35. J. A. Schumpeter, *Capitalism, Socialism, and Democracy* (London: Allen and Unwin, 1949), p.229.

36. Gaetano Mosca, *The Ruling Class* (New York: McGraw Hill, 1939), p. 119.

37. See *Monday World*, the former journal of the Monday Club, and the quarterly *Salisbury Review.*

38. See the discussion in chapter 5 of *The Conservative Nation.*

39. Peregrine Worsthorne, *Sunday Telegraph*, 15 October 1978. The need for a governing class is also one of the major themes of Worsthorne's book *The Socialist Myth* (London: Cassell, 1971).

40. It is important to note that the tradition of Social imperialism and the tradition of the middle way are frequently the same.

41. Bob Jessop *et al.*, 'Authoritarian Populism, Two Nations, and Thatcherism', *New Left Review*, 147 (1984), pp. 32–60.

42. Jim Bulpitt, 'The Discipline of the New Democracy: Mrs.Thatcher's Domestic Statecraft', *Political Studies*, 34:1 (1985), pp. 19–39; and *Territory and Power in the UK* (Manchester: University Press, 1983).

43. See P. Marsh, *The Discipline of Popular Government: Lord Salisbury's Domestic Statecraft* (London: Harvester, 1978).

44. Scruton, *The Meaning of Conservatism.*

45. J. H. Grainger, 'Mrs.Thatcher's Last Stand', *Quadrant*, 3 (December 1980) p. 6.

46. R. W. Johnson, 'Pomp and Circumstance', *The Politics of Recession* (London: Macmillan, 1985), pp. 224–55.

47. Peregrine Worsthorne, 'Too Much Freedom', in M. Cowling, *Conservative Essays*, pp. 141–54.

48. Grainger, 'Mrs. Thatcher's Last Stand', p. 5.

Chapter 6: The Struggle for Hegemony

1. Perry Anderson 'Origins of the present crisis', *New Left Review*, 23 (1964) pp. 26–53; Tom Nairn, 'The Twilight of the British State', in *The Breakup of Britain* (London: NLB, 1981), and 'The Future of Britain's Crisis', *New Left Review*, 113/4 (1979), pp. 43–70. See also Perry Anderson, *English Questions* (London: Verso, 1992).
2. Tom Nairn, 'Enoch Powell: the New Right', *New Left Review*, 61 (1970), pp. 3–27.
3. Robin Blackburn, 'The Heath Government: A New Course for British Capitalism', *New Left Review*, 70 (1971), pp. 3–26.
4. Andrew Glyn and Bob Sutcliffe, *British Capitalism, Workers and the Profits Squeeze* (London: Penguin, 1972).
5. See Colin Leys, *Politics in Britain* (London: Verso, 1989); and Stuart Hall *et al. Policing the Crisis* (London: Macmillan, 1978).
6. David Purdy, 'British Capitalism since the war', *Marxism Today*, 20:9 (1976), pp. 270–7 and 20:10 (1976), pp. 310–18.
7. Stuart Hall, 'Popular democratic versus authoritarian populism', in A. Hunt (ed.), *Marxism and Democracy* (London: Lawrence and Wishart, 1980).
8. Stuart Hall and Bill Schwarz, 'State and Society 1880–1930', in M. Langan and B. Schwarz, *Crises in the British State 1880–1930* (London: Hutchinson, 1985), pp. 7–32.
9. See S. Beer, *Modern British Politics* (London: Faber and Faber, 1965) and *Britain Against Itself* (New York: Norton, 1982); Keith Middlemas *Politics in Industrial Society* (London: Andre Deutsch, 1979). See also Bill Schwarz's assessment of Middlemas' work 'Conservatives and Corporatism', *New Left Review*, 166 (1987), pp. 107–28.
10. Nicos Poulantzas, *State, Power, Socialism* (London: NLB, 1978); and Bob Jessop, *Nicos Poulantzas* (London: Macmillan, 1985).
11. Dominic Strinati, 'State intervention, the Economy, and the Crisis', in A. Stewart (ed.), *Contemporary Britain* (London: RKP, 1983); and Stuart Hall *et al., Policing the Crisis*.
12. Stuart Hall *et al., Policing the Crisis*; 'The Great Moving Right Show', *Marxism Today* (1979), pp. 107–28) – revised version printed in S. Hall and M. Jacques (eds), *The Politics of Thatcherism* (London: Lawrence and Wishart, 1983); 'Popular democratic versus authoritarian populism', in Hunt, *Marxism and Democracy*. Most of Hall's key writings on Thatcherism are collected in *A Hard Road to Renewal* (London: Verso, 1988).
13. M. Jacques and F. Mulhern (eds), *The Forward March of Labour Halted?* (London: Verso, 1981). Eric Hobsbawm's article was first published in *Marxism Today* (September 1978).
14. Raymond Williams in *The Forward March of Labour Halted?*, pp. 142–152.
15. See especially Eric Hobsbawm, 'Labour's Lost Millions', *Marxism Today* (October 1983). Hobsbawm's essays on labour are collected in *Politics for a Rational Left* (London: Verso, 1989).

16. See Gavin Kitching, *Rethinking Socialism* (London: Methuen, 1983); Ernesto Laclau and Chantal Mouffe, *Hegemony and Socialist Strategy* (London: Verso, 1985). Strong criticism of these positions has come from Ellen Meiksins Wood, *The Retreat from Class* (London: Verso, 1986) and Ralph Miliband, 'The New Revisionism in Britain', *New Left Review*, 150 (1985), pp. 5–26. See also Ben Fine *et al.*, *Class Politics: An Answer to its Critics* (London: Central Books, 1985).

17. See the criticicims of Hobsbawm in Jacques and Mulhern (eds), *The Forward March of Labour Halted?* and Wood, *The Retreat from Class.*

18. See Patrick Seyd, *The Rise and Fall of the Labour Left* (London: Macmillan, 1987).

19. Tony Benn, 'Who Dares Wins', *Marxism Today*, 29:1 (January 1985), pp. 12–14. See also the reply by Stuart Hall.

20. This is discussed further below.

21. Patrick Hutber, *The Decline and fall of the Middle Class and how it can fight back* (Harmondsworth: Penguin, 1977).

22. Roger King and N. Nugent, *Respectable Rebels* (London: Hodder and Stoughton, 1979).

23. Bob Jessop, Kevin Bonnett, Simon Bromley and Tom Ling, 'Authoritarian Populism, Two Nations, and Thatcherism', *New Left Review*, 147 (1984), pp. 32–60.

24. Andrew Glyn and John Harrison, *The British Economic Disaster* (London: Pluto, 1980).

25. The details of company donations to political parties and other organisations are listed every year in *Labour Research.*

26. See E. A. Brett, *The World Economy since the War* (London: Macmillan, 1985).

27. See John Ross, *Thatcher and Friends* (London: Pluto, 1983; also 'Does Thatcherism have a Future', *International*, 7:2 (March 1982), pp. 4–10.

28. See H. Beynon (ed.), *Digging Deeper* (London: Verso, 1985).

29. See Geoffrey Ingham, *Capitalism Divided?* (London: Macmillan, 1984); and F. Longstreth, 'The City, Industry, and the State', in C. Crouch (ed.), *State and Economy in Contemporary Capitalism* (Oxford: Martin Robertson, 1979).

30. Ross' inclusion of construction as a sector that benefited from the policies of the Thatcher government has been questioned by Overbeek in his book, *Global Capitalism and National Decline* (London: Unwin Hyman, 1989).

31. Colin Leys, 'Thatcherism and British Manufacturing: A Question of hegemony', *New Left Review*, 151 (1985), pp. 5–25; Henk Overbeek, *Global Capitalism and National Decline*; Bob Jessop, 'The mid-life crisis of Thatcherism and the birth-pangs of post-Fordism', *New Socialist*, 36 (March 86).

32. See the analysis in Charles Leadbeater and John Lloyd, *In Search of Work* (Harmondsworth: Penguin, 1987).

33. Ben Fine and Laurence Harris, *The Peculiarities of the British Economy* (London: Lawrence and Wishart, 1985).

34. Colin Leys, 'Thatcherism and British Manufacturing'.
35. Ibid., p. 16.
36. Stuart Hall *et al.*, *Policing the Crisis*.
37. See Tessa ten Tusscher, 'Patriarchy, Capitalism and the New Right,' in J. Evans *et al.* *(eds), Feminism and Political Theory* (London: Sage, 1986) and John Solomos, *Race and Racism in Contemporary Britain* (London: Macmillan, 1989).
38. See Miriam David, 'Moral and Maternal: the Family in the Right', Gill Seidel, 'Culture, Nation, and 'Race' in the British and French New Right', and David Edgar, 'The Free or the Good', in Ruth Levitas (ed.), *The Ideology of the New Right* (Cambridge: Polity, 1986). See also Lynne Segal, 'The Heat in the Kitchen', in Hall and Jacques (eds), *The Politics of Thatcherism*.
39. Bea Campbell, *Iron Ladies* (London: Virago, 1987).
40. Miriam David, 'Moral and Maternal: the Family in the Right'.
41. Jean Gardiner, 'Women, Recession, and the Tories', in Hall and Jacques, *The Politics of Thatcherism*.
42. Peter Riddell, *The Thatcher Government* (Oxford: Basil Blackwell, 1985), p. 59.
43. Riddell's scepticism was shared by several other leading journalists, including Ian Aitken, Hugo Young and Peter Jenkins. There were others, however, notably Brian Walden, Ronald Butt and Paul Johnson, who argued that the Thatcher government introduced radical and irreversible changes.
44. Richard Rose, *Do Parties Make a Difference?* (London: Macmillan, 1984). See also Dennis Kavanagh, *Thatcherism and British Politics*.
45. Christopher Hollis, 'The Merits and Defects of Marx', in G. Woodcock (ed.), *A Hundred Years of Revolution* (London: Porcupine Press, 1948), p. 87.
46. See Grahame Thompson, *The Conservatives' Economic Policy* (London: Croom Helm, 1986); Maurice Mullard, *The Politics of Public Expenditure* (London: Croom Helm, 1987); Paul Mosley, *The Making of Economic Policy* (London: Wheatsheaf, 1984); and Jim Tomlinson *Monetarism: Is there an Alternative?* (Oxford: Basil Blackwell, 1986).
47. Bob Jessop *et al.* 'Authoritarian Populism, Two Nations, and Thatcherism', *New Left Review*, 147; 'Thatcherism and the Politics of hegemony: a reply to Stuart Hall', *New Left Review*, 153 (1985), pp. 87–101; 'Popular Capitalism, Flexible Accumulation, and Left Strategy', *New Left Review*, 165 (1987), pp. 104–22. See also Fiona Atkins, 'Thatcherism, populist authoritarianism, and the search for a new left political strategy', *Capital and Class*, 28 (1986), pp. 25–48.
48. Bob Jessop 'The Transformation of the State in Post-War Britain', in R. Scase *The State in Western Europe* (London: Croom Helm, 1980).
49. See Bob Jessop, *The Capitalist State* (Oxford: Martin Robertson, 1982), pp. 244–5.
50. See Bill Jordan, *The State* (Oxford: Basil Blackwell, 1985).
51. Stuart Hall, 'Authoritarian Populism: a reply to Jessop *et al.*', *New Left Review*, 151 (1985), pp. 115–24.

Chapter 7: The Legacies of Thatcherism

1. Antonio Gramsci, *The Prison Notebooks* (London: Lawrence and Wishart, 1971), p. 161.
2. The statecraft approach is most associated with Jim Bulpitt. The best statement of the policy implementation approach is David Marsh and Rod Rhodes, *Implementing Thatcherite Policies: Audit of an Era* (London: Open University Press, 1992).
3. See Anthony King, 'Margaret Thatcher: the Style of a Prime Minister', in *The British Prime Minister* (London: Macmillan, 1985); Philip Norton and Arthur Aughey, *Conservatives and Conservatism* (London: Temple Smith, 1987); Dennis Kavanagh, *Thatcherism and British Politics* (Oxford: Clarendon Press, 1987); and Martin Burch, 'Mrs. Thatcher's Approach to leadership in Government', *Parliamentary Affairs*, 36:4 (1983).
4. David Baker, Andrew Gamble and Stephen Ludlam, '1846...1906...1996: Conservative Splits and European Integration', *Political Quarterly*, 64:4 (1993).
5. Philip Norton, 'The Lady's not for Turning But What About The rest?' *Parliamentary Affairs*, 43:1 (1990).
6. Ivor Crewe, 'Voting and the Electorate', in Patrick Dunleavy *et al. Developments in British Politics 4* (London: Macmillan, 1993).
7. Anthony King, 'The Implications of One-Party Government,' in A. King (ed.), *Britain at the Polls 1993* (New Jersey: Chatham House), pp. 223–48.
8. See Doreen Massey, 'The Contours of Victory', *Marxism Today*, 27:7 (July 1983), pp. 16–19; and 'Heartlands of Defeat', *Marxism Today*, 31:7 (July 1987), pp. 18–23. For psephological analysis of the Conservative vote see Dunleavy and Husbands, *British Democracy at the Crossroads* (London: Allen and Unwin, 1985); R. Rose and I. McAllister, *Voters Begin to Choose* (London: Sage, 1986); A. Heath *et al.*, *How Britain Votes* (Oxford: Pergamon Press, 1985); Ivor Crewe, 'Voting and the Electorate', in *Developments in British Politics 4*.
9. The term comes from Peter Glotz. For a discussion see Andrew Gamble, 'The Great Divide', *Marxism Today*, 31:3 (March 1987) pp. 12–19.
10. See Jessop *et al.*, 'Authoritarian Populism, Two Nations, and Thatcherism.'
11. See Patrick Dunleavy and Chris Husbands, *British Democracy at the Crossroads*.
12. R. Jowell *et al.* (eds), *British Social Attitudes: the 1985 Report* (London: Gower, 1985). The 1987 report confirmed that the broad trends away from Thatcherite values identified in the earlier surveys were continuing. John Curtice argued, however, that this trend was less important for voting decisions than the level of 'economic optimism'. See 'Interim Report: Party Politics' in *British Social Attitudes: the 1987 Report* (London:Gower, 1987). See also D. Sanders

'Why the Conservative Party Won – Again', in A. King (ed.), *Britain at the Polls 1992* (New Jersey: Chatham House, 1993,) pp. 70–100.

13. Knighthoods were given to loyal Thatcherite tabloid editors such as Larry Lamb and David English. For an analysis of the press see J. Curran and J. Seaton, *Power without Responsibility* (London: Methuen, 1985).

14. See Colin Leys, 'Thatcherism and British Manufacturing', and the 1985 report of the Select Committee of the House of Lords set up to examine the results of the rundown of manufacturing on the British balance of payments. For a summary of its conclusions see Lord Aldington, 'Britain's Manufacturing Industry', *Royal Bank of Scotland Review,* 151 (1986), pp. 3–13. See also the different views collected in David Coates and John Hillard (eds), *The Economic Revival of Modern Britain: The Debate between Left and Right* (London: Edward Elgar, 1987).

15. See Ross, *Thatcher and Friends*, and *Labour Research*.

16. The concept of the social market economy was at first adopted by the Centre for Policy Studies. See *Why Britain Needs a Social Market Economy* (London: CPS, 1975). It was later employed by the SDP.

17. Martin Smith and Jo Spear (eds), *The Changing Labour Party* (London: Routledge, 1992).

18. See Scott Lash and John Urry, *The End of Organised Capitalism* (Cambridge: Polity, 1987); and Henk Overbeek, *Global Capitalism and National Decline.*

19. See Thompson, *The Conservatives' Economic Policy,* and Smith, *The Rise and Fall of Monetarism.*

20. See Maurice Mullard's analysis of the Thatcher government's record on public spending, *The Politics of Public Expenditure* (London: Croom Helm, 1987), ch. 6.

21. Between 1979 and 1987 asset sales raised £12 billion for the Treasury. See Veljanovski, *Selling the State*, ch. 1. Oil revenues expanded swiftly during the 1980s to reach £10–12 billion a year, which was larger than the public-sector borrowing requirement.

22. See Thompson, *The Conservatives' Economic Policy,* and Wyn Grant, *The Political Economy of Industrial Policy* (London: Butterworths, 1982).

23. See evidence from ministers to the House of Lords Select Committee in *Report from the Select Committee on Overseas Trade* (House of Lords, 1985).

24. Eurotunnel, and the Dartford Bridge across the Thames to relieve congestion on the M25 orbital motorway were two examples.

25. See Hans Kastendiek *et al.* (eds), *Economic Crisis, Trade Unions and the State* (London: Croom Helm, 1986).

26. John Lloyd and Charles Leadbeater, *In Search of Work* (Harmondsworth: Penguin, 1987).

27. See Bob Rowthorn, 'Britain and Western Europe', *Marxism Today,* 26:5 (May 1982), pp. 25–31.

28. See Barnett, 'Iron Britannia'.

29. See Nevil Johnson, 'Constitutional Reform: Some Dilemmas for a Conservative Philosophy', in Z. Layton-Henry, *Conservative Party*

Politics, pp. 126–55; and Gillian Peele, 'The state and civil liberties', in Drucker, *Developments in British Politics 2*, ch. 6.

30. Sir John Hoskyns, 'Whitehall and Westminster: An outsider's view', *Parliamentary Affairs*, 36 (1983); and 'Conservatism is not enough', *Political Quarterly*, 55 (1984).

31. Civil Service numbers were cut from 732 000 in 1979 to 624 000 by 1984 and 590 400 in 1988. See G. K. Fry, 'Inside Whitehall', in *Developments in British Politics 2*, ch. 4, and Patrick Dunleavy, 'Government at the Centre', in Dunleavy *et al.* (eds), *Development in British Politics 3* (London: Macmillan, 1990).

32. A number of such appointments were made. See Kavanagh, *Thatcherism and British Politics*, ch. 9, for an assessment.

33. See Kavanagh, *Thatcherism and British Politics*, and P. Hennessy *Cabinet.*

34. The Policy Unit is discussed by Fry, Hennessy and Kavanagh. See also for an insider's view David Willetts, 'The role of the Prime Miinister's Policy Unit', *Public Administration*, 65:4 (1987). Willetts revealed that the first two questions asked by the Policy Unit about every departmental paper were (i) is there a less interventionist solution which has not been properly considered or has been wrongly rejected? and (ii) is there a less expensive option?

35. For Thatcher's style as prime minister see Anthony King, 'Margaret Thatcher: the style of a Prime Minister', in A. King (ed.), *The British Prime Minister* (London: Macmillan, 1985).

36. After the speech the Conservative party's poll rating leapt nine points. For a discussion of race and the Conservative Party see Z. Layton-Henry, *The Politics of Race in Britain* (London: Allen and Unwin, 1984).

37. Two influential treatments of this theme are, Martin Wiener *English Culture and the Decline of the Industrial Spirit* (Cambridge University Press, 1981) and Corelli Barnett, *The Audit of War*, (London: Macmillan, 1986); see also David Coates and John Hillard (eds), *The Economic Decline of Modern Britain* (London: Wheatsheaf, 1985).

38. See for example David Eccles, *Popular Capitalism* (London: Conservative Political Centre, 1954).

39. See Stephen Blank, 'The Politics of Foreign Economic Policy', *International Organisation*, 31:4 (1977), pp. 673–722. See also Joel Krieger, *Reagan, Thatcher, and the Politics of Decline* (Cambridge: Polity, 1986).

40. Hugo Radice, 'The National Economy: a Keynesian Myth?', *Capital and Class*, 22 (1984), pp. 111–40.

41. Foreign investments, both direct and portfolio, increased from £38 billion at the end of 1978 to £177 billion at the end of 1985.

42. See Paul Hirst, *After Thatcher* (London: Collins, 1989). For assessments of the Thatcher government's economic record see C. F. Pratten, 'Mrs. Thatcher's Economic Legacy', in K. Minogue and M. Biddiss (eds), *Thatcherism: Personality and Politics* (London: Macmillan, 1987); Peter Riddell, *The Thatcher Era* (Oxford: Basil Blackwell, 1991); and Grahame Thompson, *The Conservatives' Economic Policy* (London: Croom Helm, 1986).

43. Sir John Hoskyns as reported in the *Daily Telegraph*, 27 July 1986.
44. Patrick Dunleavy and Rod Rhodes, 'Government beyond Whitehall', in Drucker, *Developments in British Politics 2*.
45. The phrase is Shirley Letwin's in *The Anatomy of Thatcherism* (London: Fontana, 1992). A very different view of Thatcherism is provided by Ian Gilmour, *Dancing With Dogma* (London: Simon and Schuster, 1992). See Andrew Gamble, 'The entrails of Thatcherism', *New Left Review*, 198 (1993), pp. 117–28.

Further reading

Anderson P., *English Questions* (London: Verso, 1992).

Barry, N., *The New Right* (London: Croom Helm, 1987).

Behrens, R., *The Conservative Party from Heath to Thatcher* (London: Saxon House, 1980).

Bell, D. (ed.), *The Conservative Government 1979–84* (London: Croom Helm, 1985).

Blake, R., *The Conservative Party from Peel to Thatcher* (London: Fontana, 1985).

Bosanquet, N., *After the New Right* (London: HEB, 1983).

Brett, E., *The World Economy Since the War* (London: Macmillan, 1985).

Bruce-Gardyne, J., *Mrs. Thatcher's First Administration* (London: Macmillan, 1984).

Bulpitt, J., 'The discipline of the New Democracy: Mrs. Thatcher's Domestic Statecraft' *Political Studies*, 34:1 (1985), pp. 19–39.

Campbell, B., *Iron Ladies* (London: Virago, 1987).

Clark, J. (ed.), *Ideas and Politics in Modern Britain* (London: Macmillan, 1990).

Coates, D., *The Context of British Politics* (London: Hutchinson, 1984).

Cosgrave, P., *Margaret Thatcher: A Tory and her Party* (London: Hutchinson, 1978).

Cosgrave, P., *Thatcher: The First Term* (London: Bodley Head, 1985).

Cowling, M. (ed.), *Conservative Essays* (London: Cassell, 1978).

Dearlove, J. and P. Saunders, *Introduction to British Politics* (Cambridge: Polity, 1984).

Drucker, H. *et al.* (eds), *Developments in British Politics 2* (London: Macmillan, 1986).

Dunleavy, P. *et al.* (eds), *Developments in British Politics 3* (London: Macmillan, 1990).

Dunleavy, P. *et al.* (eds), *Developments in British Politics 4* (London: Macmillan, 1993).

Dunleavy, P. and C. Husbands, *British Democracy at the Crossroads* (London: Allen and Unwin, 1985).

Durham, M., *Sex and Politics* (London: Macmillan, 1991).

Fine, B. and L. Harris, *Peculiarities of the British Economy* (London: Lawrence and Wishart, 1985).

Gilmour, I., *Inside Right* (London: Hutchinson, 1970).

Gilmour, I., *Britain Can Work* (Oxford: Martin Robertson, 1983).
Gilmour, I., *Dancing With Dogma* (London: Simon and Schuster, 1992).
Glyn, A. and J. Harrison, *The British Economic Disaster* (London: Pluto, 1980).
Greenleaf, W. H., *The British Political Tradition, Vol I: The Rise of Collectism, Vol II: The Ideological Heritage* (London: Methuen, 1983).
Hall, S. *et al.*, *Policing the Crisis* (London: Macmillan, 1978).
Hall, S., *A Hard Road to Renewal* (London: Verso, 1988).
Hall, S. and M. Jacques. (eds), *The Politics of Thatcherism* (London: Lawrence and Wishart, 1983).
Holmes, M., *The First Thatcher Government* (London: Wheatsheaf, 1985).
Holmes, M., *Thatcherism: Scope and Limits* (London: Macmillan, 1989).
Ingham, G., *Capitalism Divided* (London: Macmillan, 1984).
Jenkins, P., *Mrs. Thatcher's Revolution* (London: Jonathan Cape, 1987).
Jessop, B. *et al.*, *Thatcherism* (Cambridge: Polity, 1988).
Johnson, R. W., *The Politics of Recession* (London: Macmillan, 1985).
Joseph, K., *Stranded on the Middle Ground* (London: CPS, 1976).
Kavanagh, D., *Thatcherism and British Politics* (Oxford: Clarendon Press, 1987).
Keegan, W., *Mrs. Thatcher's Economic Experiment* (London: Allen Lane, 1984).
King, A., 'Margaret Thatcher: the style of a Prime Minister', in A. King (ed.), *The British Prime Minister* (London: Macmillan, 1985).
Krieger, J., *Reagan, Thatcher, and the Politics of Decline* (Cambridge: Polity, 1986).
Langan, M. and B. Schwarz (eds), *Crises in the British State* (London: Hutchinson, 1985).
Lawson, N., *The View from No. 11* (London: Bantam, 1992).
Layton-Henry, Z. (ed.), *Conservative Party Politics* (London: Macmillan, 1980).
Letwin, S., *The Anatomy of Thatcherism* (London: Fontana, 1992).
Levitas, R. (ed.), *The Ideology of the New Right* (Cambridge: Polity, 1986).
Leys, C., 'Thatcherism and British Manufacturing', *New Left Review*, 151 (1985), pp. 5–25.
Leys, C., *Politics in Britain* (London: Heinemann, 1983).
Marsh, D. and R. Rhodes (eds), *Implementing Thatcherite Policies: Audit of an Era* (London: Open University Press, 1992).
Middlemas, K., *Power, Competition, and the State* (London: Macmillan, 1991).
Nairn, T., *The Breakup of Britain* (London: Verso, 1981).
Norton, P. and A. Aughey, *Conservatives and Conservatism* (London: Temple Smith, 1981).
Overbeek, H., *Global Capitalism and National Decline* (London: Unwin Hyman, 1989).
Owen, G. (ed.), *The Thatcher Years* (London: Financial Times, 1987).
Powell, E., *Freedom and Reality* (Kingswood: Elliott Rightway Books, 1969).
Riddell, P., *The Thatcher Era* (Oxford: Basil Blackwell, 1985).
Ridley, N., *My Style of Government* (London: Hutchinson, 1991).

Ross, J., *Thatcher and Friends* (London: Pluto, 1983).

Savage, S. and L. Robins, *Public Policy Under Thatcher* (London: Macmillan, 1990).

Schwarz, B., 'The Thatcher Years', in R. Miliband (ed.), *Socialist Register 1987*, pp. 116–52.

Seldon, A. (ed.), 'The Thatcher Years', *Contemporary Record*, 1:3 (1987), pp. 2–31.

Thatcher, M., *The Downing Street Years* (London: Harper Collins, 1993).

Thompson, G., *The Conservatives' Economic Policy* (London: Croom Helm, 1986).

Wapshott, N. and G. Brock, *Thatcher* (London: Futura, 1983).

Willetts, D., *Modern Conservatism* (Harmondsworth: Penguin, 1992).

Young, H., *One of Us* (London: Macmillan, 1989).

Index